IN DEFENSE OF MY PEOPLE

IN DEFENSE OF MY PEOPLE

ALONSO S. PERALES
TRANSLATED AND EDITED BY **EMILIO ZAMORA**

Arte Público Press
Houston, Texas

In Defense of My People is made possible in part through a grant from the Summerlee Foundation. We are grateful for their support.

Recovering the past, creating the future

Arte Público Press
University of Houston
4902 Gulf Fwy, Bldg 19, Rm 100
Houston, Texas 77204-2004

Cover design by Mora Des!gn

Library of Congress Control Number: 2022937653

♾ The paper used in this publication meets the requirements of the American National Standard for Information Sciences—Permanence of Paper for Printed Library Materials, ANSI Z39.48-1984.

Copyright © 2021 by Alonso S. Perales
Printed in the United States of America

21 22 23   4 3 2 1

Table of Contents

Introduction xi

VOLUME I: *In Defense of My People*
Introduction 3
By Way of a Prologue, Carlos E. Castañeda 5
Author's Biographical Notes 7
Counter-Productive Ideas for Americanization in the United States 9
Mexican Americans Must Be Treated as Americans to Feel American ... 12
A Protest against Claims by James E. Ferguson 14
A Theatrical Presentation that Is Unfair to the American People 17
Mexican-American Youth, Study Law! 19
Ignorance as a Cause of Racial Prejudice 21
Mexican-American Suffrage 23
Presentations for the Advancement of Mexicans 25
To the Mexican and Mexican-Texas Communities of Alice, San Diego,
 Corpus Christi, Kingsville, Falfurrias, Cameron County and the
 Lower Rio Grande Valley 27
Two Ideals and One Goal 28
The Problem Facing Mexican Americans 30
The Evolution of Mexican Americans 35
The Mexican-American Ideal 39
Enthusiastic Defense of Mexican Workers 40
We Ask for Justice in the Raymondville Case 43
A Protest against a Real Estate Company 45
Letter to President Coolidge, Protesting the Assassinations in
 Raymondville 47

In Defense of the Mexicans 51
A Just Defense of Mexicans 53
In Defense of La Raza: An Important Letter to President Coolidge 54
Let Us Honor the Memory of the Heroes of Mexican Origin 57
Efforts on Behalf of Mexicans in Jail Accused of Entering this
  Country Illegally 59
To the Mexican Youth 61
Defending La Raza before the Committee on Immigration of the
  US Congress: Statement by Alonso S. Perales, Attorney at Law 66
The Convention of the League of Citizens in Edinburg Was Noteworthy . . 73
Perales' Address during La Gran Fiesta de La Raza in the San Antonio
  Auditorium 76
Protesting the Segregation of our Youth in Government Centers 80
Education Opportunities that We Should Exploit 82
The Sanitary Commission Met and Discussed the West Side in the
  Meeting 84
Another Protest Regarding Pensions, Prepared by Council 16 of the
  League of United Latin American Citizens 86
Defending Humble Mexicans before the Civil Service Commission
  of the Police and Firefighters of San Antonio, Texas 88
The Parent-Teacher Association 90
Requesting School Facilities for Our Children: A Judgement Sought
  Against the School Board in the District Court 92
Concerning the Home Beautification Contest 96
On the Convention of the Anti-Tuberculosis Association of Texas 98
To the Pan American Round Tables, Rotary Clubs, Lion's Clubs,
  Kiwanis Clubs, Chambers of Commerce and other Organizations
  Interested in Promoting Understanding and Cooperation between
  the Peoples of Mexico and the United States of America 99
A Protest against Poems that Are Offensive to Mexican People 103
Our Forthcoming Convention and the Future of Our School Children ... 104
The True Mission of Our League 109
The Forthcoming Elections and the Future of Our Children 114
The Next Elections and the Future of Our Raza 116
The Mexican American and the Recent Elections 118

The Mexican American and the Recent Elections II 120
How to Request School Facilities for Our Children 122
The Education of the Youth Is Obligatory: Chapter 18 Civil Statutes
  of Texas Compulsory Education 128
Mexicans: Educate Your Children 133

VOLUME II: *In Defense of My People*

Commentary on Volume I, *In Defense of My People* 137
En Defensa De Mi Raza: My Opinion on the First Volume and its
  Author, José de la Luz Sáenz 140
A Brief Statement on the High Purpose of *En Defensa de Mi Raza*,
  Juan Sauceda 142
A Protest in Support of a Mexican-American Legionnaire 144
Issues Facing Our Race in the United States, I 147
Issues Facing Our Race in the United States, II 149
Issues Facing Our Race in the United States, III 151
Issues Facing Our Race in the United States, IV 155
A Letter Praising Dr. Herschel T. Manuel 158
Presentation by Alonso S. Perales on the Radio Program "La Voz
  de La Raza," June 8, 1932 160
Societies as a Means for Progress 162
Cooperation 164
The Importance that We Give the Adult Schools 166
Impressions of a Trip to Mexico 168
The Formal Petition for the Construction of a Distinctly Mexican
  Square, Presented by Representatives of LULAC at the Last
  Meeting of the Centenary Commission 170
LULAC Protests an Incident, Mexican Texans Forced to Pull a Car
  with Ropes 173
Perales Congratulates Calleros and His Colleagues 174
Attorney Valls Stands Up for the Mexican People, the Strong and
  Noble Attitude of the District Attorney, His Heart Swells with
  Resentment Towards the Reproach from El Paso, "We Don't Ask for
  Privileges, But Equal Rights before the Law" 176
Mayor Quin Responds to a Letter from Perales 180

To All the Councils of the League of United Latin American Citizens 181
Mexicans Are Not to Be Classified as Colored in Texas; an
    Objection by Maverick and LULAC Members 182
The Issue Has Ended 185
Mr. Cleofas Calleros in San Antonio 187
Our Nation Will Protest the Classification of Mexicans, the
    Mexican Chamber of Deputies Will Prepare It 189
More Actions in Support of Mexicans 191
The Bureau of the Census Declares Mexicans as Whites 193
Several Clubs Discuss the Case of the Shanties and Sheds in
    San Antonio 198
The Animated Words of Attorney Perales 200
Again, the Classification of Mexicans, It Appears in the Social
    Security Form 203
The Classification of Mexicans as Whites 206
Telegram 210
The Words of Alonso S. Perales through KMAC Station on the
    Occasion of an Artistic Contest 212
The Poll Tax or Voting Tax 214
A Letter from San Antonio Councils 16, 12 and 2 of the League of
    United Latin American Citizens to Manufacturers and Businessmen
    and other Persons from San Antonio Requesting a Higher Daily
    Wage for Mexican Workers 219
Mexican Visitors Bring Much Benefit 222
Perales Congratulates the Junior Chamber of San Diego, Texas 224
The Insult against Mexicans Is Repeated in San Angelo 226
Summary of Resolutions by Attny. Alonso Perales, Delegate of
    Council 16 During the Ninth Annual Convention of the League
    of United Latin American Citizens, Houston, Texas, June 5 and 6,
    1937 229
Echoes of the Grand General Convention Celebrated in
    Houston, Texas 231
Notes on the Immigration Laws of the United States of America 233
Speech on Behalf of the Mexican Community of San Antonio Upon
    Accepting a Community Center Constructed by the City 235

Congressman John N. Garner (Now Vice President) before the
Immigration Committee of the US Congress, Advocating against
Restricting the Entry of Mexicans into this Country .... .237
Office of the Minority Leader of the US House of Representatives ..... .238
Defending La Raza before the Immigration Committee of the
US Congress .... .240
Echoes of the Special LULAC Convention Held in Corpus Christi ..... .244
A Letter from Dr. Herschel T. Manuel, Professor of Educational
Psychology at the University of Texas .... .246
Protesting the Segregation of Our Raza in New Braunfels .... .251
Perales Addresses the Mayor and the Commissioners of
New Braunfels .... .253
The True Origin of the League of United Latin American Citizens ..... .256

Notes .... .277

Introduction

Historians specializing in the twentieth century history of Mexicans in the United States recognize Alonso S. Perales for his singular leadership during the initial phase of the Mexican civil rights movement of Texas. They also give him credit for being the most important co-founder of the League of United Latin American Citizens (LULAC), the leading and longest running civil rights organization in the Mexican community of the twentieth century.[1] Other historians, especially those who study US history, may be less acquainted with his writings, most of which remain relatively unknown because he wrote them in Spanish. This includes his first two book-length serial publication that appeared in 1936 and 1937, *En Defensa de Mi Raza*, or *In Defense of My People*.[2] The present, translated and edited version of Perales' two-volume work makes available to a wider audience his significant contributions to the history of Mexicans and their cause for dignity, equal rights and respect. Scholars and social studies curriculum writers and teachers in our public schools should take notice of this now more accessible history, and appreciate its importance as a subject in itself and as a means to better understand the histories that rhyme alongside it.

Alonso S. Perales

Perales was born on October 17, 1898 in the South Texas town of Alice to Nicolás Perales, a shoemaker from Mexico, and Susana Sandoval, a Texas-born homemaker. Nicolás died when Alonso was six. Six years later, Susana passed away, leaving the young Perales to fend for himself, until Crecencio Treviño, a barber from Texas, and Eugenia Naranjo, a homemaker from Texas took him in. They raised the young Perales as their own and saw him graduate from the official high school in Alice, becoming the first Mexican-American student to have done so. Alonso S. Perales died in San Antonio on May 9, 1960. Perales was a precocious child. According to family lore, he showed an early self-awareness and concern for the well-being of the largely impoverished Mexican working families in the area. About the time that the Treviño-Naranjo family adopted him, he would occasionally pause and stand above the cotton plants and openly exhort fellow cotton pickers to strive for better and more dignified labor. Perales may have bothered, and possibly embarrassed, the workers with his brash commentary, but this does not seem to have concerned him. His loving Perales-Sandoval and Treviño-Naranjo parents raised him to be confident and outspoken, and inculcated in him the working-class values of hard work coupled with a hopeful vision for a better future. This was evident in his determination to get ahead in life, especially when he attended a business school in nearby Corpus Christi. Perales served as an officer with the American expeditionary forces in France and, after his return, he worked for an oil company in Mexico and the US Censor Committee in the San Antonio Post Office.

Perales set out for Washington DC in 1920 to do his undergraduate and legal studies. He worked as a clerk in the Commerce Department and, prior to obtaining his law degree, joined the US diplomatic corps with assignments in Mexico, the Caribbean and Central America. He worked as a clerk for several diplomatic delegations and subsequently became a translator and legal advisor. The world of diplomacy provided Perales with valuable experience in mediation, international norms and the preparation of foundational documents such as constitutions, treaties and agreements for reconstituted governments that the United States was propping up, often with military force. The rarified air of international relations also nurtured a confidence in his leadership and legal abilities and strengthened his abiding belief in the rule of just laws.

During one of his trips to Texas, he met Marta Carrizales Pérez, an educated and, by all accounts, lovely bookstore owner from Rio

Grande City. They married in 1922. Marta became his caring partner, the mother to their three adopted children, and his constant and closest political associate in what she called "*la causa*," or the cause for Mexican rights. With time, along with his network-building work throughout Central and South Texas and prolific writing in Spanish-language newspapers, Perales built a reputation as an intelligent, confident and outspoken leader—in both the Spanish and English languages of Texas. In the 1920s, he joined with other young civic leaders in initiating a civil rights cause and established LULAC, the organization that was to lead the Mexican fight for dignity, equal rights and respect.[3]

Perales kept an incredibly busy schedule that included family responsibilities, legal work, writing for Spanish-language newspapers, speaking engagements, attending local and regional meetings, testimonials before congressional and legislative bodies, and preparing letters of protest to persons and institutions that endorsed racial segregation or were in a position to correct cases of discrimination. Representative records—including letters, reports, articles, extended public service statements and testimonials, most of which Perales published as newspaper articles between 1920 and 1937—appear as entries in his two-volume book.

Perales advanced the civil rights cause as a representative of LULAC and other civil rights organizations that he co-founded, including the Committee of One Hundred Citizens and the League of Loyal Citizens. Some of his important achievements during the early 1920s included the continuous recruiting of new members and local councils or chapters, and tending to the work of LULAC at annual conferences and smaller meetings throughout the state. Perales also served as the head of the Nicaraguan Consulate in San Antonio for twenty-five years, an accomplishment made possible by the contacts that he made in Central America as a member of the US diplomatic missions of the 1920s and 1930s.

Perales testified before congressional committees on immigration, consistently arguing that the United States could formulate all the policies that it wished, but public officials and powerful lobbying groups like the American Farm Bureau Federation could not use racially demeaning arguments to justify their actions in favor or in opposition to Mexican immigration. To do so would undermine the work of the Mexican civil rights organization, especially its advocacy for improved relations between Mexicans and Anglos and for advancing the principles of justice, fairness and equality embodied in the nation's Constitution. Perales also became a major figure in the discourse over the Good Neighbor Policy in Latin America, usually challenging such groups as the Pan American Round Table of Texas for their hypocrisy in calling for better relations in the Americas but doing little or nothing about accommodating Latin Americans at home.

During the 1930s and 1940s, Perales and other Mexican civil rights leaders merged their pan-Americanist appeals with calls for civil rights legislation. He worked closely with members of the San Antonio delegation to the Texas Legislature to propose civil rights legislation based on the official designation of Mexicans as whites but also as a pan-Americanist initiative during the 1930s and a wartime measure in the 1940s. These efforts as well as his interventions with federal officials failed, but the civil rights leadership shifted their attention to Mexican government officials. This cooperation turned into a working relationship between Mexican civil rights organizations and the Mexican consulates in soliciting, investigating and settling complaints of discrimination by Mexican nationals and Mexican Americans. Perales also began to call for civil rights legislation from hemispheric platforms, including the 1943 Inter-American Bar Association Conference in Mexico City and the inaugural meeting of the United Nations, for which he served as a member of the Nicaraguan delegation. These accomplishments occurred after 1937, the date of the publication of his second volume of *En Defensa de Mi Raza*, but they are relevant to his longstanding civil rights work.

Perales received numerous recognitions for his work. Aside from his appointment to the Nicaraguan Consulate in San Antonio and the Nicaraguan delegation to the United Nations meeting, El Comité Patriótico Mexicano, a federation of thirty-four "civil and cultural" organizations from San Antonio, gave him a hero's welcome for his participation at the UN meeting and especially for his contributions in

INTRODUCTION   xv

the preparation of the UN Charter. The Spanish government awarded him the rank of Commander in the Spanish Order of Civil Merit for his public service. The Edgewood ISD named an elementary school after Perales and LULAC delegates to their 1990 national convention paid tribute to him and his work. The Law School at the University of Houston administers a scholarship under his name, largely made possible by Arte Público Press and Law Professor Michael A. Olivas, the editor of a recent anthology that celebrates his life and work. Perales was especially proud of his membership in American Legion Post No. 2 and the Knights of Columbus (Fourth Degree), No. 786.

The Book *En Defensa de Mi Raza*

The book's title greets the reader with the popular Latin American self-referent of "La Raza" that Perales turns into the possessive "mi Raza," or "Nuestra Raza," meaning my or our people. José Vasconcelos, the Mexican historical figure, makes a similar, famous declaration that now stands as the motto encapsulating the guiding spirit of Mexico's Universidad Nacional Autónoma de México, "*Por mi Raza hablará el espíritu.*" The differences between the two are as memorable. While Vasconcelos points to spiritual redemption of a people somewhere beyond their present, Perales, with the customary bravado of a righteous civil rights leader, confidently shifts our attention to his ongoing and enduring defense of a people that are his people. Vasconcelos was assuring his own Raza of a wondrous and reconstituted Mexico earned under the fire of an exhausting social revolution. Perales was not yet imagining a restored and comforting future for his people in the United States; he was absorbed in his own insurgency and living out the meaning of his old German cognate, Adalfuns, "ready for battle."

En Defensa de Mi Raza contains 106 records plus the front matter that includes prologues and introductions by Perales and leading civic and civil rights leaders of the time. The entries include mostly articles that Perales published in Spanish-language newspapers, including reports on conferences, acts of discrimination and violence against young male adults in legal custody, correspondence with other LULAC and civic leaders, as well as articles on prejudice, discrimination and the civil rights cause.[4] The book contains other entries such as letters that Perales wrote to government officials and civic leaders calling for interventions and assistance on behalf of aggrieved Mexicans. The last and smallest group of entries are articles that fellow civil rights leaders and Spanish-language newspaper editors wrote about his civil rights work.

When the articles were located in newspapers and archival collections, they appear as verbatim entries, otherwise, the editor has included the translated Spanish versions that Perales shares with us. The entries that Perales originally published in English and that he included in their original form—for example, sample applications for government service and a series of letters between LULAC leaders that credit Perales with being the principle founder of LULAC—also appear in verbatim form. Together, the materials introduce the readers to a rich collection of Mexican records compiled and mostly authored by the leading Mexican civil rights leader of the twentieth century. The book speaks to the Mexican discourse over prejudice, discrimination and inequality, as well as the process of asserting self-worth and collective pride, the righteous, willful acts of protest, claims for moral and constitutional rights and conciliatory and aggressive appeals to reason.

The reviewers that Perales selected to introduce the book—one Mexican American and three Mexican nationals with long residence in Texas—placed their attention on him, especially his tenacious and honest leadership. Carlos E. Castañeda, the renowned borderlands historian from the University of Texas at Austin and a major civil rights figure in his own right, was the first among the invited reviewers to comment on the 1936 volume.[5] The book, according to Castañeda, sought to motivate the youth to assume leadership positions in the fight for the dignity and rights of Mexicans. Castañeda's focus, however, was on Perales, the author "with the moral strength to protest the injustices before civil authorities, the public and an entire people during the last eighteen years.[6] "We are not exaggerating," Castañeda added, "when we say that he is the defender of his *Raza*" and "although he is not the only one to have fought for our dignity and rights in recent years, no one else has done as much."

Manuel Urbina, a popular teacher, minister and political figure from San Antonio with a flair for the dramatic in his writings, also paid tribute to Perales' dedication to public service.[7] Young people had to emulate him if Mexican communities ever expected to rid themselves of the racial oppression that lorded over them. With Perales in mind, he added,

> Conditions will change in the Imperial State only when we can count on a significant number of Mexicans without an exaggerated sense of self. They should also have a deep understanding of history, sociology, economics, law, etc. and, above all, a genuine love for our racial brothers.

According to Urbina, the situation was desperate for Mexican communities because prejudiced Anglos seemed to be acting with impunity. Mindful of the corrosive and far-reaching consequences of racial thinking, Urbina warned of global calamities: "Anglos are slowly instilling into the hearts and minds of thousands of people the idea of future world wars that bring destruction, ruin and the death of entire nations." Only persons like Perales could defend his people and help the world avoid the destructive effects of racism.

José de la Luz Sáenz, a teacher, author of a World War I diary, and one of Perales' closest confidants, also heaped praise on his character and abilities. Like the other reviewers, the native son from Realitos, Texas, counseled the youth to look to Perales as the kind of leader that they should strive to become. He also urged them to read his book to appreciate the demanding political work of a civil rights leader, "You will find in his articles and letters many ideas emerging out of the different moments that pressing circumstances have dictated to him."

Juan Sauceda rounded out the introductions of the book.[8] He also offered a generational view of the cause and the need for youth to join it. Sauceda used Perales' techniques of pointing to Mexican historical and cultural figures to validate and inspire the fight for the rights of Mexicans. These allusions to a glorious Mexican past were not limited to the collective fight. They were also necessary in the personal struggles for growth and development among the youth. According to

Sauceda, "The sincere interest that you express in improving your immediate social condition will serve as the best and most welcomed crown of recognition that you will be extending to the work of the descendant of Ilhuicamina, Cuauhtémoc and Juárez."[9]

Perales compiled thirty-six excerpts from letters of support that he received from fellow civic and civil rights leaders, government representatives, scholars and private citizens and residents that offer further evidence of the reception that the two volumes received.[10] Renato Cantú Lara, the Mexican Consul in Los Angeles, reminds us that Perales was addressing race and color as the central issues in the lives of Mexicans: "Clearly there are few like you who have studied the racial issues that the color of our skin has raised in this country." Sumner Welles, the Under Secretary of Foreign Relations, added weight to the claims for equality in a way that only a government official could do: "There is no room for harboring racial prejudice in our country, especially when men and women of your racial background have done so much to build it up to its current world standing." Enrique Ortega from San Antonio, lacking the standing of a Sumner Welles, but making it up with an abundance of praise, stated, "The book has significant historical value and all persons of Mexican origin in the United States should read it to strengthen their eventual unity and obtain through legal means a change in their humiliating condition."

Prudencio Gutiérrez, the president of LULAC Council 60 from Houston spoke with equal fervor: "I do not have enough words to congratulate you for your great work for the advancement of *Nuestra Raza* and the well-being of our youth so that future generations can live without the obstacles that have hindered our way." Dr. Herschel Manuel, Professor of Educational Psychology at the University of Texas, repeated a common observation when he said, "I congratulate you for the great service that you have extended to your people. As you know, I admire you and appreciate your courageous work. You have been a strong and able leader." Urbina may have noted the most moving statement in a separate article in *La Prensa*. The book, according to Urbina, made a deep impression in my spirit, not only because of its just ideas and, in some ways, for the international concepts (in relation to the good understanding that should exist between Anglos and Mexicans in Texas) but also for its clarity, frankness and sincerity, as well as the loyalty that the author expresses for his community and his Raza.[11]

Complementary Writings

Perales published other works, including "El México Americano y la Política del Sur de Texas, Comentarios," a reproduction of an article by O. Douglas Weeks, a University of Texas at Austin Government professor, with limited commentary by Perales.[12] Weeks' purpose, abetted by Perales the publisher, was to explain race and class as determining variables in the social relations between Mexicans and Anglos in South Texas, especially in the border region between Laredo and Brownsville and extending northward to the Nueces River, which empties in Corpus Christi. Three groups, according to Weeks, made up the Mexican class structure. The first class included the landed and politically influential descendants of the original settler communities from places like Laredo, Rio Grande City and Brownsville. They had strong cultural attachments to the colonial past and contemporary Mexico, but also identified themselves as citizens of the United States by immersing themselves in the commercial and political activities of South Texas. In counties where they predominated, they wielded political influence.

The second group included urban-based and educated persons, some of whom were products of the first class and actively seeking incorporation into American society. Weeks suggested that these aspiring Mexicans—including Perales—represented the future for the community, given that they were adept at operating in the Anglo world and embraced life in the United States. The third group included the larger impoverished working class of native citizens who were culturally isolated in low-wage occupations and segregated communities.

Weeks offered demeaning descriptions of the group as a class and as a racial group. Perales did not challenge this view, suggesting that he agreed with one of Weeks' central conclusion, that political bosses in rural areas and segregationists in the cities could maintain a caste-like system because the majority of the Mexicans did not understand

English, would not identify as American and were ignorant of the obligations and responsibilities of civic culture. Perales' commentary ended with the observation that Weeks "has told the truth," a "truth" that Perales and his civil right associates expressed on other occasions, including disparaging descriptions of the Mexican working class. Although Perales does not include these negative views in Weeks publication, he did incorporate the work of other non-Mexican academics and government officials who affirmed his views of Mexican communities and their obvious need for effective leadership.

Perales' last book-length publication, *Are We Good Neighbors?*, is a compendium of articles, speeches and reports of discrimination by some of the leading Mexican and Anglo civic and civil rights leaders in the state, including Perales himself.[13] Published in 1947, the book takes stock of the Mexican condition soon after the Second World War, a period that historians describe as a time of recovery from the Depression years. The expanded wartime economy had provided new and better paying jobs that helped working families recuperate from the hard times of the 1930s. Mexicans, according to Perales and other contributors, had made use of improved employment opportunities but had not recovered like Anglos and African Americans. Recent research confirms this view. Mexicans joined the movement out of agriculture, a low-wage industry, but remained disproportionally concentrated as farmworkers beyond the 1940s.[14]

One of the book's contributors, Carlos E. Castañeda, added that Mexicans entered urban-based, high wage firms at a lower rate. He pointed this out from his first-hand observations as a former Regional Director of the Fair Employment Practice Committee (FEPC), the government agency responsible for enforcing President Franklin D. Roosevelt's executive order that prohibited employment discrimination based on creed, race and national origin. Several contributors to the book also pointed to Mexico's interventions on behalf of Mexicans in the United States. They suggested and outright declared that racial thinking was so ingrained that not even an expanded economy, the FEPC or the greater diplomatic awareness and admission of racism as a hemispheric issue worked to improve the Mexican condition relative to Anglos and African Americans.

Other notable books appeared around the same time as *En Defensa de Mi Raza*, but none was like Perales' two-volume work. Manuel Gamio, the Mexican anthropologist, archaeologist and sociologist, for instance, produced a magisterial study of Mexican immigrant communities in the United States.[15] His 1930 publication, *Mexican Immigration to the United States*, explains the causes of the immigrant flows and studies the conditions under which immigrants lived and worked. Gamio provides a valuable companion to *En Defensa de Mi Raza*, especially when he shares the voice of the immigrants that describes and responds to their living and working conditions and contemplates the vagaries and choices in their demanding working-class lives.[16]

Paul S. Taylor, the labor economist from the University of California, Berkeley published two books that also serve as supplementary readings to Perales' book. His studies on economic development and Anglo-Mexican relations in Dimmit and Nueces Counties, Texas demonstrated that the racialization of social relations had created a caste-like structure that concentrated Mexicans in lower-wage occupations, especially in agriculture. Perales noted a seemingly permanent relationship between the dominant Anglos and the largely subordinate Mexicans. More recently, Texas historian David Montejano revisited Taylor's massive archival collection and provided a longer history of racial oppression and Jim Crow conditions in urban areas extending into the 1970s. One of Montejano's contributions was an impressive examination of migratory labor as a Mexican strategy for surviving the hardships of an impoverished existence.[17]

Ignacio Muñoz, a journalist from Mexico who claims to have participated in the famous 1915 San Diego revolt in South Texas, provides a perspective on the history of Mexicans in Texas that is different from Perales' focus on civil rights. Muñoz, instead, recounts militant action.[18] Similarly, Emma Tenayuca, the nineteen-year-old chair of the Communist Party and her husband, Homer Brooks, the secretary of the Texas Communist organization, published a manifesto-like essay in 1937 that offered a different vision of Mexican politics. Tenayuca and Brooks essentially reissued the position of the

Communist Party on African Americans with the appropriate revisions to make it applicable to the Mexican experience.[19]

Two important government publications that reveal the labor exploitation and hardship that Mexican urban and rural workers endured in the 1930s can help the reader understand and appreciate Perales' ire and political resolve.[20] The authors of *The Pecan Shellers of San Antonio* and the *Mexican Migratory of South Texas* provide quantitative and qualitative data that underscore the challenges that poor Mexican families faced on the eve of the United States' entry into the Second World War.

The more contemplative and imaginative works by novelists Teodoro Torres and Conrado Espinosa provide accounts of the same kind of immigrant families that Perales includes in his work. In *El Sol de Texas,* Espinosa provides a sensitive account of the difficulties that immigrant families face as they long to return to their homeland. One family returns to Mexico while the other stays in Texas. Torres' novel, *Patria Perdida*, tells the story of upper-class political refugees. The wife dies in the United States and her husband Luis takes her remains to be buried in her hometown in Mexico. Luis, the protagonist, becomes disillusioned with post-Revolution Mexico and decides to live the rest of his life in the exterior, in his own piece of México *de afuera*, on a ranch he had purchased in Missouri.[21]

José de la Luz Sáenz, one of Perales' closest friends and fellow civil rights leader, advances one of the most important claims for equal rights that Perales restates in his two volumes; that is, that Mexicans deserve better treatment after serving in the military and making the ultimate sacrifice on the battlefields. Sáenz, like Perales, also underscored the contributions by Mexicans as workers and as important figures in the history of Texas.[22]

Studies on Mexican history, culture and folklore seen through the keen eyes of Mexican origin persons were also available in the 1930s and 1940s. The best known among these was by writer Jovita Gonzalez. She prepared an important thesis on the Mexican communities of Cameron, Starr and Zapata counties in the 1930s and wrote other histories as well as renditions from the Mexican oral tradition, many of which Sergio Reyna compiled and edited in 2000.[23] Elena Zamora

O'Shea made her contribution to the publication record with *El Mezquite*, a historical novel that records the long history of South Texas from the vantage point of the hardy Mexican tree of the region.[24]

The foregoing publications, as noted earlier, are contemporary to Perales' two-volume compendium and provide social, political and literary context to his work. Perales' record of publications, are not limited to the two volumes and the pamphlet in which Perales comments on Weeks article and *Are We Good Neighbors?* He published extensively in Spanish-language newspapers, including long-running columns on religion, the civil rights movement and the Mexican community. Many of the articles that do not appear in the two-volume work are available in the Perales Papers at the University of Houston. Others can be located by searching the Spanish-language press.[25]

Ideas, Beliefs and Understandings

Historians who have studied LULAC conclude that Perales and his fellow civil rights leaders were ideologically conservative. They offer at least three general explanations. Mexican civil rights leaders allegedly slighted Mexican nationals while focusing their challenges against discrimination and inequality on behalf of US-born Mexicans, the group with a special claim on constitutional rights by virtue of their nativity. They are said to have accepted the official designation of Mexicans as whites, presumably because they embraced the prevalent racial hierarchy and sought to abandon or set themselves apart from African Americans. Third, historians have pointed out that civil rights leaders like Perales often called for political and cultural accommodation, that is, an exaggerated form of loyalty to the nation in return for social incorporation.

Attributing such ideas to LULAC has painted the organization and the cause that it pursued as conciliatory, conformist and lacking an otherwise uncompromising or radical approach to change. Applying these ideas to complex issues in shifting political settings, however, remind us that public statements or even official declarations of guiding values or beliefs do not always define political behavior. It is true that LULAC favored the US-born, but leaders like Perales also encourage Mexican nationals to join if they sought naturalized citizenship. Mexican civil rights leaders also frequently spoke on behalf of all Mexicans and, on some occasions, would question the racial edifice and segregationist building blocks that sustained it. Moreover, they claimed constitutional rights based on personhood, jurisdiction and human rights dictated by international norms. In other words, leaders like Perales often spoke in general terms, with a big-tent approach.

It is also true that the representatives of LULAC and other Mexican civil rights leaders, like everyone else who was caught up in the world of racialized social relations, would sometimes express or suggest disdain for African Americans. However, they mostly used the official designation of whiteness as a strategy to challenge racial discrimination. Lastly, the exchange of social incorporation for demonstrable loyalty was more complicated than it appears. Civil rights leaders typically agreed on the dictates of reformist-driven Americanization campaigns, but they also insisted on full equality in accordance with the egalitarian principles in the nation's foundational documents.

On balance, the ethnic brand of politics that the Mexican civil rights movement advanced took a conciliatory and cautious approach that reflected a moderate or conservative orientation and that sought to minimize the appearance of disloyalty in a racially charged political environment. At the same time, leaders like Perales offered bold denunciations of cases of discrimination and called for significant change in the face of persistent segregation and even violence against Mexicans. These departures from the moderate or conservative mold that historians use to describe the civil rights movement also reflected moral and ideational sensibilities that expressed themselves as outrage against the view that Mexicans were culturally deficient and lacking a sense of self-worth.

Perales' book reveals the ideas, beliefs, moral thinking and constitutional guarantees that explain the content of his voice of protest in the social context within which he acted. However, we should also read him for what he said and what he did; that is, we should first draw meaning from the obvious. His articles and letters on violence against young males while in legal custody in Raymondville are cases in point. Perales spoke with palpable anger against the authorities for disregarding the rights of the men that they assassinated while transporting them to Brownsville. The wanton violence and the impunity with which such men acted also suggested widespread disdain against Mexicans in Texas. Perales' protests against violence before state and federal officials also give credence to and gain trustworthiness from secondary publications by such authors as Mónica Muñoz Martínez, who has studied the state-sanctioned violence and its generational consequences of pain and grief for the families of the victims.

Readers can formulate their own interpretations with the use of records in *En Defensa de Mi Raza*. For example, they can reconstruct the circumstances of the killings, understand Perales' arguments for the rights of the victims and sense his anger. They could also identify and offer possible explanations for consistencies and inconsistencies between Perales' articles on the killings and his letters of protest to state and federal government officials. Another comparison could place these documents side by side with the letters that he writes to a white veterans' organization from Falfurrias to protest their refusal to admit a decorated Mexican-American veteran into a patriotic celebration. The purpose here would be to evaluate Perales' argumentation and ire, as well as his inclination to see different types of discrimination as part of the same general problem of widespread disdain for Mexicans.

Perales' writings also provide readers opportunities to identify ideas, beliefs, motivations, concerns, understandings and objectives within different contexts. A case in point is the issue of whiteness. He believed that the official designation of Mexicans as whites allowed them to challenge discrimination based on race. Civil rights leaders usually questioned racial discrimination on moral or constitutional grounds. However, they also used whiteness to argue sameness and, on occasion, to distance themselves from the caste-like category of "colored." In 1936, when faced with the possibility that the government might deny them the "white" designation, Perales and fellow civil rights leaders from El Paso, San Antonio and Laredo showed how zealously they would defend their fragile, protected status.

Texas officials suddenly began to remove Mexicans from the white category in their vital statistics report to the federal government. The change turned out to be a technical mistake that the head of the US Census Bureau corrected after a number of protests from Mexican leaders. The public fight, however, demonstrated that civil rights leaders were deeply troubled that they would be associated with Blacks. Although there is no evidence that LULAC and other Mexican civil rights organization officially adopted anti-African American views, readers could interpret their protests to mean that they harbored prejudice against Blacks. An alternative interpretation is that they reacted to what they believed to be a major assault on their whiteness and a decision to move them to a permanent underclass, coming as it did less than five years after the courts ruled against the Mexican plaintiffs in the *Salvatierra v. Del Rio ISD* (1930).

The court had rejected their whiteness claim and ordered the school to continue segregating Mexican youth on pedagogical grounds. In the Salvatierra case, Mexican youth registered lower attainment levels and would allegedly delay the development of Anglo students if placed in the same classrooms. Perales, one of the attorneys for the Mexican parents, saw this as a major loss on two levels. The decision had allowed the continuation of racial segregation. It also nullified the Mexican claim to whiteness.

Perales' exchange of letters with Nat M. Washer, President of the Americanization Committee for Bexar County, reveals another aspect of Perales' strategic ingenuities. He often staged public debates to state his views on important issues on his own terms. He did this when Washer published an article on the Americanization program that appeared in a San Antonio English-language newspaper. Perales took him to task in the Spanish-language press by pointing out the deceptive proposition embedded in acculturation campaigns that if Mexicans embraced an admittedly amorphous national culture, society would incorporate them. Perales noted that the Americanization efforts and, presumably, the self-Americanizing process already occurring in Mexican communities, could never succeed while reformists like Washer continued to disregard discrimination as an obstacle to their social incorporation. Mexican readers must have admired Perales' bilingual and debating abilities, as well as his suggestion that the Americanization program was more interested in reassuring Anglo fears of alien cultures while simultaneously keeping "foreign" groups at bay.

Conclusion

Concluding this preface in preparation for reading Perales' *En Defensa de mi Raza* requires that we visit his statements of purpose. His primary political interest that is evident in the book was to help Mexicans equip themselves intellectually, spiritually and materially to defend themselves against discrimination and to participate effectively in the civic culture of the nation. Social advancement was not possible, according to Perales, if Mexicans did not "meet our civic duties." Meeting responsibilities, such as voting, participation in parent-teacher organizations and beautification campaigns, however, were not enough. Mexicans also had to embrace "the moral obligation" of advancing their interests and demanding equality in order to reach "the place that corresponds" to us in Texas and other parts of the country. The exchange, in other words, proposed acculturation into the civic culture of the nation as well as social incorporation on an equal basis. The key to the exchange was an educated community that was alert and ready to struggle to gain and sustain dignity, equality and respect.

Perales used his book to assist in this exchange by addressing and debating issues, clarifying moral and constitutional arguments for change, providing philosophical meanings for identity, history and culture, and proposing political directions for the civil rights movement. He was especially concerned that readers, especially the youth, see him as an honorable and trustworthy person who was devoted to the nation and his people. Perales maintained that he had never served for personal gain nor material interest and implied that the youth should understand that this ethical commitment was as important as his devotion to his Raza.

Marta, his wife, deserves the last word on her husband: "He was a great man and I say this to the whole world, an honest man and a warrior. He was the light that guided the confused, all of them. I was his companion for thirty-eight years and a witness to his struggles, victories and disappointments. I admired him."[26]

Emilio Zamora

IN DEFENSE OF MY PEOPLE

VOLUME I

In Defense of My People

For Generations to Come...

I dedicate this book with deep devotion and care for my nation and my people, and to the Mexican youth of the United States who are witnesses to our struggles and suffering and who will soon become adults, calling on us to recount how we, as citizens, sought a better future.

Introduction

I believe that as citizens of this nation and descendants of a noble people of importance, we should meet our civic obligations, including offering our lives for the nation when necessary. At the same time, we should expect and insist that this country respect our inalienable right to life, progress and the pursuit of happiness just as it does for all its citizens. This is what I thought in 1919 when I began to work for the good of the nation and just treatment of my people, and it continues to be my firm conviction after seventeen years of honest and selfless struggle. I expect that we will continue this cause with reason and respect for the law of the land, even if we are only expressing our gratitude and respect to the founders and heroes of the nation who contributed mightily to its noble and lofty ideals.

I also believe that Mexican-origin residents have the pressing need and moral obligation to progress in the full sense of the word so that we can assume our rightful place in the Lone Star State. This is why I emphasize our responsibility to be forthright, and to act with faith and vigor in our efforts to advance our intellectual, economic and social well-being. Nothing less than meeting our civic duty and demanding our rights will guarantee our full and rapid advance. Moreover, we must contribute to our progress by capitalizing on the opportunities at hand. If we cannot move forward, let it be due to a lack of opportunity and not to indifference and apathy.

I have been sincere in this effort, not thinking about myself or any form of compensation except for the sublime and profound satisfaction of serving my nation and hoping to see my people progress. I have served my nation fully because I truly believe that the citizen who reveres and defends the guiding principles of the nation does more for it than the person who disregards these principles.

I sincerely hope that this book inspires and encourages our Mexican youth, because our people will expect them to assume the responsibility of carrying out our work in the future.

To conclude, I want to express my sincere and profound appreciation to all my good and fine friends who have supported me.

The Author

By Way of a Prologue
Carlos E. Castañeda[1]

The circumstances that Mexicans have faced in Texas continue to be dreadful. The ignorant and prejudiced Anglo Saxon has violated their rights and trampled their dignity regardless if they are Mexican nationals or American citizens. Mexicans face constant social, economic and political discrimination, and they mostly suffer in silence or protest quietly, which encourages even more outrages, insults and violations of their rights.[2]

This sad situation, however, has given rise to a person with the moral strength to protest the injustices before civil authorities, the public and an entire people during the last eighteen years.[3] He has not wavered in defending the dignity and rights of *La Raza* before the powerful; he has labored as the champion of the Mexican in Texas and in all the other states of the union. A native of the small but welcoming community of Alice and the son of humble yet honest parents, Perales has fought since an early age for the right to be who he is and to educate himself. With admirable determination, he completed his elementary and secondary grades, and showed even greater resolve by educating himself in the same university where Washington received a bachelor's degree and by securing admission into the bar of Texas in 1925.

The tireless fighter that he is, Perales continues his campaign for the rights and dignity of Mexicans and Mexican Texans. We are not exaggerating when we say that he is the defender of his Raza. He has not acted alone, but no one else has done as much.

We should commend Perales for compiling the many articles, letters and speeches that he prepared while defending our Raza and for selecting an appropriate and significant book title. He has sought understanding and unity between two great peoples without offending the sensibilities or dignity of either. Perales has followed the lesson of the great historical figure of the Americas, "Respect for the rights of others is peace."[4] The Mexican Texan is American before the law and should have all the rights and privileges that the Anglo Saxon enjoys. The constitution and laws of this country guarantee the same rights to all its citizens regardless of race, color or creed. This is his message in defending our Raza. His collection of writings and speeches carry bitter truths and enduring lessons for our Mexican youth in Texas. The author's candor, his fairness in this significant effort on behalf of Mexicans and his unwavering faith in the success of our just cause is no less than a living inspiration to the Mexican Texan youth. They will see in his life and thought the ideals of a great people that has been denied its rights by the ignorance and unjustified prejudice of many.

With the vision of a prophet, Perales understands that the solution to the problem rests in the education of our children. To succeed, however, our society must grant them all the necessary opportunities. This is why the author has directed most of his attention to the educational needs of our children. Parents, as well as the youth, will find in this book wise counsel that will serve them well in the future. The ideals and purpose of this selfless fighter in *En Defensa de la Raza* should serve as inspiration and example for the youth of tomorrow.[5]

Author's Biographical Notes

ALONSO S. PERALES. Born in Alice, Texas, on October 17, 1898. Son of Nicolás Perales and Susana Sandoval Perales. Married to Marta Engracia Pérez of Rio Grande City, Texas. A graduate of the primary grades in Alice, Texas and Washington High School, Washington, DC. Attended the College of Arts and Sciences at George Washington University. Graduated from the School of Economics and Government and the School of Law at the National University, Washington, DC, with degrees in Economics and Government and Law. Admitted to the Texas bar in September 1925. I served in the US military during the First World War and the Department of Commerce two and one-half years later. I served as Secretary to Sumner Welles in the US diplomatic corps; Special Representative of the President of the United States in the Dominican Republic, 1922; Aide to the US Delegation to the Conference on Central American Affairs, Washington, D.C., 1922, 1923; Aide to the Inter-American High Commission, Washington, DC, 1923; Counsel and Translator with the US Delegation led by General John J. Pershing in the Tacna and Arica Arbitrations, 1925 and 1926; Special Aide to the American Delegation at the Sixth Pan American Congress, Habana, 1928; Counsel to the United States in the Mexico American Reclamations Commission, Washington, DC, 1928; Counsel to the American Electoral Mission, Nicaragua, 1928; Special Aide to the American Delegation at the International Conference of Conciliation and Arbitration, Washington, DC, 1929; Aide to the American Delegation to the Congress of Presidents, Deans, and Educators, Habana, 1930; Legal Consultant to Captain A. W. Johnson, US Envoy Extraordinary and Minister Plenipotentiary in Nicaragua and President of the National Board of Elections of

Nicaragua, 1930; Legal Counsel to the Electorate Mission of the United States, Nicaragua, 1932; Aide to the US Delegation to the Northern and Central American Conference on Radio Communications, Mexico, Federal District, 1933; and Nicaraguan Delegate to the Conference on Foreign Trade, Houston, November 1935. I also served as the Honorary Consul of the Republic of Nicaragua in San Antonio; General President, co-founder and active members of the League of United Latin American Citizens (LULAC); Director of the Anti-Tuberculosis Society of Texas; Director and member of the Executive Committee of the Association Against Tuberculosis in Bexar County; Member of the Chamber of Commerce of San Antonio and the Council of Presidents of the American Legion of San Antonio; and Honorary member of the Missouri Pacific Latin Booster Club, Sociedad Benevolencia, Sociedad Modelo and Club Vesper, San Antonio, Texas and Sociedad Mutualista Benito Juárez, Pearsall, Texas.

Counter-Productive Ideas for Americanization in the United States[6]

San Antonio, Texas
November 4, 1919

Mr. Nat M. Washer,[7] President
Americanization Committee for Bexar County
San Antonio, Texas

Dear Sir:

With great delight, I have read an interesting article published in last Sunday's issue of the *Express*, entitled: "Sowing Americanism to Raise Better Citizens."

While the article in question provides a complete detail of all the means now being used to carry out the plan of Americanization, there is still one more subject of which no mention has been made and which constitutes a very important factor if the present plan of Americanization would be a success; to wit, discrimination of Mexican Americans.

The writer, an American Citizen by birth, of Spanish descent and a member of the United States Army, makes the above statement based upon his own personal observation and experience. Prior to my entering the military service of this country I often found it difficult to find a decent place to live due to the fact that I am a Mexican although an American citizen.

Sometime ago a schoolteacher friend of mine, also a Mexican American who had recently returned from the battlefields of Europe, was entrusted the supervision of a school in a neighboring town. Upon his arrival there, the County Judge of that community accompanied him to a hotel with the intent of securing him an apartment for the duration of the school term. However, very much to the surprise of the Magistrate, the hotel refused him service and explained that his business did not admit Mexicans, regardless of citizenship.[8]

A few months ago, several Mexican American boys, who were born and reared in Alice, Texas, arrived from France after participating in all the battles fought by the famous 90th Division. Upon receiving their discharge in San Antonio, they went to visit their relatives in Alice. While in that city they decided to play a game of billiards, but they had hardly finished selecting their cues when the proprietor of the establishment told them to leave the premises—this in spite of the fact that they were still wearing the uniform of the United States Army.

Last but not least, two Mexican Americans from San Antonio were denied the privilege of bathing at the Hot Wells Bathing Pool on the grounds that Mexicans were not allowed.[9] All these injustices have been committed upon persons of unquestionable character both from an intellectual and racial viewpoint. While discrimination is sometimes necessary due to the habits and conduct of some people, in my opinion the discrimination should be INDIVIDUAL AND NOT COLLECTIVE, as has been the case in many instances. Distinctions are often justified when directed against individuals, but not an entire race.[10]

Theodore Roosevelt, the late Colonel and President, stated in a speech delivered on January 27, 1917, that American citizenship means complete loyalty to the United States of America. This means that there is no such thing as a semi-citizen, that is, a half-American and half-foreign person.[11] Knowing this, we should also remember that the rights attached to being American-born belong to every American citizen and, as such, no one should discriminate against a race with an unimpeachable history. We cannot be American if only allowed half of the rights and prerogatives guaranteed by the Constitution of the United States.

In conclusion, I would say that unless the necessary precautionary measures are taken to banish the unjustified feelings—among some people—toward the Mexican Americans, any efforts on behalf of the Americanization Campaign now underway throughout the country will be futile in so far as the Americanization of Mexicans is concerned. Unjust treatment, far from inspiring loyalty, incites treachery.

Respectfully Yours,
Alonso S. Perales

Mexican Americans Must Be Treated as Americans to Feel American[12]

Washington, DC
March 16, 1920

Editor, *The San Antonio Express*
San Antonio Texas

Colonel Louis M. Maus discovered an interesting truth when conducting a psychological study of the Mexican people in Texas under the auspices of the International Reform Bureau, Washington, DC.[13] He found that the majority of the Mexicans born and raised in the United States do not believe that they are Americans. While in San Antonio, Colonel Maus noted the following on February 17, 1920:

> I believe that Mexicans in this country are American citizens and they should know that their ideas and thoughts emanate from the United States rather than Mexico. They should turn toward the country of their birth and forget that they are Mexicans, as most of them feel today.

"The purpose of the survey," said Colonel Maus, "will be to see what measures can be taken to help the Mexican people in the United States achieve a more complete Americanism."

Colonel Maus is correct. The goal of the International Reform Bureau is truly reasonable and altruistic. Moreover, Colonel Maus should know that numerous Mexican Americans approve of his mission in Texas, especially since he can explain why Mexican Texans feel more Mexican rather than American.

Mexican Americans have not fully Americanized because of a lack of understanding between them and some Anglo Americans. Anglo Americans do not always see them as Americans. They often treat Mexicans unfairly, meaning that they deny them rights and privileges guaranteed by their American citizenship. The Texas Legislature recently proposed a bill with the idea of separating Mexicans from Americans in the schools and other public establishments. This led to a protest by the Mexican government before the State Department of the United States.[14] Even without such a law, businesses throughout the state frequently deny them services. Given these circumstances, no one should be surprised that Mexican Americans do not favor their country of birth. We must not forget that when the United States entered the war a great number of these poorly treated sons of America, fully conscience of their duties and obligations to the nation, responded immediately to their government's call and left for the European battlefields to fight for the noble and worthy ideals that their nation had ordered them to defend. Many never returned. Although it is true that some failed to meet their responsibility by avoiding military service, the facts that we are treating here explain their sense of civic responsibility.

Dr. Frank Crane notes in his "Ten Points of Americanism":

> Teach that in America there are no classes. Birth, race or circumstance does not fix one's station in life. What any man or women may become depends entirely upon the individual.[15]

If Texans practiced Dr. Crane's advice on Americanism, they would surely be creating a better understanding between the two races, providing especially valuable aid to the work on Americanism.

Mexican Americans are ready and willing to accept their responsibilities as American citizens. Would society allow them to enjoy the rights and privileges to which they are entitled in the same way as their fellow Anglo American citizens?

A Protest against Claims by James E. Ferguson[16]

Mexicans who come to this country are loyal and honest workers. The whole world understands this better than our former governor. They are people of social and cultural worth. Mexican citizens are not the only ones who have protested the harmful accusations that ex-Governor Ferguson has made in his newspaper. Citizens from this country have also condemned his views.

Mr. Alonso S. Perales, currently in Washington, DC, has responded to Ferguson by stating that the ex-governor was obviously mouthing off unfounded claims. Mexicans who come to the United States are loyal and honest workers who make real and important contributions to agricultural and industrial enterprises, and are thus especially useful to society.

Mr. Perales forwarded to *La Prensa* the translation of a letter that he sent Ferguson and that we are now pleased to share:

I have before me [notes Mr. Perales] a copy of the article that you published in the December 16, 1920 issue of the *Ferguson Forum*, that in part, states as follows:

> During the war, when we needed Mexicans to harvest our crops, almost all of them hurried back to Mexico. Now that the war is over, they have returned demanding one-third of our cotton for picking it and murdering our citizens because somebody objects to the damn greasers riding in a coach with the white people.
>
> We have a law to separate the blacks from the whites. We should also segregate Mexicans in order to avoid problems. We are not going to give the Mexicans more privileges than

the Negro, who is in many ways far more superior to make a good citizen.

The Mexican people have not improved one bit culturally and they are more bloodthirsty than ever.

They come to the United States for one purpose only. They want our money and we have spoiled them by paying them more for one day's work than they could get for a whole week in their country.

We proclaim before the world that we do not propose to recognize the Mexican as our equal, socially or otherwise.

My faith in justice calls on me to address you with the sole purpose of rebuking your views and emphatically refuting your claims regarding the merits the Raza Mexicana (the Mexican race). Yours truly is an American citizen by birth, knows Mexicans perfectly well and, for that reason, is in a position to demonstrate the errors in your article and, if you will allow me, to educate you on the matter.

Even though the incident that occurred on the Missouri, Kansas and Texas train, near Granger, is truly lamentable, it is also an exceptional case, and you should not use it to disparage the honorable Mexican race. You should be aware that Mexicans are not the only ones who have persons of weak character. They exist in all the nations of the world.[17]

The segregation of the Mexican race that you seek is an injustice. At times, it may be necessary to set apart some persons because of their individual behavior or habits, but we cannot—even under the circumstances near Granger—segregate a group. Mexicans are not coming to kill our citizens. Frankly, they come to work. They have been a great help to farming in Texas and, in the process, they have made major contributions to the development of the state. I know that the majority of Texans would agree that Mexicans are loyal and honest workers and not the bloodthirsty people that you say they are.

Fortunately, the entire world knows the Mexican level of civilization and they would reject your unjust claims. I agree that the majority of Mexicans have not had the good fortune of educating themselves, but this is due to a lack of opportunities and not because they cannot learn. The lives of prominent Mexicans like the late Felipe Angeles, known around the world for his accomplishments, and Francisco León de la Barra, recently appointed president of the French-Austrian Court of Arbitration established by the Treaty of St. Germain, demonstrate the intellectual capacity of the modern Mexican race.[18] Thousands of other Mexicans are currently bringing honor to their country in foreign lands.

When you proclaim before the entire world that you do not intend to consider Mexicans as your equals, socially or otherwise, you should use the singular "I" rather than the plural "us," even though there are a good number of persons who, like you, hate Mexicans. The truth is you cannot count on the support of the majority of good and sensible Americans. Because of this, you lack the authority to speak for the great American nation.

It is truly a shame that you find pleasure in disparaging la Raza Mexicana in your newspaper while honorable organizations like the Pan American Union, the Pan American Round Table, the Pan American Federation of Labor and the Chambers of Commerce of the United States seek to establish ties of friendship and to promote understanding between our peoples.

Respectfully,
Alonso S. Perales

A Theatrical Presentation that Is Unfair to the American People[19]

Washington, DC
May 15, 1923

Editor of the *Washington Post*
Washington, DC

Dear Sir:

As an American citizen who is proud of his racial origin and on behalf of every Mexican living in and outside the city of Washington, I protest most emphatically against the presentation of the satirical comedy entitled "The Bad Man" now appearing in a local playhouse. It is an injustice to the Mexican people in general and an outright insult to the official representatives of the Mexican government and to all the other Spanish-American diplomatic officials living in Washington who, although not Mexicans, also resent the attacks made upon our race because of the blood and language ties that bind us. This is unjust. First, the presentation is very much overdrawn. Second, such exhibitions tend to create the wrong impression that all the Mexicans are bandits. It is undeniable that bandits exist among our race, but neither can we deny that every nation on earth, including the United States, has produced abnormal characters.

To underscore my point: it is a well-known fact that the United States has criminals. Statistics show that 4,097 lynchings occurred during the last thirty-six years. Counting the number of bank robberies that have occurred throughout the country would be a challenging task. Suppose that Mexicans or any other group of Spanish-Americans would represent you in their theaters as the typical "Daring American Bank Robber" or "The American Lyncher." Would this not make your blood boil? Why? Because Spanish-Americans who did not know better would consider you robbers and savages. No greater injustice would be committed on you!

It is truly deplorable that while well-intentioned American institutions and organizations are sparing no effort to foster better understanding between the Spanish and Anglo Americans and a mixed Mexican-American commission is conferring in Mexico City to improve relations, an American theater hinders their work by staging the lowest type of individual found among Mexican people.

Alonso S. Perales
Georgetown University Law School

Mexican-American Youth, Study Law![20]

An illustrious English jurist implored that, "the heavens allow for the study of law to inspire a deep affection for liberty and justice." I offer my own interpretation:

> "I hope that the study of law by young Mexican Americans brings justice to our racial brothers."

The frequent attacks on Mexicans-American citizens and Mexicans along the border region, especially in Texas, show that few persons are defending our people in this country. That is, we lack Mexican-origin lawyers who are so inspired by the love of justice and pride in their noble heritage as to provide our racial brothers a proper defense in the appropriate courts. I do not have to provide a detailed account of the assaults because they have been occurring for a long time. It is enough to consider an incident involving vicious criminals who took Elías Villarreal Zárate out of the Weslaco jail in November 1922 and murdered him in a savage and cowardly manner.[21] Why? Because of an altercation that the unfortunate young man had with someone named Sullivan! Since the victim was a Mexican citizen, his government acted with everything at its disposal to insure justice. However, they still have not resolved the matter. What would have happened if he had been an American citizen? Even if the case had attracted public attention and reached a court of law as is usual in these cases, I doubt that we would have seen justice. The fact is that Mexican Americans are worse off than the citizens of Mexico are.

Mexican citizens can depend on someone to come to their defense in the United States, at least in the diplomatic arena.

One could ask, why study law and practice in Texas if our formidable and well-intentioned efforts are in vain against the racial prejudice that we face? We must address this point. Are we or are we not the descendants of Cuauhtémoc and Hidalgo and are we not entitled to participate in the cosmopolitan North American nation like everyone else?[22] It would not reflect well on us if we remained satisfied with being North American citizens at the same time that society denies us the rights and privileges that our citizenship guarantees us. One of these privileges, my dear Sirs, is to obtain complete justice when others violate our rights. It would be unworthy of us to accept being treated like "greasers" when rights and privileges are at stake and to be called "American citizens" only when the country of our birth asks us to meet the obligation of military service when we are at war. They only need to treat us like those before to have us feel like American citizens. I am referring to the experiences of the English, French, Italians, Germans and others.

With this said, let us study the law of the land. This will prepare us to fight more effectively for our well-earned rights in the arena of reason.

We need Mexican American attorneys, not rogues or panderers, but true defenders of our race to insure that everyone respects our rights. They could work closely with the Mexican Consuls and in that way promote the rights of our Raza and defend Mexican Americans in the manner they should be.

Washington, DC
March 3, 1923

Ignorance as a Cause of Racial Prejudice[23]

A careful analysis of the current situation leads us to conclude that racial prejudice against Mexicans and members of the Hispanic race is partly due to the ignorance of people that—unfortunately for those of us who live here—prevails in Texas. The fact that Anglo Saxons see Mexicans, without exception, as inferior shows a lack of cultural and educational refinement.

I do not intend to become an apostle of socialism, I only wish to declare and advocate for what everyone is due. Society should judge Mexicans for who they are as individuals, and not as members of a group with shared origins, for "We are all the same, regardless of our origins."[24]

The Mexicans and Hispanic race are usually welcomed and respected in the northern and eastern parts of the country. Of course, small minds also live there, as no rules are without exception, and they continue to place persons who are as white as can be on the fringes of civilized society and culture. The northern and eastern regions have many schools, colleges and universities where Anglo Saxons learn the history and psychology of the honorable Hispanic race. Culture is accessible to everyone, rich and poor, and as a result, when Anglo Saxons are educated on and well informed of the capabilities and virtues of our race, they realize that they cannot indiscriminately put down or slander Spaniards or Hispanic Americans. Instead, they welcome them, at least out of the respectful recognition that they were the founders in this continent and the illustrious heroes in Hispanic-American history.

Individuals who study to understand us better also acknowledge the high level of civilization achieved by the Indians who inhabited most of the continent centuries before the Spanish conquest. They know the circumstances surrounding the discovery of America and do not deny that the apostles who planted the first seeds of knowledge were not Anglo Saxons, but Hispanos. They know who they are—Juárez, Hidalgo and Cuauhtémoc. They also know the names of Ramón y Cajal, Francisco León de la Barra, and many others who have raised the name of the La Raza Hispana.[25]

Things are very different in Texas. You cannot assume cultural refinement here. The hostile attitude among many Anglo Texans leads us to this conclusion and, slowly but surely, the law of prejudice overpowers us.

In addition to the frequent humiliations that our fellow Mexicans endure, Mexicans of all social classes often find it difficult to construct their homes in the residential districts of San Antonio and other such places. Consequently, we cannot be as optimistic as we would want, we simply cannot do this. The truth is that our situation is not at all good.

Not long ago, I heard a prominent Anglo-American attorney from San Antonio give an eloquent speech before a Mexican audience. He said more or less the following: "My friends, I respect and admire the Mexican race because I know their history. All of you should be proud to be descendants of Hidalgo and Juárez."

Soon after he spoke, I stated that we appreciated the comments by the learned attorney, but regretted that he did not speak before an Anglo-American audience, since we already know our political history and much more. We would prefer that Anglo-Americans who do not know us and hate us without reason take the time to understand us for their own good and for the sake of our race. We want them to "give everyone their due," that is, recognize the abilities and qualities of the deserving and noble Mexican race.

San Antonio, Texas
August 20, 1923

Mexican-American Suffrage[26]

I am very pleased to see that after extended observation and careful study the ideals that I have proposed and supported in my articles during the last six years are coming to fruition.

The Mexican-American community of Texas is organized and ready to exercise its constitutional rights. This is what leaders from numerous organizations have been saying. We must now wait for concrete evidence to support such claims, because, as the saying goes: "Things are easier said than done."[27]

Since the elections are near, we should remember that our voting rights are very important for those real and promising ends that we seek. This means that we should vote intelligently and intentionally for our general welfare and not simply because "So-and-so asked for our vote," or because friends suggest we vote for this or that individual! When we listen to them, we become their pawns and give away our vote to others and not to our own. Worse, sometimes we unknowingly end up supporting bitter enemies.

US citizenship guarantees the Mexican residents of Texas the right to vote. We should examine candidates for public office closely, especially the ones who seek office to write, execute and interpret the law. Our assessments should make certain to us that the candidates we support not only meet the legal requirements for the positions that they seek, but that they are the true friends of our race as well. Simply put, we need to make sure, to have no doubt, that once these persons win, they will demand our constitutional rights. We should also insist on the **equal protection under the law** guaranteed by the fourteenth amendment of the Constitution.

There is no need to give a detailed account of the facts; people are familiar with those cases in Texas involving Mexicans who lost their freedom and even their lives without receiving due process. We have an urgent need to inform ourselves thoroughly about persons who seek to become the legislators and other public servants of tomorrow. If our examination of the candidates shows them to be unacceptable, you, the descendants of Hidalgo and Cuauhtémoc, must insist that it is a thousand times better not to vote. Thus, we should recognize that suffrage provides us the means to exercise our constitutional rights.

Presentations for the Advancement of Mexicans

Mr. Alonso S. Perales and Profesor Sáenz Will Speak on Education, Government and Political Rights[28]

Mr. Alonso S. Perales and Profesor J. Luz Sáenz, both natives of Texas living in San Antonio, will soon begin their speaking tour throughout Texas on education, government and constitutional rights before audiences of Mexican Americans and Mexican nationals.

Sáenz and Perales have won the admiration of the people they serve because they are genuine advocates for our race.

Mr. Perales stated the following in an interview with the English-language press:

> Unfortunately, our fellow Anglo-Saxon citizens have neglected the Mexican Americans from the border states of Texas, New Mexico, Arizona and California. Civic organizations seem to care about everyone except Mexicans. If this changes, I would ask that they help us advance as much as possible, like they have done with the Irish, Armenians, Russians and other racial groups that make up this nation.
>
> Some people may say that if we are truly sincere, we should not expect help from anybody and that we should act alone. Anyone who understands the social sciences, however, knows that it is very difficult for a people to advance without leaders or other such sources of encouragement.
>
> Other people less worthy than us have received help in the enjoyment of their citizenship. We have shown our merit as a race. Why do they not help Mexican Americans? It is true that we do not have Anglo-Saxon or Celtic blood running through

our veins, but it is no less true that, with the exception of the Indians, we are the true Americans. No one is more "one hundred percent American" than we are, and I challenge anyone to prove me wrong. We have demonstrated our worth as a race. We have proven to the world that if granted equal opportunities, we can match and, in some instances, surpass the descendants of other races in the arts and sciences.

The American citizens of Mexican origin are determined to catch up with the more advanced Anglo-American citizens and, once this occurs, we will not lag behind. We will march alongside everyone else.

One of our greatest misfortunes is the lack of leaders, but we are starting to produce them. We will soon have enough to lead our race in this country. We want to better our condition educationally, economically, politically and socially so that we may become better citizens and enjoy the full blessings of liberty and progress available to citizens of the United States.

San Antonio, Texas
August 2, 1924

To the Mexican and Mexican-Texan Communities of Alice, San Diego, Corpus Christi, Kingsville, Falfurrias, Cameron County and the Lower Rio Grande Valley[29]

Now that we are back in our homes, we wish to express our gratitude for the support and courtesies extended to us during our Pro-Raza tour. We are very pleased that our cause found resonance in the towns noted above. This demonstrates that we are not alone. Many more are now convinced of the urgent need to do whatever we can to improve our intellectual, economic, political and social condition and insist that society respect our fundamental rights as the Constitution of the United States of America guarantees them to others in this country, regardless of citizenship. In sum, we understand the idea of progress.

To better demonstrate our pleasure and gratitude for the success of our labor, and to make available our opinions and views to the largest number of our racial brothers, we will soon publish our presentations in *La Prensa* of San Antonio and other newspapers that will allow us.

Alonso S. Perales & J. Luz Sáenz
San Antonio, Texas
September 1924

Two Ideals and One Goal[30]

Editorial from *El Monitor*, Falfurrias, Texas, August 28, 1924

Last week, J. Luz Sáenz and Alonso S. Perales presented talks at the Teatro Plaza, the former on education and the latter on constitutional rights.

A large congregation responded well to the intrepid fighters who with all the confidence and love in their souls gladly offered their work and intelligence for the advancement of our race.

They addressed issues of transcendental importance to the intellectual and moral progress of the race. The fruit of their labor will take time to ripen, but if we continue with faith and resolve, some day we will reach our high and noble ideals.

If our people do not claim their rights and demand respect, we will always be subject to attacks and other injustices and will never rid ourselves of the cultural imperfections that prejudiced people attribute to us. They insult and slander Mexicans because they have carried hate and bitterness in their hearts for a long time.

One of them, ex-Governor Ferguson, claims that our people lack civilization. If he spent time studying our culture and achievements, as well as the life and works of our great men, he would see how his complete ignorance of the Mexican people explains the cowardly insults that he hurled at us.

We are sure that the American people do not believe him, since it is well known that Mexico is not the backward nation that ignorant persons imagine it to be. Mexico is a civilized and progressive nation that, not unlike other major countries on this earth, have learned persons who represent it well throughout the world.

This is why we need to praise the efforts of our hard-working defenders who contribute to the advancement of our community with their intelligence and resolve. They help us understand our civil rights and instill a love of learning and education so that others will no longer see us as pariahs and can grant us respect.

Our leaders will probably face much grief and disappointment because some people laugh and mock persons like them who are enamored with the ideal.[31] Some of us will show our appreciation, and this will provide them comfort when they feel the heartaches and face ungrateful people in the cause.

Onward, walk in faith, because you will eventually receive the credit that you deserve.

The Problem Facing Mexican Americans[32]

As promised recently to my racial brothers, I have the pleasure of publishing the first in a series of articles on our situation in this country, especially in the state of Texas. I will also address the fundamental rights that the Constitution of the United States of America guarantees us.

In 1920, the International Reform Bureau of Washington, DC, directed Colonel Louis Mervin Maus to conduct a detailed study of the educational, economic and social condition of Mexican Americans and Mexican nationals in the border states of Texas, Arizona, New Mexico and California. The colonel completed his mission and submitted a report upon his return to Washington, DC, where I had the opportunity to meet him. He kindly gave me a copy of the report once he heard of my interest in the matter. Among other things, he says the following:

> A few US citizens know a little about the number and true character of Mexicans in the border states of Texas, New Mexico, Arizona and California. They know even less of their educational, economic and social condition. No two countries in the world are so close geographically and so distant in goodwill, friendliness and mutual understanding than the United States and Mexico.
>
> Speaking in general terms, Americans see Mexicans as a partly developed race, even at the edge of civilization and lacking many of the basic elements that are so necessary to produce good citizens and stable governments. They call them "greasers" and know them as bandits and professional

revolutionaries. Americans will rarely acknowledge their many qualities. Mexicans have suffered our country's opinion of them.

My thirty years among Mexicans living in our border states and in Mexico allow me to state categorically that Americans have been sadly deceived about their true character. The Mexican peon, that is, the working class, makes up ninety percent of Mexico's population; they love peace and are hospitable, they are kind, treasure the home and family and they are always ready and eager to work if given the right opportunities. Many men and women from among the educated and well-to-do classes would bring prestige and honor to any country. We should not judge the Mexican people because of a few infamous and unscrupulous leaders who have kept the country in a permanent state of revolution since Mr. Porfirio Diaz stepped down from the presidency.

The Mexican people feel that we have injured their sensibilities in our personal relationships. Americans have never learned that courteous and urbane behavior is very important to the Mexicans, and that our inability to see this partly explains their prejudice towards us. Despite wonderful opportunities in the Philippines, we failed to learn the lesson that the brusque and aggressive conduct of the Anglo Saxons offends the courteous Latin races.

It is true that our Hispano-American inhabitants of the states along the border have not marched alongside the ambitious and industrious Anglo Saxon with whom they have lived since 1848, but, in their defense, we should confess that the federal, state and local governments have almost never extended help or other forms of incentives to them. To the contrary, we have ignored them, treated them like foreigners and, on numerous occasions, expressed less regard for them than the Indians and even the Negroes after their emancipation.

We have given them such little consideration as individuals that even in our times few of them consider themselves citizens of the United States despite being born here. This was evident during their registration for the Great War. Thousands of Mexican Americans from the border region did not return their registration forms, and when local authorities asked them for an explanation, they responded frankly that society had never treated them like American citizens. Later, thousands of them left for France where they gave ample proof of their bravery in the trenches and in the line of fire. Many of them are now among the honored heroes in the fields of Flanders and France. Hundreds of them returned home wearing impressive medals for their heroic actions.

Speaking in general terms, I have found that Mexicans from the border have not Americanized much. This is even the case among the families that have lived in the region since the war against Mexico. Few adults know how to read, and they are not much different in their customs and living habits from the recent arrivals from Mexico. They are naturally timid and shy. They live in separate neighborhoods and have little to do socially and commercially with the English-speaking inhabitants who keep them at arm's length.

Since North Americans ostracize them—as people are inclined to say—they have few opportunities to learn our language and become useful American citizens.

This explains why the Spanish-speaking inhabitants from the border region need help from Americans equal to the millions that our government has spent annually in assisting the Indian people. The Bureau of Indian Affairs has established wonderful schools and colleges that offer the best education and well-deserved care to young Indian boys and girls. In the middle of the Mexican communities of New Mexico and Arizona, schools provide food, clothing, a trade and a formal education to the Indian youth. In the meantime, society abandons the Mexican youth and leaves them helpless. For generations, they have been kept uneducated and without a knowledge of English in a country where they are supposed to be citizens.

There is general agreement in the area of race that Indian blood mostly runs through the veins of the Mexican *peón*. Consequently, is there a special reason why the government should not give them the same consideration that it gives American Indians? Our US-born Mexicans have almost all lived as strangers since the United States annexed Texas, and it is time that a country that spends hundreds of thousands of dollars to help foreigners should start doing their charitable work at home. With this in mind, I suggest that the federal government legislate and make available the necessary funds for the construction and maintenance of schools in each of the states of the border region to nurture and educate young Mexican men and women, and that each one of the states have a capacity of one thousand schools.

The schools would not only improve the situation of our native Mexican community, but also prepare Mexican youth to teach in Mexico. Aside from the standard curriculum, the schools should offer courses in agriculture and the trades. The students should be fully prepared with training in stenography, typing, telegraphy, wireless communications, bookkeeping, aviation and other useful trades. The schools should also offer a course in domestic science so that our young women can learn to cook, wash, preserve and assume other responsibilities that are appropriate for women.

This is our general condition, as understood by a learned North American and genuine friend of our race.

I now take the liberty of reproducing statements by Mr. O. R. Vázquez, from New York that *La Prensa* from San Antonio published in May 1922:

> We, the Mexicans who have migrated to this country, fleeing religious and political persecution and searching for a livelihood not available in our country, suffer horribly when people trample our rights under the American flag. Our well-being and development would be the same as the European

immigrants if we received help and protection from our race in the United States. Unfortunately, Mexicans who are born here find themselves in a lower political, social and economic position. They are not in a position to help us or to contribute to our well-being and happiness in the United States. They do not guide us, nor do they teach us English, the laws, the social practices or American customs because the schools have never taught them the language, laws and customs. If they do not have opportunities in the political, commercial and laboring spheres, we will quite obviously not have them either. If they are insulted, segregated and abused, we the immigrants will also be offended and denied social contact with other races.

No one who has studied and thought about our situation in Texas can deny that neither Colonel Maus nor Mr. Vázquez have deviated one bit from the truth. Their observations demonstrate that they understand our problem well.

Descendants of Hidalgo and Cuauhtémoc, how long will we remain indifferent to our condition? When will we begin to resolve our problem? Mexican-American compatriots, how much longer will we be satisfied to live as pariahs? After listening to Colonel Maus and Mr. Vázquez, do you not think that it is time to commit to evolve as a people? How do we do it? I will address this in my next article.

San Antonio, Texas
October 1924

The Evolution of Mexican Americans[33]

Seventy-six years have passed since Texas became part of the American Union and Mexican Americans still wear the clothes of servants.[34] Our challenge is to improve our condition and our responsibility is to resolve the problem. In my humble opinion, the solution involves three factors: **Education, Unity and Politics**. I will now address the first one.

Everyone knows that **Education** is one of the most important issues in human development because intellectual growth brings economic progress and this makes social evolution possible. Therefore, we should urgently seek to educate our children so that we no longer perform pick and shovel work, so that they can become persons with skills and with a future. This is what other races do in this cosmopolitan nation. Why can we not do the same? The day when our earning power matches that of our fellow citizens of different racial backgrounds is the day when our standard of living will be equal to theirs. We do not care if they continue insisting that they only know us as "Mexicans" because they honor us when they do this, and this should make every conscientious Mexican-American proud.

The second issue is **Unity**. Everyone knows that unity means strength. Mexican Americans who live in the United States should organize. We must be able to count on our leaders to be intelligent, active, sincere and honorable. They must also act with confidence and enthusiasm for the good of our race and our nation, and they must not talk endlessly. All our efforts will be in vain if they do not emerge. Why do we propose such standards? I will explain. Our leaders must be intelligent so that they can fully understand the importance of the phrase **Consistency in Principles**. Upon my return from Washington, I had the opportunity to observe persons who only *seem* to act like leaders. Despite declaring that they are fighting enthusiastically for the well-being of our race, when they enter politics (the most effective weapon that we have to fight for our rights) they support the candidates of an organization that is a determined enemy of Mexicans. These same persons claim to be our leaders and defenders of our race! Where is their **consistency in principles?** In order to demonstrate that this organization from San Antonio is the enemy of our race, I will take the liberty to reproduce the following statements that its official organization published on September 15, 1923.[35]

> Even though white American men have always run the city of San Antonio, they never have been elected by a majority of white votes. This is why the city has always been under the influence of foreign voters (Mexicans) who pay no attention to who occupies public office (The ignorant juveniles that they are, they call us foreigners, not understanding that if we vote, we are obviously as American as they are!). Because of this, foreign influences (at least those among them who differ with the underlying principles of our state and federal governments) have dominated San Antonio, known as one of the largest cities in the state. We are sure that no one can deny this, except persons who are more interested in personal gain than in the well-being of the state, the county or the city.
>
> The Mexican vote is always a deciding factor in every San Antonio election, and the white man who controls the Mexican vote wins of course. The newspapers once again noted "the battle that was just won by white, patriotic Americans." As you would expect, every candidate, regardless of background, receives some American support in all of the local elections. Regardless of who the candidate may be, the votes of the foreigners (Mexicans) or the Negroes decide the results of the elections in San Antonio!
>
> Things are going to change in San Antonio one of these days. The Battle of the Alamo was a victory and a symbol for its defenders despite the fact that the heroes of the bloody conflict died in combat. San Antonio was the opening wedge, but

in the battle of San Jacinto, Sam Houston and his small group of valiant Texans thrust their weapon very deep. This famous battle will be repeated in San Antonio when, for the good of its people and this district, this city sends the foreign element on a "Marathon for tall timber."[36] That day will come as sure as the dawn itself. So let us prepare ourselves for the work ahead and the victory that might come slowly but that will be ours.

So there you have the view of our people. Despite those declarations, many enthusiastic "defenders of our race" were not satisfied with solely giving their individual votes, and dedicated themselves during the campaign to openly call on the Mexican community to vote for the so-called worthy candidates of this organization . . . perhaps to better ensure our political and social improvement!

There it is, Gentlemen. This is the reason why it is indispensable that our leaders be intelligent, patriotic, sincere and honorable men with a racial pride that surpasses their personal ambitions. Persons who are proud of their racial origin will most certainly never abandon a noble cause like ours to join the enemy. We should come together. It is urgent that we study and understand persons who pretend to be our leaders, for the banner of our desperately needed unity should include nothing less than patriotism and justice.

The third factor in the solution of our problem is **Political Action**. Mexican Americans should take a greater interest in our government. Ours is a Republican government, and, in the words of the great President Lincoln, it calls for "a government of the people, by the people and for the people." Accordingly, those of us who are citizens of this country are as American as the best among them. Not one person with blood from some other race has the right—even if the person is audacious—to tell us that we are not "one hundred percent American." As I have already said, based on ethnicity, history and geography, nobody—except for the pure American Indian—can dispute the claim that we, the descendants of Hidalgo and Cuauhtémoc, have the right to call ourselves one hundred percent American. I challenge anyone to disprove this.

Politics, I repeat, **Politics** is the most powerful weapon to defend our rights and improve our situation. We should study the candidates for public office in municipal, state and national elections since we are offering them the responsibility to govern us. Thus, it is necessary that these men be educated, sincere, fair and honorable. Once in power, they should be ready to demand justice for our race. Mexicans, regardless of citizenship, do not ask for favors, nor do we beg for sympathy—but we do ask for **justice**. This is our goal and our dream.

To demonstrate why we should study the candidates, I give you the case of ex-Governor James E. Ferguson. In 1921, this man unjustifiably made denigrating and inflammatory comments about our race. Once aware, I did not hesitate to challenge them from Washington, DC. I told him in a letter that his attacks were unjust and that he was ignorant about the merits of Mexicans as a group. In August of this year, he responded that he stood by his statements from 1921, and added that his wife did not *in the least* need the Mexican vote to win.

When this man became governor, how many Mexicans do you think completely overlooked his views about our race and supported him? With men like Ferguson in power, will our ideas on advancing as a people remain distant possibilities? How many Mexican Americans will support Mrs. Ferguson next month, despite her husband's attacks on our race?

Gentlemen, here is why we need to study the candidates. We now have an opportunity to demonstrate, with facts, that we are proud to have Mexican blood in our veins.

Next November, conscientious Mexican Americans will have an opportunity to register a protest against the unjustifiable attacks that Mr. Ferguson directed against our race. Mexican Americans who are truly proud of their ethnic roots should go to the polls on November 4 and vote against Mrs. Ferguson. That is the best way to fight our enemies!

Gentlemen, when we have educated, enlightened and organized ourselves and taken a greater interest in our government, we will have evolved. Furthermore, we will have recovered the good name of our worthy and noble Mexican race.

San Antonio, Texas
October 1924

The Mexican-American Ideal[37]

I have no doubt that upon reading my writings some will ask themselves: What is the Mexican-American ideal? Do they seek Americanization? Do they want to reject their race? Are they pleading with the Anglo Saxons to mix socially? These are the answers: Conscientious Mexican Americans always see ourselves as the most American, and we challenge anyone to demonstrate otherwise. We do not seek to renounce our race. On the contrary, we are proud that Mexican blood runs through our veins. We do not ask, much less plead, that Anglo Saxons allow us to mix with them. We simply long for progress and want no one to deny us.

We want Anglo Saxons to respect our well-deserved rights and privileges. We want equality of opportunity in all spheres of life and equality before the courts of law. We wish to see persons of Mexican-origin who violate the law go before competent courts, and that Anglo Saxons not lynch them. This was the fate of Elías Villarreal Zárate in Weslaco, Texas, in November 1922. We ask that when we decide to attend a theater, restaurant, dancing hall or other such business that caters to the public, proprietors do not drive us out for racial reasons, as is often the case. In short, we ask for justice and the opportunity to progress. That is our objective. That is our ideal.

San Antonio, Texas
October 1924

Enthusiastic Defense of Mexican Workers[38]

Made by a Texas lawyer who witnessed the attack on braceros of our race in a journal in Washington, DC

Lawyer, Alonso S. Perales, recently named Legal Consultant to the American-Mexican Reclamation Commission, has come out in defense of Mexican workers in an article that appeared in *The Washington Post*.

He responded to an editorial that was calling for the restriction of Mexican workers migrating to the United States and describing them as persons who do not Americanize and tend to live in the slums. Perales told the editor of *The Washington Post* that he is misinformed and that his attacks on our race are baseless. His defense appears in the following letter that he sent to the Washington newspaper.

Washington, DC
August 31, 1926

Editor, The Washington Post
Washington, DC

Sir:

Referring to your editorial of August 24, 1926, entitled "Restrict the Peons," allow me to say to you that I accept your noble aim to protect the American laborer, but I cannot help but condemn the unjust attack you have made upon the defenseless Mexican *peón*.

It is perfectly legitimate and patriotic for you to protect the American laborer with the utmost zeal, but when you go to the extent of supporting your contention by libeling the Mexican *peón*, you force me to enlighten you on the subject.

You state that many of these Mexican laborers make the slums of the cities their homes. If some choose the slums, this does not mean that all of them do the same. By the way, Mr. Editor, is it not the case that social workers tell us that the slums harbor representatives of nearly all the races of the world? Why single out the Mexican *peón*?

You also state that, ". . . the Mexican of the laboring class . . . shows no disposition to become American." Americanization organizations make no effort to Americanize the Mexican laborer. The reason is obvious, Mr. Editor: blood ties do not exist and race prejudice is very strong.

You further state that "The Mexican *peón* is poor material and often becomes a tax upon the community that harbors him." Many American employers have praised the Mexican laborer very highly for his honesty, trustworthiness and efficiency. The only instances that Mexican laborers have been in danger of becoming a tax upon a community has been when unscrupulous American labor contractors have deceived the defenseless workmen and left them stranded on American soil.

In conclusion, you state that "His contribution to the country's wealth and welfare is more than offset by his undesirable qualities," and that "the immigration restriction law should be applied to him." Mexican laborers do not have those undesirable qualities that you and other prejudiced writers have attributed to them. Do you know that the State of Texas alone—to say nothing of the other states on the Mexican border—produces one-third of the average yearly cotton production of the United States, or 4,000,000 bales, amounting to approximately $320,000,000? The Mexican peons that plant and pick nearly all of this cotton are the ones that you have seen fit to attack in your editorial.

I trust you will see your way clear to publish this letter for the information of the public and in justice of the Mexican *peón*.

Yours truly for the sake of more truths and less falsehoods in the preparation of editorials.

Alonso S. Perales
(A lawyer from Texas)

We Ask for Justice in the Raymondville Case[39]

Attorney Alonso S. Perales has authored the following letter to the Lady Governor of Texas in response to the events that transpired in Raymondville, Texas. He is currently in Washington working in the Latin American offices of the Department of State as a member of the Plebiscite Commission headed by General John J. Pershing in Arica, South America.

Washington, DC
October 24, 1926

Your Excellency
Miriam A. Ferguson
Governor of Texas
Austin, Texas

Excellency:

I have the honor to share with Your Excellency a news item from the Associated Press that I read today in two local papers. Your Excellency reported to Washington on October 23 that Tomás Nuñez and his two sons, the persons assassinated in Raymondville on September 7, were American citizens and not Mexicans.[40]

Assuming that the news from the Associated Press is true, yours truly, an American citizen by birth, of Mexican origin and citizen of Texas, takes the liberty to say to Your Excellency that the assassination of the defenseless citizens is a misfortune for our state and our nation.

The information that I have at my disposal notes that state officers assassinated three American citizens by birth and of Mexican origin and two others while in their custody and that after this occurred no one convicted them. If true, these circumstances will make the case a singular one in the annals of Texas criminology. I am sure that Your Excellency understands that the conditions surrounding the loss of life of these American citizens requires a careful investigation to establish responsibility and to punish the guilty. If, as claimed, unknown persons attacked the victims from the nearby woods, the officers appear to have failed in their responsibility to extend to them the protection guaranteed under Article XIV of the Constitution of the United States of America. Meanwhile, we expect that in the interest of justice for all American citizens of Mexican-origin and also in the interest of justice and the good name of our state and our nation, Your Excellency would want to remove or seek to remove the officers who held the victims in custody when they were assassinated.

I am very confident that Your Excellency's righteous principles, along with her repeated declarations that she wishes to be fair with all the inhabitants of Texas, without distinctions based on race or color, will lead her to take the immediate, serious and impartial steps that this case requires.

I have the honor of addressing Your Excellency, with much respect.

Alonso S. Perales

A Protest against a Real Estate Company[41]

This concerns the McAllen Real Estate Board and its unjustifiable attempt to deny Mexican-origin persons the purchase of lots in selected additions of the growing city of McAllen.

We recently informed our readers of a protest by Professor Samuel J. Treviño, Mexican Consul in McAllen, against the McAllen Real Estate Board for denying Mexicans and American citizens of Mexican origin the sale of lots in additions under construction in the city. We now have to add a new protest by Mr. Alonso S. Perales who has shown on numerous occasions that he always comes out in defense of Mexicans.

The attorney's protest states the following:

Washington, DC
January 29, 1927

McAllen Real Estate Board[42]
McAllen, Texas

Sirs:

I have before me a newspaper from McAllen that reports that you recently approved a resolution prohibiting the sale of real estate to persons of Mexican origin, without consideration of citizenship. This writer, American citizen by birth and of Mexican origin, takes the opportunity to protest your unjustified insult against the dignity of the Mexican-origin inhabitants of McAllen and the entire Mexican race.

I will not waste our time educating you on the merits of the Mexican people as a race. Nevertheless, I will briefly point out that, the Mexican citizen as well as the Americans of Mexican background have clearly helped McAllen become the city that it is.

Neither the social sciences nor economics contain a single principle or doctrine that supports your unjust and arbitrary attitude.

It is truly lamentable that while good Mexican and American citizens, as well as organizations throughout the country, are working to improve relations between the Mexican and American people you would defy such a noble cause by deliberately and unjustly insulting my well-deserving Mexican race.

Respectfully,
Alonso S. Perales

El Fronterizo, Río Grande City, Texas, February 5, 1927.

Letter to President Coolidge, Protesting the Assassinations in Raymondville[43]

Washington, DC
February 14, 1927

Your Excellency
Calvin Coolidge
President of the United States of America
White House

Excellency:

This writer, American citizen by birth, takes the liberty of addressing you with the following:

On or about September 7, 1926, the Sheriff of Willacy County, Texas, arrested Tomás Nuñez, a Mexican citizen, his two sons, Bonancio and José Núñez, American citizens Inocencio González, also an American citizen and Mat Solar, an Austrian, on suspicion of being implicated in the death of two American deputy sheriffs of said county. Information in my possession indicates that law enforcement officials grilled the five prisoners and took them to a certain spot outside of Raymondville, Texas, and slayed them. The officials then returned to Raymondville and reported that unknown parties ambushed them, they returned fire and the prisoners died in the crossfire. A fact worthy of notice in this connection is that although all five prisoners were slain none of their custodians was harmed.

Open-minded observers in Texas who are familiar with the details of this incident believe that the officers of Willacy County or someone with the knowledge and consent of said officers killed the five prisoners. If, as alleged by the custodians, unknown parties fired upon them and the five prisoners died as a result, nothing short of a miracle could have saved the officers from some injury.

The death of the two officers of the law allegedly killed in Raymondville shortly before the slaying of the five prisoners is regretful.[44] However, it was well within the power of the authorities of Willacy County to apprehend, try, convict and punish the killers "in the manner prescribed by law," but not otherwise. In this connection, permit me to invite your attention to the first section of Article XIV of the Constitution of the United States:

> Nor shall any state deprive any person of life, liberty or property, without the due process of law; nor deny to any person within their jurisdiction the equal protection of the law.

In a letter addressed to Mr. W. T. Galliher, chairman of the Citizens' Committee of the Thousand, under date of January 5, 1927, President Coolidge said, among other things:

> All first-class governments [should] make an honest and intelligent effort to have the laws respected. The standard of citizenship suffers much when individuals do not observe the laws.[45]

On January 8, 1927, the local newspapers quoted a White House representative defining the policy of the United States with respect to Mexico and Nicaragua as follows:

> The first duty of government is to protect lives and property. This is a paramount obligation. This is why we establish governments, and governments neglecting or failing to perform it become worse than useless. The government of the United States has determined to perform to the extent of its power toward its citizens on the border. This government

does not care, nor has it ever cared, about the methods used to extend this protection.

The effective protection of American lives and property is the sole point upon which the United States is tenacious.[46]

Hence, it is to be hoped that just as our government has on several occasions carried the foregoing principles into effect by landing armed forces in foreign countries to protect the lives and property of American citizens, so it will likewise see its way clear to protect the lives of American citizens within our own country. We, American citizens of Mexican descent, have implicit confidence in our federal government's sense of duty, justice and fair play.

We, American citizens of Mexican origin, absolutely trust our federal government's understanding of duty and justice.

I wrote to Miriam A. Ferguson, Madam Governor of Texas, on October 24, 1926, requesting an investigation of the incident that I have been addressing. I have not received a response and, as far as I know, she has done nothing to assign responsibility to the murderers, or to punish them.

On January 25, 1927, I sent the same appeal to our new governor, Dan Moody, but I have not yet received a response from him.[47]

In January 1927, a complaint by the relatives of the Núñez victims led the grand jury of Willacy County to conduct an investigation, but it chose not to prosecute the presumed murderers. Of course, the intense prejudice that exists in Willacy County against persons of Mexican origin, regardless of citizenship, explains this. Some claim that Sheriff Raymond Teller's brother employed members of the grand jury and that others are his relatives by marriage. I trust, therefore, that Your Excellency, by virtue of being the President of the United States of America, would call on the US Justice Department to conduct a thorough and impartial investigation of the assassination of these defenseless (and obviously innocent) American citizens, whose deaths have brought sadness and suffering to their homes.

I do not have to remind Your Excellency that this kind of investigation would not only place the responsibility of the crime where it belongs, but it would also assure all American citizens of Mexican-origin from Texas that the constitution protects their right to life, liberty and happiness.

I also take the liberty of attaching two newspaper clippings reporting that on the fifth of this month, a jury of the federal court in Corpus Christi, Texas, found the aforementioned Sheriff Raymond Teller and some of his deputies guilty of peonage. The five victims that I have noted had been in their custody.[48]

Respectfully,
Alonso S. Perales

Explanation: The federal government sent Sheriff Teller and his deputies to prison because they had held two young Anglo Saxons against their will, which constitutes peonage. Their punishment had nothing to do with the assassination of Mexicans that I have been discussing.

Note: The author has sent similar letters to the following high public officials to inform others about the injustices committed against Mexicans in the state of Texas:

    The Honorable Dan Moody, Governor of Texas
    The Honorable Morris Sheppard, Senator of the United
        States of America[49]
    The Honorable John Nance Garner, US Representative of
        the Fifteenth Congressional District
    The Honorable John C. Sargent, Attorney General of the
        United States

In Defense of the Mexicans[50]

Washington, DC
February 15, 1927

Delta Development Company
McAllen, Texas

Sirs:

I have before me a newspaper from McAllen with news that you have recently announced the sale of lots in College Heights in local papers, including the *McAllen Press*, and that you have declared that Mexicans cannot buy said properties in the subdivision as an incentive to buyers.

The undersigned, a citizen of the United States of America and a Texas native, hastens to vigorously protest the deliberate and unjust affront that you have directed against the residents of Mexican-origin from McAllen—both Mexican and American citizens. I am not going to waste my time trying to enlighten you on the merits of the Mexican people as a race since this is something that Anglo Texans should know by now. Neither do I wish to lecture you on sociology or economics. However, I do challenge you to dispute the following facts:

1. Mexicans pick most of the cotton, as well as the fruits and vegetables produced in the Lower Rio Grande Valley. They do all the work, although it is also true that they receive the smallest share of the industry's profits. In fact, the chambers of commerce of Texas are making titanic efforts at this moment to

keep Congress from placing a quota on Mexican immigration. The chambers openly declare that Mexican workers are very important to the economic development of Texas. Despite this, you have decided to show your appreciation of the Mexican community by insulting them deliberately and unfairly.
2. Mexico represents the major foreign market for the sale of goods and products from Texas. Despite this, you have decided to show your appreciation of the Mexican community by insulting them deliberately and unfairly.
3. When American citizens visit Mexico, Mexicans offer them genuine hospitality and courtesies. Despite this, you have decided to show your appreciation of the Mexican community by insulting them deliberately and unfairly.
4. A large number of American citizens of Mexican origin who live in the Lower Rio Grande Valley—including McAllen—bravely defended our country in the battlefields of the Great War. Others gave their lives for the nation. Despite this, you have decided to show your appreciation of the Mexican community by insulting them deliberately and unfairly.
5. Last but not least, the educated world knows that the Mexican race is as important as other groups.

If not for my loyalty to my native state and my country, I would do everything that I could to keep Mexican immigrants from coming to Texas and I would encourage the ones that are here to leave the country. Maybe then you would learn how to act appropriately and courteously towards a noble race of worth.

Alonso S. Perales

A Just Defense of Mexicans[51]

Not too long ago McAllen newspapers announced that a large real estate company from the area refused to sell lots to Mexicans out of plain disdain. Not surprisingly, Mexican newspapers from Texas have been critical. They have argued that the restriction harms our people.

Since we have commented on injustices of this kind on other occasions and have in our possession a copy of a letter that attorney Alonso S. Perales, an American citizen and native of Texas, sent to the Delta Development Company, we offer a review of some of the more interesting aspects of the case. Our views are not limited to this case but apply to many others in which our compatriots have been victims of flagrant injustices resulting from a racial hate that is inconsistent with claims of being civilized.

Perales has been vigorous and truthful in defending our people. With his latest wise thoughts, he clearly demonstrates that Texas would not sustain its wealth without Mexicans. Perales adds that while the real estate company treats our compatriots unjustly, they and only they are making the land of Texas bear fruit. Their strength and perseverance as workers is the best measure of the importance of our race.

In Defense of La Raza: An Important Letter to President Coolidge[52]

Mr. Alonso S. Perales, our dear friend who lives in Washington and, as our readers already know, has often filled important positions in this country's government as a native of Texas, has distinguished himself with his patriotism and his love for our race. He sends us a translation of a letter that he sent Calvin Coolidge, the President of the United States:

Washington, DC
April 30, 1927

Your Excellency
Calvin Coolidge
President of the United States of America
The White House

Excellency:

According to newspapers from the capital, Your Excellency stated the following on US relations with Mexico, China and Nicaragua to the members and guests of the United Press in New York on the evening of April 25, 1927:

> We live under a system that guarantees the sanctity of life and liberty through public order and protects the rights of pri-

vate property under the principle of due process. We have placed every possible safeguard on the individual in order to protect them from any invasion of their rights even by the government itself. Ours is a peculiarly American doctrine that all civilized countries accept in principle if not in practice. It rests on the concept of inalienable rights guaranteed to all persons everywhere and the understanding that the chief function of government is to provide instrumentalities to secure and protect these rights.[53]

We have adopted these ideals because we believe that they are of universal application and square with the eternal principles of what is right. They will not continue to prevail unless we are always prepared to make great efforts and large sacrifices for their support.

I agree with Your Excellency that our government has the duty to protect the lives of American citizens on foreign soil. I regret, however, that he has not also underscored the fact that our government has the obligation to protect the lives of American citizens and foreign-born persons in our own country. I take the liberty of directing your attention to my letter of February 14, 1927, in which I informed you of the killing of Tomás Nuñez, American citizen, Inocencio González, American citizen and Mat Zoler, Austrian, in Willacy County, Texas, around September 7, 1926. They were in the custody of county officials. They did not arrest or hold anyone accountable for these crimes and they seem to have closed the case, although numerous American citizens of Mexican origin and Mexicans have not forgotten the incident.

In view of the death of these men in Texas, it seems that we have only proclaimed the principle of guaranteeing the sanctity of life and the freedom of the inhabitants of the United States, for if we observed it in practice, why would our government allow such crimes to go unpunished? I prefer not to think this, Mr. President, but in light of these and many other outrages in Texas that go unpunished and our government's firm conviction to protect the lives of American citizens in other countries with the use of armed force, American citizens are much safer in Nicaragua and China than in the United States.

Respectfully,
Alonso S. Perales

[Note: On September 1927 *La Prensa* and other newspapers in Texas published two articles written by Perales which were written in McAllen, Texas, on education, organizing and other basic elements related to the evolution of Mexican Americans in Texas.]

Let Us Honor the Memory of the Heroes of Mexican Origin[54]

Profesor José de la Luz Sáenz, the well-known teacher of Mexican youth in Texas and a veteran of the World War, has initiated the honorable campaign to erect a statue in San Antonio. The statue will be in memory of the Mexican American and Mexican heroes who died in the battlefields defending the stars and stripes with valor and the singular stoicism of our race. Since the project is highly transcendental not only for Mexican Americans but for the entire Mexican race, I do not hesitate for one instant to embrace with all my heart such a laudable plan. At the same time, I urge all of my racial brothers to do even more: the idea is to raise fifteen thousand ($15,000) dollars through a public campaign. The project requires and deserves our support and determined cooperation. Let us unite so that we can complete it. May we respond immediately and generously and, in the process, remember the American citizens of Mexican origin and the Mexicans who we wish to honor for offering their lives, some in fulfilment of a sacred duty to our nation, and all to vindicate themselves as responsible members of our noble and admirable Mexican race.

We should also remember that at this moment Mexican Americans are using the law to fight so that our people receive the respect and consideration that they deserve. The idea of securing and honoring the memory of the heroes of Mexican origin is truly beautiful and sublime, since the commemorative monument will also remind persons who express hate towards our raza that Mexican Americans—regardless of their roots—can faithfully meet their responsibilities as citizens and die bravely and heroically in defense of their nation. The Mexican citizen also knows how to fight bravely and heroically like others in the pursuit of an honorable ideal on the battlefields!

Descendants of Hidalgo and Cuauhtémoc, let us give ourselves to this! Give your unwavering support to the campaign! Honor the memory of the Mexican-origin heroes of the Great War!

Managua, Nicaragua
June 30, 1928

[Note: On August 1928 *La Prensa* and other newspapers in Texas published four articles written by Perales in Managua on education, organizing and other basic elements related to the evolution of Mexican Americans in Texas.]

Efforts on Behalf of Mexicans in Jail Accused of Entering this Country Illegally[55]

Washington, DC
May 3, 1929

Honorable John N. Garner US Congress
Washington, DC

Dear Mr. Garner:

I have read in *La Prensa* of San Antonio, Texas, that a large number of Mexicans living in Texas, including many women and children are being detained. Authorities have accused them of entering the United States illegally and placed them in decrepit jails with everyday criminals. Leaving aside the immigration laws that have led to these arrests, I write to ask that you kindly use your good offices to convince the federal authorities responsible for executing such laws that they observe the following:

1. Be compassionate with the women and children, allowing them to remain in their homes in those cases when the male head of the family is arrested for entering this country illegally; if the women and children cannot be allowed to remain in their homes, they should be housed in an adequate detention facility until they are able to demonstrate their right to live in the United States;
2. In cases when the male head of the family but not the rest has the right to reside in the United States, his family should be

housed in an adequate detention facility until they are able to demonstrate their right to live in this country; and
3. Women and children who do not have a male head of the family and are accused of entering illegally into the United States should be housed in an adequate detention facility until they are able to demonstrate their right to live in this country.

Be assured that this writer and the entire Mexican people will forever appreciate any effort that you take to remedy this painful situation.

Sincerely,
Alonso S. Perales

[Notes: The author sent an identical letter to Honorable Morris Sheppard, Texas States Senator Mr. Garner and Mr. Sheppard responded accordingly and all was resolved satisfactorily.

On August 1929, *La Prensa* and other newspapers in Texas published six articles written in Washington, DC, on the unification of Mexican Americans.]

To the Mexican Youth[56]

Since the start of classes is approaching and the studious youth are turning their attention to school—the foundation for their future—I find it fitting to advise them again that after graduation from this country's secondary schools, they should pursue professional studies and not allow the lack of resources to discourage them.

Washington, New York, Chicago and other urban centers have great universities where you can attend in the evenings. Thousands of young men and women educate themselves in this manner. Some study to be medical doctors while others prepare themselves to be lawyers, engineers, diplomats or US commercial agents in other countries, etc. The students work in various types of jobs, but the government employs most of them from 9:00 in the morning to 4:30 in the afternoon. They attend the university every day, from 5:00 p.m. to 7:30 p.m.

I find Washington the most agreeable place to study because it is peaceful and interesting, and suitable for the life of the student. It is also very important because our government and the diplomats from all the nations in the world engage each other there. Young Mexican Americans have the best opportunity to find government employment since it requires American citizenship. Those who come to Washington to work in government during the day and pursue professional studies at night should do the following:

1. Graduate from a secondary school where they reside;
2. Learn English and Spanish well, at the very least English;
3. Enroll in a stenography or typewriting class and learn to be a competent stenographer;

4. Take a civil service examination. In order to obtain detailed information about where and how to take an examination for stenographers, consult the United States Civil Service Commission, Washington, DC, or the postmaster in your city; and
5. As soon as you receive an assignment, come to Washington to take your position and enroll in a university.

Young Mexican citizens can prepare to be stenographers and translators and try to secure a position in Latin American legations and embassies in the capital or in New York or Chicago, and secure employment in commercial houses that do business in Latin America. You should then enroll in a university. Mexican American youth as well Mexican nationals should know that they secure well-paying jobs if they know both English and Spanish well rather than only one of them. Knowing both languages can benefit stenographers and typists as well as interpreters and translators.

We have good law, medical, engineering and foreign service schools. Young people who do not wish to be attorneys, doctors or engineers but commercial agents or members of the diplomatic and consular corps can enroll in one of the capital's major schools on international affairs and prepare for that kind of work. You can study European and Latin American political and diplomatic history, economics, political science and the political and social history of the United States, as well as accounting, business administration, languages, trade and transportation in the United States, US foreign relations, US government, maritime law, comparative government studies, comparative jurisprudence, etc. etc.

Once students graduate, they can establish contacts to represent the commercial houses in other countries or they can take an examination to provide their services to the diplomatic and consular service or departments of commerce in their respective countries.

Some may ask why so much preparation is necessary to become a commercial agent or to become a part of the diplomatic and consular offices. They can consult the February 18, 1929, presentation by the Honorable Frank B. Kellogg, ex-Secretary of State of the United

States, on the tenth anniversary of the establishment of the School of International Affairs at Georgetown University:

> I will briefly refer to a department at the university that interests me very much. I refer to the School of International Affairs. I believe that it is the first school of foreign affairs established in the United States. Its program includes all the learning and understanding necessary to prepare young people from this country for one of the most important areas of government service.[57]
>
> I know of no other branch of service that requires a broader education and understanding. I will not try to describe the expansive instruction that this and other schools offer, but will say that they teach international jurisprudence, maritime law and municipal government, and an understanding of our government structure and other governments throughout the world, foreign languages, foreign relations, commercial treaties, tariffs, exports and imports and the general ramifications of foreign trade.
>
> No more than twenty-five years ago, we had no specially trained foreign service. The offices of consul, secretary of embassy and legation, ambassador and minister were political patronage, and almost all, if not all, of these came from civil life, many of exceptional ability, to be sure, but no training whatever in the complex and intricate problems arising in our dealings with foreign countries. At the present, all officers below the grade of minister are from the trained personnel, and twenty-seven out of fifty-two ambassadors and ministers entered the service after examination and ascended to their present position after many years of faithful and efficient service.
>
> Our foreign trade currently reaches ten billion dollars annually. It includes the thousands of Americans who travel throughout the world, our maritime trade and the enormous amount of money that our people and foreign countries invest. Our diplomatic corps must have intimate knowledge

not only of all branches of business and commerce but the principles of international law and the rights of businesses and protection of our citizens. Above all, they must acquire a good understanding of the hundreds of treaties that we have with most of the countries in the world on diplomatic and consular rights, friendship and commerce, arbitration, extradition and naturalization. It became evident about twenty-five years ago that the United States could not compete with other nations that had a well-prepared foreign relations branch. Beginning in 1906, we began to classify different officers of foreign affairs and assign the necessary responsibilities to verify—through an examination—the preparation of the applicants for foreign affairs. However, we did not take measures for the education and preparation of young persons for this service. The Department of State took action in the fall of 1907 when the consuls, vice consuls and secretaries of foreign affairs received thirty days of instruction in the department. This was the minimum by law. Since then, the department has established a school to teach the recently appointed officers in foreign affairs. The school's purpose is to provide a fuller and more comprehensive instruction.

The experience of the whole world has shown us the advisability and the necessity of such a trained personnel. To be sure, the transition from the old system to the new did not come suddenly nor without opposition. From an experience of twelve years in the Senate and, as Ambassador and Secretary of State, I am sure that foreign relations has received the most sympathetic support from the Congress of the United States.

The State Department and our country owe a debt of gratitude to the Georgetown school for blazing the way towards a comprehensive service training for foreign affairs.

As is evident, we live in an era of material progress, competencies and specialization. If we are to compete with the other races of this nation, we must prepare ourselves and specialize in a profession.

Now then, a daytime program of work and evening classes is a very demanding task, but it is not impossible. It is a matter of willpower, good health, determination and perseverance. The thousands of young men and women that graduate year after year from these educational institutions serve as irrefutable evidence that it is possible beyond any doubt to complete one's professional studies as I have demonstrated.

I would be very pleased to see Mexican youth commit to finishing their secondary schooling and then come to one of these large urban centers for professional training. We need more leaders that can bring standing and prestige to our Raza.

Alonso S. Perales
Washington, DC
September 3, 1929

Defending La Raza before the Committee on Immigration of the US Congress: Statement by Alonso S. Perales, Attorney at Law[58]

MR. ALONSO S. PERALES. My name is Alonso S. Perales. I am a lawyer. I was born in Alice, Texas. I am an American citizen.

MR. CHAIRMAN AND HONORABLE MEMBERS OF THE COMMITTEE, if you will allow me to incorporate this statement that I have here in the record, I will make but a few remarks, and then I will be ready to answer any question you may ask. I do not want to indulge in any long flight of oratory here.

MR. GEORGE J. SCHNEIDER, ACTING CHAIRMAN. You know, the regulation of the committee is 10 minutes for any one speaker. Can you give us the substance of what you want to say?

MR. PERALES. I will give you the substance. If this can appear in the record, I will not exceed the time very much.

MR. SCHNEIDER. I agree that it should be.

MR. ERNEST W. GIBSON. I agree.

MR. PERALES. First, Mr. Chairman and members of the committee, I want to state that I am not here to oppose the Box Bill nor the Johnson Bill or any other bill that promotes the welfare of the American people. At the same time, I am not going to discuss the economic side of this problem.[59] However, I do wish to refer to the statements made by some sponsors of the quota bill, to the effect that the Mexican people are an inferior and degenerate race. Since I am a Mexican by blood and just as proud of my racial extraction as I am of my American citizenship, I feel it my duty to deny that the Mexican race is inferior to any other race. I have cited sources here in support of my statement [at this point, Perales raised a typed statement from the table].

Some persons also claim that authorities should restrict Mexicans because they do not become American citizens. I am one of the founders of an organization known in Texas as the LULAC.

Mr. Canales, the gentleman who preceded me is also one of the founders and foremost leaders of this organization. The main objective of the organization is to develop within the members of our Raza the best, purest and most perfect kind of a true and loyal citizen of the United States of America; and to state with absolute and unmistakable clearness our unquestionable loyalty to the ideals, principles and citizenship of the United States of America.

Now Gentlemen, others also ask that if we are not an inferior race, why is it that we have not produced outstanding men? Well, if I may answer that in a general way, I will say that we have, despite our handicap as a race, produced a few outstanding men. I give you as an example Mr. Mata, one of the most eminent surgeons in the world.[60] Another important figure is Francisco León de la Barra, a Mexican attorney who currently serves as an arbiter for several international reclamation commissions. Why have we not produced such distinguished persons in Texas? The problem in Texas has mostly involved racial prejudice. We have received little encouragement to advance and become useful American citizens. On the other hand, some have tried to keep us down. Because of this, we have established an organization known as the LULAC and we have been very successful in the process.

That is all I have to say, and I will be very glad to answer your questions.

MR. GREEN. Are you an American citizen?

MR. PERALES. Yes, sir.

MR. GREEN. Are you a member of the bar?

MR. PERALES. Yes, sir.

MR. GREEN. Your testimony suggests that you have our country's interest at heart. Is this so?

MR. PERALES. Yes, sir.

MR. GREEN. Would it not be better for Americans if we Americanized the immigrants in our country instead of letting more come in? We should first look to America and not to the country of origin.

MR. PERALES. As to the methods that we should pursue to do what you suggest, I do not favor one over another. I believe I have been clear. I would support any measure that seeks to promote the well-being and happiness of the American people. Therefore, if the sponsors of this bill or any other bill **can prove** that Mexican citizens are a threat to the American workers because they come to work for **less money** to do the same work, then I would say that the restriction is justified. On the other hand, if you cannot offer solid evidence to support your reasoning, YOUR SOLE REASONING for restricting the Mexicans, and if you are depending on **fictitious** reasons, that is, that Mexicans belong to an inferior and degenerate race, I say, Gentlemen, you are completely mistaken. This is precisely why I have prepared a detailed statement to have entered into the record.

MR. GREEN. I can appreciate the Gentleman's views, especially since we share a racial origin.[61] I am probably more distant from our origins than you, but I believe that our first responsibility is to Americanize and protect all those who are here. All American citizens are in the same condition relative to the ones that are coming here. This does not only apply to the Mexican people but everyone who is coming to the United States. My point of reference is the four of five million unemployed. Conditions are staggering in some parts of our country, our natural resources are depleting rapidly, and the population is growing rapidly every second and hour of the day. In other words, our population has increased by 20,000,000 in the last ten years, and I believe that our first duty is to our own, our American property and our American institutions. We should not open the doors to foreigners so that they can undermine our norms and increase the number of workers in all fields.

MR. PERALES. You are correct. I have nothing to add if you are confining your attention to the economic side of the problem. I am an American citizen and, naturally, I support everything that is good for our country.

MR. SAMUEL RUTHERFORD. Do you have cause to believe—based on the language of the bill—that we are offering another purpose?

MR. PERALES. Than the economic one?

MR. RUTHERFORD. Yes.

MR. PERALES. Based on my experience in Texas, I have reason to believe that the motivation among American citizens of Teutonic or Nordic extraction may be to exclude people that do not belong to these races. Mexicans descend from the two great races, the Indian and the Spanish. Obviously, they are not part Nordic or Teutonic. When two races come in contact prejudice emerges and, naturally, the dominating one tries to exclude the other. I am inclined to believe that this is one of the reasons motivating many of the declarations before this Honorable Committee.

MR. SCHNEIDER. Are there any other questions? If not, we will excuse the witness. Thank you, Mr. Perales, for agreeing to appear and offer us this information.

MR. JOSÉ TOMÁS CANALES. Will you allow me to make a statement? This Gentleman served with General Pershing in the Tacna-Arica incident. I would like to place this in the record.[62]

MR. SCHNEIDER. Do we have any more witnesses who may wish to testify before the Committee this morning? If not, the Committee will enter into Executive Session for a few minutes.

The Committee entered the following statement by Mr. Perales into the Committee's record.[63]

MR. PERALES. Members of the Committee, I am very glad to have the opportunity to share with you the following material related to the Box Bill.

I understand that persons who favor restrictions on Mexicans characterize them as a degenerate and inferior race, incapable of assimilation or of good citizenship. Such an indictment is false and represents a grave injustice directed at a worthy race. The truth is, Gentlemen, an ingrained, deep-rooted racial prejudice has inspired the vile slander against the Mexican people.

Race prejudice has existed since the beginning of time. This is why I am not surprised that the persons who support the Box Bill want to restrict the entrance of Mexicans into this country.

In support of his claims, Perales cited the findings of psychologists Allport and Moss on the racial question to support his arguments regarding the problem of racial prejudice that has always existed throughout the world and the baseless and unfair accusations of racial inferiority and degeneracy levelled against Mexicans. After doing this, Perales stated:

I will now address the psychological aspect of racial prejudice. Now then, in light of the accusations that persons have directed against my race, I think it proper to state who the Mexicans are. I will not do it myself. I will allow persons of your racial background, authorities on the subject, to speak to you.

Perales followed by referring to several authors, including Caspar Whitney, Frank Tannenbaum, George McCutcheon, McBrice, Hermann Schnitzer, Carleton Beals, L. Spence, Robert M. McLean, O. Douglas Weeks and L. M. Maus. All of them will declare that the Mexican race is a worthy race.

* * *

Tuesday, January 30, 1930[64]

The immigration committee convened at 10:30 a.m., Honorable Albert Johnson presiding.

THE CHAIRMAN. We will proceed, Gentlemen. I have a telegram addressed to William Green, President of the American Federation of Labor, and referred to the committee yesterday. It is dated San Antonio, Texas, January 28, 1930.[65]

Mr. William Green,
President, American Federation of Labor
Washington, DC

As Honorary President, of the San Antonio LULAC Council, and supported by Manuel C. Gonzales, General Vice President of this same league throughout Texas, I wish to inform you that any testimony that may be offered today or tomorrow before the House Immigration Committee by J. T. Canales of Brownsville, Texas, a member our League, but employed by Southern Texas Growers, Ben Garza, President of the league and Alonso S. Perales, of 2121 New York Avenue NW, Washington, DC, Honorary President of the League, is not an official act of the League nor has it ever been discussed, endorsed or supported by the general membership or any division thereof. The Honorary President under our laws has no authority to speak for us or the League on that subject. I hope this will be made clear to the committee because there are about 20 or more subordinate councils in this state that know nothing about the activities of these gentlemen or the hearings of the committee on the subject of immigration, and, further, because the problem of immigration from Mexico is foreign to the general purposes and aims of the League, which is an organization exclusively based upon principles of Americanism clearly specified. Please advise Mr. Perales at his home address of the full contents of this telegram, as we wish to make it a matter of record in the League.

Clemente N. Idar
Manuel C. Gonzales

[Hearings before the Committee on Immigration and Naturalization, House of Representatives, Seventy-first Congress, January 28 and 30, 1930, page 218. Hearing No. 71.2.6.]

The Convention of the League of Citizens in Edinburg Was Noteworthy[66]

Special from *La Prensa*

Edinburg, Texas, May 5. As reported by *La Prensa* and according to its convention program, LULAC held its annual meeting in this city on the third and fourth of this month. It was completely successful. About one thousand persons attended, including a large number of Anglo Saxons.

Mr. Herschel T. Manuel, Professor from the University of Texas, delivered a brilliant defense of the Mexican youth in Texas schools. We will translate his address into Spanish and make it available at the appropriate time. Colonel Sam A. Robertson spoke about the "Irrigation by Indians before the Spanish Conquest."[67] His presentation was also very interesting and will appear in Spanish soon. Others also spoke, including, Mr. Dozier C. Abney, the mayor of the City of Edinburg; Alonso S. Perales; Fidencio Guerra, the young student of medicine from McAllen; Ed E. Couch, Hidalgo County judge; Mr. Thompson, District Judge and attorneys Neal A. Brown, McWhorter and Ruben R. Lozano and Professor J. O. Loftin.[68]

Mrs. Celia I. de Guerra, the young Mary Lubbock, the young García y Herrera women, the Attorney Rubén R. Lozano and several other persons that the correspondent cannot remember performed the artistic part of the program very well.[69]

The conference organizers served a delicious lunch at midday and an elegant dance entertained the participants at the country club in the evening.

An Animated Speech by Perales

The convention made an impression on the participants. Perales, General President of the league, explained the basic principles of the organization, and offered a vigorous defense of the Latin American residents of this country, especially Texas. While noting concrete cases of injustice committed against Mexicans, he spoke about the murder of several Mexicans and Mexican Americans in Raymondville in 1926. This included Elías Villarreal Zárate, lynched in Weslaco in 1922, and Alejo Quintanilla, murdered a few miles from Edinburg while being transported to jail by a deputy sheriff and an attorney whose names the orator said he was ready to reveal.[70] He added, "In none of these cases were the evil-doers punished, which demonstrates that the legal authorities did not provide the unfortunate victims the equal protection under the law guaranteed by the Constitution in the United States of America. Where is the justice for the Mexicans in Texas?"

Perales followed by referring to the segregation of our children in the public schools of Texas and said that aside from constituting an injustice, it did great harm to the purpose of the league, since the organization proposes to develop loyal citizens. He added that if upon taking the case of segregation in Del Rio to the Supreme Court of the United States the justices decided that the segregation of Mexican youth in the schools of Texas was legal and just, he would be the first to reject his American citizenship.[71] Manuel C. Gonzales from San Antonio stood up at this point and interrupted the orator, saying, "No, no, my country right or wrong." José T. Canales from Brownsville rose up almost at the same time and also challenged Perales, noting that he was out of order and that it was best that he stop speaking.

The Orator Maintains What He Said

Attorney Perales explained that he stood by his declaration that he would reject his citizenship before he would allow fellow Anglo Saxon citizens to treat his race unjustly and make him out to be disloyal. He supported what he had just said by citing the case of Mexican Americans who avoided military service during the Great War but were obligated as American citizens to fight for their nation in Europe. Perales explained that some Mexican Americans had not met their responsibility because Anglo Saxons treated them badly and made them feel like foreigners. The entire audience gave Perales a booming ovation when he finished, indicating they agreed with everything that he had said.

Moments later, Perales took the floor again and said: "A moment ago I stated that if the supreme court of this country decided that it was right and just for school officials to segregate our Mexican children from the Anglo Saxons in all the schools of Texas, I would give up my citizenship. I did not mean that I would be disloyal to my country by doing this but that I would proceed to change my citizenship. As long as I keep my birthright, I will continue to be, just as I have always been, a loyal and one hundred percent citizen of the United States of America. I served my nation in the military during the Great War and later served in the Department of Commerce and the diplomatic corps in Washington and in foreign lands. The gentlemen who interrupted me a while ago to make me appear disloyal to my country can examine my record of service in the respective federal departments whenever they wish, and I challenge them to demonstrate that they are more loyal American citizens than me."

His Critique Was Just

The audience again gave him a long and loud applause and once the session ended, all the distinguished Anglo Saxons approached him and extended their warm compliments. They underscored their approval to all that he had said because it was the truth and nothing but the truth, and very fair. His many Latin American friends also congratulated him profusely.

[*La Prensa,* San Antonio, Texas, May 7, 1931]

Perales' Address during La Gran Fiesta de La Raza in the San Antonio Auditorium[72]

Respectable Audience:

I very much appreciate the opportunity that Mr. Ignacio E. Lozano, the organizer of this grand celebration, has given me to speak to you.[73]

We gather here with two purposes. First, we commemorate Columbus Day (Día de la Raza).[74] We also offer our grain of sand in support of the suffering humanity.

It is especially fitting, ladies and gentlemen, that we should come together year after year to pay homage to the heroes of our race, especially because of the egoism that reigns among humankind. This vanity sometimes finds its most serious expression when it denies some peoples the respect and importance that they are justly due.

A few days ago, I received a small publication on civics that sought to familiarize the new citizens of this country with our institutions and the workings of our government. I read from one of its sections:

> In 1789, when the Constitution took effect, persons from the British Isles represented the majority of the population, just as they do now. It was not an accident that the English language would be the universal language or that we would inherit the political institutions from the British Isles. People from other nations were present, not only in their persons, but also in terms of influence. The Dutch in New York, the Swedish in New Jersey and Delaware, the Germans in Penn-

sylvania, the Scotch Irish in the mountainous region of the Alleghany and in the South, the Irish Catholic on the coast and the French in Louisiana. Anyone familiar with American history has heard of these communities and the role that they have played in the development of a virgin continent.[75]

We find the following in another section:

The Anglo Saxon are more numerous than any other race in the United States. Their defining characteristics are deeply rooted and permanent and, as a whole, are of inestimable value in the formation of nations. Consequently, it is useless to suppose that the Anglo Saxon would not be an important element. No doubt, they are the foundation of the new race that is now taking shape. Other communities will also contribute with their important qualities, and strengthen and invigorate Americans for centuries. The persons known as the "Native Americans" have great attributes that we will discuss later. On the one hand, they probably surpasses fellow citizens from other races. Also, they have much to teach people from various European regions, especially regarding the essential characteristics of a complete man, including the imagination, adaptability, art, music, dressing attire, thorough investigations and discipline. Any Americanization plan that tries to erase the singular racial disposition of the French, Italian, Slav, German, Irish and Scandinavian instead of intelligently incorporating their racial talents into the American mix of tomorrow would be making a mistake. The history of Great Britain demonstrates that this can be done. The Anglo Saxon himself . . . as well as almost all peoples . . . are the product of a long historical process in which a variety of races have been fused into only one. Such an amalgamation is occurring today in the United States.

As you can see, the material that I have just read does not mention the Hispanic race. Why is this? Why do they ignore our Raza?

As we all know, exactly 441 years have passed since Cristopher Columbus discovered America. According to historians, Christopher Columbus was Genovese and, possessing an adventurous spirit, he requested and obtained permission and the necessary funds from the Spanish crown to cross the Atlantic in search of new lands. Equipped with three boats and eighty-eight men, he departed on his dangerous and daring adventure and finally discovered this continent after two months and nine days.

Other historical events regale the Spanish race. We also know of the work of the Jesuits, the principal Christian missionaries in India and North America. Their educational and civilizing campaigns among the Indians of South America and the social regard of the Spanish towards the conquered inhabitants of this continent reflects no less than the glory and splendor of Spain. According to the English historian Herbert G. Wells, their schools were the best in Christendom for a long time. "The Jesuits," according to Wells, "raised the level of intelligence, quickened the conscience of all Catholic Europe and stimulated Protestant Europe to competitive educational efforts." Sir Francis Bacon, the distinguished English philosopher added: "As for the pedagogic part, consult the schools of the Jesuits, for nothing better has been put in practice."[76]

On the other hand, Spain's approach towards the conquered communities, I repeat, made the Spaniards the most important, noble, just and democratic conquerors in the world. They assimilated the Indians, gave them not only their religion, their language and their culture, but also their blood. And that is why those of us who carry in our veins the noble blood of Hidalgo and Cuauhtémoc celebrate with joy and well-founded pride El Día de la Raza, a Spanish and Indo Hispanic race that is as good as any because of its historical lineage and its intellectual and moral values. Ladies and gentlemen, may the heroic deeds of our ancestors help us challenge persons who show malice towards our race and seek to instill in us an inferiority complex by ignoring the great virtues and heroism in our history to the point of occasionally saying that we belong to an inferior and degenerate race.

It is lamentable that egoism can reach such an extreme form among humankind. Nevertheless, the whole world should know that we have unimpeachable proof of the importance and glory of our race. We could demonstrate this even if society denied us our earned sense of worth and burned the histories of the world—and the winds of time and the roar of the machine gun destroyed the magnificent temples that the Spanish and the indigenous people of Latin America built.

Protesting the Segregation of our Youth in Government Centers[77]

San Antonio, Texas
August 27, 1935

Honorable Lyndon B. Johnson
National Administration for Youth, Texas Director
604 Littlefield Building
Austin, Texas

Dear Mr. Johnson:

We understand that the Federal Emergency Relief Administration will establish centers for women, that the centers will include young, single women between sixteen and twenty-five years of age who are receiving relief support, and that each one of the young women will spend three months in centers of one hundred persons. We also know that the centers will offer special instruction in the vocational and literary fields and that the government will establish five centers—one in Dallas, one in Houston, one in Austin and two in San Antonio. The person in charge of the two camps in San Antonio believes that the program should separate the young Mexican and Anglo American women.[78]

I write to praise the good work that you are about to start, but I also wish to strongly protest the planned segregation. LULAC seeks to develop among the members of our race the best, purest and most perfect kind of true, loyal and progressive citizen of the United States of America, but we will surely fail if we do not receive the valuable and indispensable cooperation of our fellow Anglo-American citizens. As you know, Mr. Johnson, the segregation of these young women would make both groups more racially aware than they are already, and this does not even account for the mental confusion and uncertain attitudes that this segregation would cause. We are sure that you will agree that this would not help make the members of either group better Americans, nor would it extend the cordial relations that we fortunately have between our communities.

We are confident that for the good of our community and our country you will reconsider this and that instead of having two centers in San Antonio, you only establish one so that the members of our two great races from our beloved state of Texas can associate and fraternize freely—without unfavorable experiences of any kind. In this way, they would stand as symbols of the affection, friendship and good understanding justified by good and powerful reasons, and perfect the true democracy that the founders of this republic so wisely sought to establish.

Sincerely,
Alonso S. Perales, President
Education Commission, Council No. 16
League of United Latin American Citizens

Education Opportunities that We Should Exploit[79]

An Institute for Teachers of Adult Education is operating in Austin, and its purpose is to prepare teachers for effective teaching during the next academic year. Dr. Herschel T. Manuel, faculty member at the University of Texas and a good friend of our race, is the director and Dr. Carlos E. Castañeda, Latin American Librarian at the University of Texas, collaborates with him. Almost five hundred teachers from all parts of the state of Texas participate in the institute, including a large number of teachers of Mexican origin.

Two years ago the federal government, in cooperation with the state government and local school boards, initiated in Texas as well as in the other states of the union an instructional program for adults with two purposes. First, it provides employment to thousands of teachers and other persons trained to teach. Second, the program teaches adults that did not have the opportunity to educate themselves well during their youth and who day by day hope to acquire the knowledge necessary to better enjoy life, and be more intelligent and informed citizens. The adult night schools include English instruction, civic education, history, hygiene, Spanish, geography, arithmetic and many other subject areas. Attendance is free.

Dr. L. A. Woods, the superintendent of Public Education in Texas, and Mr. George Fern, director of the Program for Adult Education in the State, participated in the institute this year. Joining them were representatives of the Federal Emergency Relief Administration, including its director, Mr. Adam R. Johnson, as well as Dr. H. Y. Benedict, the University of Texas president, and Dr. Manuel.

The success of the institute has been very gratifying. The adults have responded with genuine enthusiasm. Mr. Aubrey Williams, an official with the Federal Emergency Relief Administration, estimates that one million, seven hundred thousand adults throughout the nation participated in the classes during March, and that five thousand unschooled adults learned to read and write in English last year. Mr. Williams calculated that approximately ten to twelve million persons in the nation still cannot read or write, or if they are able, they cannot read or write well. This tells us that the federal government, the state governments and educational institutions are more interested than ever in this very important and constructive work, and they are prepared to resume the activities in September.

We are encouraged and pleased with the future of our race in this country because our community has cooperated well in this great educational project. Judging from reports of the work in Alice, McAllen, Raymondville, Del Rio, Kingsville, Laredo and other communities, Mexicans have embraced with trust and enthusiasm the idea of educating themselves.

May we respond to this year's wonderful opportunity with even greater enthusiasm?

San Antonio, Texas
August 28, 1935

The Sanitary Commission Met and Discussed the West Side in the Meeting[80]

Led by its president, Dr. Arthur R. McKinstry, the Sanitary Commission of the San Antonio Chamber of Commerce met on Friday at the Bluebonnet Hotel, and decided to forward a petition to the mayor and city council members, the judge and commissioners of Bexar County and school officials. The petition requests the establishment of a politically independent sanitation department to more effectively address the problem of sanitation.

During the meeting, they read an editorial that appeared in one of the local newspapers Friday afternoon. The writer cited a report produced by the United States Public Health Service on the sanitary conditions in the city of San Antonio.[81]

> There may not be another city in Texas where medical service against venereal disease is more needed than in San Antonio. This is due primarily to the unusually large Mexican population and the proximity of a large military camp.

Alonso S. Perales, a member of the Sanitary Commission of the Chamber of Commerce of San Antonio, stated the following:

> I wish to offer the same clarification that I recently made when this commission met jointly with the board of the Chamber of Commerce in the Plaza Hotel to discuss this important issue. I very much regret that the Sanitary Commission of the United States of America did not communicate

with me when they prepared their report. I would have suggested that they tell the WHOLE TRUTH.

Perales added,

> The reason for the high incidence of venereal diseases in San Antonio is not due to the large Mexican population, but to the existence of a large district of houses of ill repute on the west side of the city **against the will of the Mexican community**. On numerous occasions, the Mexican community has asked the mayor and the members of the city council to close these houses and they have refused to do it. It is obvious that if such places did not exist in this city, we would not have venereal diseases. We are, thus, victims of the inattention of our city officials and the indifference of many of our friends and fellow Anglo American citizens. The same problem occurs with the miserable housing in Mexican neighborhoods, the same ones that the federal report cites. The *corrales* and *jacales* are in a horrible and unhygienic condition. Despite this, the city officials of San Antonio and the owners of said *corrales* and *jacales* expect that the Mexican renters live in them.[82]

The participants in the meeting included Dr. T. J. McCamant, Director of Sanitation of the City of El Paso, Texas; the Reverend Arthur R. Mckinstry, President of the Sanitation Commission of the Chamber of Commerce of San Antonio; Dr. Thomas Dorbandt, Dr. W. B. Russ and the Reverend A. C. Tranchese. Rabbi Ephrain Frisch, Alonso S. Perales, Engineer Terrell Bartlett, Attorney Oscar Powell, Mr. P. G. Lucas, Dr. E. V. DePew, Dr. T. N. Goodson, Mayor C. G. Sinclair from Fort Sam Houston and Mr. R. William Archer, General Manager of the San Antonio Chamber of Commerce also participated.

[*La Prensa*, San Antonio, TX, November 15, 1935.]

Another Protest Regarding Pensions, Prepared by Council 16 of the League of United Latin American Citizens[83]

On the initiative of Alonso S. Perales, LULAC Council No. 16 decided unanimously at its evening meeting of November 13 to send telegrams to Governor James V. Allred and local state representatives protesting the unfair distinctions made against citizens of Mexican origin by the Old Age Assistance Program approved by both sides of the legislature. They also resolved to notify the general president of LULAC of this action and to request that he address all the councils in Texas by telegram recommending that they send their own protests to Governor Allred and their state representatives.

When we interviewed Perales on this issue, he offered the following opinions:

> The unfavorable distinction that the pension law makes against citizens of Mexican origin is especially unjust since we all know that the citizens and residents of the state of Texas, without consideration of race or color, will be generating the funds for the pensions. As such, it would not be fair that a citizen of Saxon origin receive a pension of thirty dollars and a citizen of Mexican origin only ten or fifteen.
>
> It is not true that a pension of thirty dollars would be a luxury for some Mexicans, especially in these days of crisis when very little can be bought with a dollar. To speak of economic problems through a sociological lens and to talk of standards of living is fine in normal times but not during a Depression. If Mexicans have a lower standard of living than Anglo Americans, it is because employers pay them little for

their labor and not because they are satisfied with the norm. In other words, Mexicans in Texas are victims of exploitation.

Our fellow Anglo American citizens should behave differently. They should support the advancement of Mexicans instead of trying to keep them in the backward state where they have placed them. Pay them salaries and daily wages that are equal to Anglo Saxons and they will see how their standard of living will also rise.

[*La Prensa*, San Antonio, TX, November 15, 1935.]

Defending Humble Mexicans before the Civil Service Commission of the Police and Firefighters of San Antonio, Texas[84]

We have just finished hearing the witness declarations in the complaint presented by Profesor Manuel A. Urbina and other men. The complaint concerns an official who has acted arbitrarily and, what is worse, has not only viciously insulted the complainants and persons who accompanied them, but our entire race, our noble Raza. Furthermore, he has done this in front of women and children.

We are willing to overlook the arbitrary behavior of said official in reference to his unjust arrest of the esteemed Profesor and we are willing to forget that the official fired his gun in front of the assembled group. But we are not willing to tolerate and vehemently protest the filthy and vulgar language that he directed at everyone that was present, including women and children and, truth be told, towards our entire race, according to the declarations of the witnesses. We have demonstrated beyond any doubt that the officer in question was arbitrary and criminal. The witnesses, although poor, are honorable and responsible persons. Furthermore, I have been surprised that some of members of this Honorable Commission have questioned the witnesses concerning their citizenship. I wish to state for the record that according to the Constitution and the laws of our country, Mexican citizens have well-defined rights, and one of these is the right to bring charges against abusive public officials, and the word of those Mexican citizens is as good and valid as the word of American citizens. Things also work the other way around. The word of American citizens is as good before Mexican courts as is the word of Mexican citizens. Thus, the Commission should not doubt the word of three humble but honest Mexican citizens who come to make a declaration against the officer in question simply because they are citizens of Mexico or they believe that the Italian war against Ethiopia is one of the greatest injustices of our century. They have a constitutional right to say what they think despite the stated view by the aforementioned officer that he did not care at all for the constitution of the United States of America.

Members of the Commission, the truth is that the officer abused his authority, and it is time that we stop these abuses. I am sure that the four witnesses are not interested in firing the officer and denying his wife and children their daily bread. However, they do expect the Honorable Commission to impose a punishment so that the defendant and his colleagues in the police force finally learn that Mexicans, like the rest of the citizens and residents in our cosmopolitan city, have rights that all public officials and employees should respect. THEY HAVE TO RESPECT THEM regardless of their classification. One other thing, THEY SHOULD AND MUST RESPECT Mexican women, as humble as they may be.

I repeat, we have offered an abundance of evidence to establish **beyond a doubt** the just accusations by the complainants and, as such, this Honorable Commission should find the accused GUILTY and impose an appropriate punishment, in fairness to the victims of the abuse and for the good of this community.

The Parent-Teacher Association[85]

Educators established the Parent-Teacher Association in Washington, DC, on February 17, 1897.

The objectives and goals of the association are:

First: Promote the well-being of children in the home, school, church and the community; elevate the standards of home life, and secure laws that are more suitable for the care and protection of children.

Second: Strengthen relations between the home and the school so that parents and teachers can cooperate intelligently in the education of the children, and develop among educators and the public a united effort that can secure for all the children the greatest advantages in their physical, mental, moral and spiritual education.

As is evident, the basic principles of the association are truly sublime insofar as they seek the protection and advancement of our children. Latinos should ensure that all the schools that educate our Mexican children have a Parent-Teacher Association.

Our children of today will be the adults of tomorrow, and the future leaders of our race will come from among them. The stature of those leaders will depend on the care that we place on their intellectual and moral development. In other words, if we give them a good education and build their character during the first years of their lives, they will become productive leaders, which is precisely the kind of persons that will insure the more rapid progress of our community in Texas. Now then, this preparation represents a real challenge to the

Parent-Teacher Association as it addresses issues such as citizenship, juvenile protection, the education of parents, recreation, hygiene, savings, the education of the children, etc.

The association has branches in all the states of the American union, including the District of Columbia and Hawaii. On April 15, 1931, the total number of members reached 1,511,203, and the number of organizations 22,000. During the 1930-31 academic year, 17 colleges and universities offered courses on this movement of parents and teachers. The official organ of the association is *Child Welfare* and it has a circulation of 666,000. The association also prints and distributes pamphlets on numerous subjects related to children. All of this shows that the Parent-Teacher Association is a serious and valuable organization that deserves the support and cooperation of all parents that have children in school.

San Antonio, Texas
December 1935

Requesting School Facilities for Our Children: A Judgment Sought Against the School Board in the District Court[86]

[From *La Prensa*, San Antonio, Texas, January 30, 1936.]

The plaintiffs represent the South Side School Patrons League and LULAC Council No. 16 is intervening in the case.

The case by C. C. Hudson and other members of the South Side School Patrons League against the Independent School District of San Antonio and members of the school board began on Tuesday, at two in the afternoon. The legal action seeks to prevent the school board from proceeding with the construction plan that it has prepared and is about to put into effect. The plaintiffs are asking for an order from the District Court to prevent the action of the school board. They maintain that the school board is obligated to build a secondary school in the southern part of the city. The school board maintains that such a school not be built because there is no need for it there; and that additional schools should be built on the west side of the city to relieve overcrowding. Approximately 4,000 children attend half a day the only school that is available.

The Hicks, Dickson and Lange Law Firm represented the school board and Charles M. Dickson and N. A. Quintanilla, members of the firm, handled the case.

The school board bases its views on their studies. Experts from the University of Texas came to San Antonio recently to study the situation themselves and make recommendations.

Attorneys Robert W. B. Terrell and J. C. Hall represent the plaintiffs.

LULAC Council No. 16 is seriously interested in securing adequate school facilities for children from the west side of the city and began fighting two years ago to secure these accommodations. The council intervened in the case with attorneys from the Davis, Wright and Perales Firm, with Alonso S. Perales serving as the lead attorney. The request for the intervention by LULAC was presented by Matías C. Trub, President Council No. 16, Pablo A. Meza, President of the Committee on School Facilities, Perales, Florencio R. Flores, Lieutenant Colonel Francisco L. Chapa, Max García, Wenceslao Martínez, attorney Pablo G. González, Gregorio R. Salinas and E. F. Gariel, all members of Council No. 16.

The members of LULAC maintain that the court should deny the petition by the members of the South Side School Patrons League. The simple reason is that a committee of experts from the University of Texas conducted a careful study of the situation and advised that the southern part of the city does not need a school, but that the west side of the city really needs many elementary schools and that the board should build them there.

J. C. Hall argued on behalf of South Side School Patrons League on Tuesday, and Perales represented Council No. 16. Perales first read the petition of intervention and followed by saying, among other things, the following:

> One of the major goals of LULAC is to develop among the members of our race the best, purest and most perfect kind of true and loyal citizen of the United States of America. With this in mind, it is clear, Your Honor (speaking to the judge), that we are seriously interested in the education of our children. Clearly, it is our responsibility to fight—we have been doing this since two years ago—and to convince the San Antonio School Board to build more elementary schools on the west side of town, otherwise we will not be able to produce those pure and perfect types of true American citizens that we seek to develop. We conducted a careful and sensible study on the existing school situation and found that we need at least eighty-four more classrooms to educate our children.

We have come to the school board once, twice, three times and many more requesting more spacious school facilities. Finally, the school board officially assured us that they would give us the school facilities since they were also convinced of the urgent need. Also, the committee of experts from the University of Texas, as well as a committee of the very school board led by Superintendent J. C. Cochran agreed and made the same recommendation. Lastly, the school board determined that the funding was available and that the construction of the schools would begin right away. We thought that the matter was settled, but here comes the gentlemen from the South Side School Patrons League asking the District Court to order the school board not to use the funding to build schools where **they are needed**, but to spend it where **they are not needed**, namely, in the south side of the city.

Referring briefly to the purely legal side of this case, I respectfully declare that this Honorable Court does not have jurisdiction over it for the simple reason that the decisions of the courts consistently stand as follows:

First: The school boards have the power and discretionary right, as well as other forms of authority to spend school funds for the reasonable and necessary maintenance of the schools. Judgment: Adams vs. Miles (Civ. App.) 300 S. W. 211.

Second: The court rendered a decision on the judicial supervision of a school board in Barton vs. Vickery (Civ. App.) 189 S. W. 1103. It decided that when residents in a school district complained before the school board and appealed the case with the Superintendent of the County Schools, the Superintendent of Public Instruction for the state and the Education Board of the state the District Court had jurisdiction over the actions of the school board. The conditions included a failure to secure relief from the school board and the board's abuse of its discretionary authority. In the case before us, the plaintiffs are not in a position to prove that the San Antonio School Board has abused its discretionary authority when it refused to build a school in the south side of the city. According to the opinion of the experts of the University of Texas and many other persons, the school is not necessary. The members of LULAC are requesting protection in the event that the school board refused to provide the school facilities that we urgently need and to which we have a right according to the Constitution and laws of our nation.

Perales continued by citing several other verdicts that supported his argument and concluded with the following words:

Finally, Your Honor, in light of the reasons that we have presented, we humbly and respectfully pray before this Honorable Court that it refuse the plaintiffs the injunction that they seek. This will allow the Honorable School Board to continue with their decision to build the schools on the west side of the city. This will insure that our Mexican children will be properly educated and placed in the position to enjoy all the prerogatives of liberty and civilization assured to all citizens in our country.

Concerning the Home Beautification Contest[87]

A little more than a month ago, the mayor of the city of San Antonio issued a proclamation for a contest to beautify properties. It reads as follows:

WHEREAS, San Antonio has the distinction this year of having its 218th birthday, and to it goes the honor of having preserved the typical Spanish atmosphere of beauty, legendry, romance and song brought to South Texas by its early Spanish settlers, and

WHEREAS, the San Antonio Real Estate Board stands ready by means of its annual beautiful yards contest to contribute its share of community service to help promote civic pride and community health, and being especially anxious to make San Antonio the outstanding "City Beautiful" in Texas for 1936— "The Texas Centennial Year"—and in its efforts will be assisted by the City Federation of Women's Clubs, assuring for San Antonio an extensive campaign to enhance beautification which will materially add to the enjoyment and pleasure of its 1936 Centennial visitors, and

WHEREAS, such a program always finds the hearty approval of the City Fathers and deserves the active cooperation of every citizen and homeowner of San Antonio.

NOW, THEREFORE, I, Phil Wright, Acting Mayor of the City of San Antonio, issue this proclamation and dedicate the forthcoming months of March, April and May to be a period of home beautification and call upon every citizen in San Antonio to stand behind the San Antonio Real Estate Board in this noble civic moment and wherever possible assist to make San Antonio in 1936 one of the most "attractive" cities in America.

What a most beautiful and constructive initiative for our community!

Since the San Antonio Real Estate Board has asked for the support of Council No. 16 of LULAC, this nucleus of enthusiastic and sincere citizens has not hesitated in responding to the call. The members of LULAC are interested in all activity that seeks the progress and well-being of the Mexican community in this country.

We have a magnificent opportunity to demonstrate to our fellow Anglo-American citizens and neighbors that we are willing to cooperate in any civic affair that seeks to improve, dignify and beautify our community. Let us respond to their call.

We cannot fall short. To fail would be a terrible moral disaster for the Mexicans of San Antonio. LULAC wants to see all our racial brothers in the dignified and decorous position that they are due. We would otherwise feel so ashamed and demoralized.

[*La Prensa*, San Antonio, Texas, April 11, 1936.]

On the Convention of the Anti-Tuberculosis Association of Texas[88]

The Anti-Tuberculosis Association, whose president is Dr. Elva A. Wright of Houston, will host a very important Convention in Harlingen, Texas, on April 17 and 18. The purpose of the meeting will be to address in a comprehensive manner the issue of tuberculosis, that is, its presence, the methods used against it, what the Association is doing to counteract it, etc. Dr. Wright wants the Mexican community to take an interest in this problem and attend the convention.

Statistics demonstrate that a high percentage of people who suffer from tuberculosis, especially in South Texas, live in Mexican communities.

This is the reason why the Anti-Tuberculosis Association of Texas and its chapters from various counties do most of its great work among members of our race.

It is time that our leaders from Texas demonstrate more interest in our own problems. Many Mexicans are constantly declaring that they care about the progress and well-being of our community. I know of no better opportunity to demonstrate their sincerity than by participating in meetings like the one the Anti-Tuberculosis Association of Texas will be organizing.

[*La Prensa*, San Antonio, Texas, April 14, 1936.]

To the Pan American Round Tables, Rotary Clubs, Lion's Clubs, Kiwanis Clubs, Chambers of Commerce and other Organizations Interested in Promoting Understanding and Cooperation between the Peoples of Mexico and the United States of America[89]

I write to request that you consider a most important matter that calls for immediate remedial action on the part of all groups that are sincere when they state that they want the friendship of the Mexican people. I refer to the frequency with which Anglo American citizens injure or murder Mexican citizens in Texas, instances so frequent that it has become a custom for Anglo American landowners to deprive Mexican citizens their share of the harvest.[90]

I have in mind some very recent cases, including the one in which law enforcement officials from Zavala County brutalized brothers Nicolás and Simón Hernández. We also have the case of Modesto Herrera. Frank Bradshaw assaulted Herrera while he was walking home with his two older children. Herrera died, leaving a wife and ten children in a very difficult situation. An investigation has shown that when friends took the unfortunate and defenseless victim to a public hospital in Austin, they denied him medical attention.

Nicolás was shot three times and left to die. Fortunately, a friend took him to a private hospital and saved his life, for the time being. His condition is critical and he may die. Hospital representatives also say that Nicolás is permanently disabled. Zavala County does not have a public hospital, and the County Commissioners refused to pay the hospital bill despite the fact that the victim is penniless and an officer of the law deliberately and unjustly caused the injury. Authorities have not arrested anyone and, even if they do, the courts will probably not convict him. The person who killed Herrera is free with a horrendously low bail of one thousand dollars. We will now see if persons unjustly and without cause can deprive peaceful and defenseless Mexicans of their lives without being brought to justice at the capital of our state.

Regarding the cases in which large farms deny Mexican citizens their share of the harvest, they are so many as to constitute a legion. Almost all the cases are like the following: an Anglo American farmer enters into a contract with a Mexican that calls on the latter to harvest the crop and the former promises to pay with part of the yield. When harvest time arrives, the Anglo American, on the slightest pretext, will run the Mexican away from his farm without giving him any of the crop. Or else, he will offer an amount that is ridiculously lower than what the Mexican deserves.

I know that you will immediately respond by saying that aggrieved Mexicans can find remedy in court. Ordinarily, this would be correct. However, racial prejudice has created an abnormal situation in almost all of the towns and cities of Texas. **Public opinion does not favor Mexicans** and, as a result and with few exceptions, they lose before they can defend themselves against Anglo Americans.

The situation, such as it is, can only be resolved with the practical approach of changing public opinion, that is, by building empathy towards Mexicans in the hearts and minds of our fellow citizens and Anglo American friends of Texas. This is precisely where your organizations can provide a great service. It is your responsibility. You profess a desire to promote relations between our two great races and that you are interested in Pan Americanism. It behooves you, therefore, to take up this problem and solve it. You can do it. Your organizations are influential in your communities. You can write articles for your local newspapers and magazines and offer lectures to your local clubs and organizations, making special note of the virtues and good reputation of the Mexican people. In that way, you would promote among your readers and audiences empathy towards us. You should not be so concerned that people call you Mexican lovers to disregard the opportunity to champion the well-meaning Mexican cause. You can respond to anyone who calls you this by stating that you are TRUE, GENUINE AMERICANS AND NOT HYPOCRITICAL PAN AMERICANS. The **true Anglo American friends** of the Mexican people should rise up and openly insist on the just treatment of Mexicans in Texas. You should also call on society to treat them as human beings, not as slaves and outcasts. We need persons of Anglo American descent to defend us in the courts and the press. We are already doing our part to warrant recognition and respect. Our efforts, however, will be for nothing without your support and cooperation.

In order to defend the Mexican cause, you can cite the irrefutable facts. Mexico once owned this territory. The independence of Texas would not have been possible without the assistance of persons of Mexican extraction who gave their lives for the cause of freedom and justice. Moreover, Mexicans have helped to make Texas what it is today. Lastly, Mexico is Texas' best trade partner. Even if we were to view the matter from a purely economic standpoint, Mexico could reward the people of Texas for treating them fairly. After all, Mexico offers her own remedy—she buys from Texas more goods than Texas buys from her. If the people of Texas do not treat Mexican nationals justly and fairly, Mexico might stop buying from Texas, or perhaps the United States altogether. I am not saying that Mexico will do this, I am merely pointing out what Mexico might do if we Texans wear out her patience.

In this regard, I think it is appropriate to point out the official trade figures. We imported $42,326,000 worth of Mexican goods and exported $65,576,000.

All of this has relevance to the bad treatment that Mexican citizens receive in Texas. I will follow with a brief account of the situation of American citizens of Mexican origin. It is identical to the case of Mexican citizens.

LULAC, a civic and patriotic organization that I co-founded and promote, seeks to produce among its Mexican members the best, purest and most perfect kind of true and loyal citizen of the United States of America. Obviously, in order to meet our objective, we need adequate school facilities for our children. However, the majority of the towns and cities of Texas provide inferior school facilities to Mexican children. In some places, like Ozona for example, our children do not receive secondary schooling because school officials do not allow them to attend alongside the Anglo American students. What is true regarding school facilities is also the case with other conditions that are necessary for the advancement of our citizens. An indisputable fact is that racial prejudice in Texas significantly inhibits persons of Mexican origin, regardless of whether they are citizens of Mexico or the United States. Despite this, we Texans often hold banquets to express with flowery speeches our feelings of goodwill and international solidarity. We do this without recognizing that we can win the hearts of the Mexican people by granting them justice in Texas instead of holding these empty banquets and offering superficial expressions of goodwill.

In conclusion, if we are to ever understand the true meaning of Pan Americanism and establish a solid form of legitimate and genuine Americanism in our state, we have to end this unfortunate situation. We can accomplish this with a campaign, initiated and carried out in a permanent and resolute manner by Anglo Saxons. This movement would seek to replace the problems of prejudice and injustices against Mexicans with sympathy, friendship and justice.

San Antonio, Texas
May 1936

A Protest against Poems that Are Offensive to Mexican People[91]

San Antonio, Texas
May 20, 1936

Honorable Robert S. Menefee President, San Antonio School Board

Dear Mr. Menefee:

On behalf of LULAC Council No. 16, I strongly protest the publication of two poems, "The Tortilla Makers" and "Peons," on pages 65 and 66 of *If Crickets Hear* (a book of original poems published by students of Thomas Jefferson High School). I have attached them.

I am sorry to have to tell you that the poems are not fair to the Mexican people and do great harm to the cause of international cooperation and good will.

We would greatly appreciate it if you removed the poems before the book begins circulating.

Sincerely,
Alonso S. Perales, President
Justice Committee
LULAC Council No. 16

Our Forthcoming Convention and the Future of Our School Children[92]

The seventh annual LULAC convention will take place in Laredo, Texas on June 6 and 7. The organization includes American citizens of Mexican origin and it seeks to promote the intellectual, economic, political and social advancement of Mexican Americans and La Raza population in this country. In other words, we wish to see Mexican Americans progress faster than ever and educate themselves as well as possible. We want to see that they meet all their obligations as citizens and learn to respectfully but firmly demand respect for their constitutional rights. Ideal citizens meet their obligations as citizens and know how to defend their rights. We are also very interested in the progress of **all** our race. This writer has the honor of being the past General President and one of the founders of LULAC. I am, and have always been, an active member of our league for the simple reason that I believe that it is the best organization to support the progress of Mexican Americans and our race as a whole in the United States. We established LULAC in Corpus Christi, Texas, on February 17, 1929. Three groups of citizens came together to form the organization, namely, League of Latin American Citizens, with nine councils (established on the initiative of yours truly in Harlingen, Texas, on August 14, 1927), the Corpus Christi Council of the Orden Hijos de América and the Orden Caballeros de América, consisting of only one council from San Antonio.

LULAC has put its principles into action and, to the extent that the public has recognized the work of the organization, its popularity has grown. For example, one of our representatives, Mr. Ben Garza of Corpus Christi, past general president and a co-founder of our organization, testified before the Congressional Committee on Immigration in January 1930 and refuted the charge that Mexican immigrants live almost their entire life here and never seek American citizenship. The idea was to place a quota on Mexico much like with other countries.

Our league again demonstrated its courage when school officials from Del Rio, Texas, sought to segregate our children in public schools. In this case, our league cooperated with the Comité Pro-Defensa Escolar de Del Rio (the Del Rio School Defense Committee).[93]

The case reached the US Supreme Court and, although the outcome was not as good as we expected, we gained much since the United States Court of Appeals for the Fourth Circuit declared that it was unlawful to segregate students in the public schools of Texas simply because they were of Mexican origin.

On the other hand, our league has done good work in the civic arena. In addition to constantly preaching the gospel of education, we seek to insure that our members vote intelligently and elect persons to public office who will give us our just due. Our league is not a partisan organization. We advise Latin Americans to be good citizens, to pay their poll tax and vote intelligently and conscientiously to elect persons who will govern us effectively and honestly. We also advise them to be especially careful not to place in office persons that hate our race. Our organization never endorses, nor can it endorse, candidates, and members have the absolute freedom to vote as they choose. As far as our civic-social work is concerned, it is enough to read the activities report of Council 16 of San Antonio, Texas, from June 1935 until June 1936 to understand the importance of our league to the progress and well-being of our race in this country. The following are the standing committees of Council 16: Education, School Facilities, Young Explorers of America, Legal assistance, Health, Houses of Prostitution, Homes, Recreational Centers, Poll Taxes and Justice. If every city in the State of Texas established a committed and hardworking organization like Council No. 16, or any other civic organization of men and women **fully determined to work enthusiastically and continually for the common good**, our race in Texas would quickly advance. We would move up swiftly and establish ourselves as a progressive community. Parenthetically, on the subject of progress, we must be convinced that our progress is necessary to gain the recognition and respect that we demand as citizens or residents of this country. It is obvious that if we continue to pull our children out of school when they reach the third grade—as most of our people customarily do—and fail to maintain our persons and properties in a clean manner, we will not obtain what we seek. In other words, people constantly see us as ignorant and dirty. Our obligation, therefore, is to demonstrate that this is not true, **and the only way to do this is through action, not words.** Let us educate ourselves as much as possible, all the while insuring the cleanliness of our persons, homes and vacant lots. Our personal appearances and the look of our homes have much to do with how others see us.

The annual Convention at Laredo will be engaging, interesting and instructive because the planning committee, made up of two select groups of men and women and led by Mrs. R. G. García and Mr. Juan G. Villarreal, spared no effort to make the forthcoming convention the best and biggest gathering in the history of our League. Delegates will arrive from numerous Texas cities, including many Latin Americans and Mexican citizens who sympathize with the ideals of LULAC. They know our goals and objectives and are using the opportunity to demonstrate in clear fashion their adherence to the constructive and grand effort that that we are making in the Lone Star State.

During the evening of Saturday, June 7, we will host a royal banquet in one of the main hotels of Laredo and hear an address by the distinguished attorney Mr. Juan A. Valls, a Latin American who has earned the respect and esteem of everyone who know his vast learning, righteousness and honesty.[94]

On Sunday, starting at two in the afternoon, a very interesting literary and musical performance will take place in the auditorium of the Louis J. Christen School.

Dr. Herschel T. Manuel, psychology professor from the University of Texas will speak on the important topic of "Children of all the People." He is well known and liked in the Mexican community of Texas because he has distinguished himself with his profound knowledge of the challenge of teaching children, and especially the issue of school facilities. He authored *The Education of Mexican and Spanish-Speaking Children in Texas* and other related studies. Dr. Manuel stands out as a vigorous defender of Mexican children and advocates in plain language and without equivocation for school facilities that are equal to the Anglo American children. It will be very interesting to hear what he has to tell us on Sunday afternoon, June 7. Everything will work out, especially because Dr. L. A. Woods, the State Superintendent of Public Education who has also distinguished himself with his just and equitable approach to many school issues, will follow Dr. Manuel. His important position in the school system of Texas means that he can help, especially with a determined pursuit of equal school facilities for our children. LULAC has already tested him and he has not disappointed us. Dr. Woods has always responded to our requests for help. In 1934, he helped us convince Goliad school officials to admit Mexican children into their high school, and he is now working with us in persuading school officials from Ozona to do the same. It will be interesting to see how Dr. Woods responds to the scientific and masterly presentation of facts, figures and photographs that Dr. Manuel will use to demonstrate that school facilities assigned to the Mexican children in Texas **are inferior**. This issue speaks to our constitution and by-laws, that is, ALL children, regardless of race, religion or political affiliation have the right to **equal school facilities.**

Gustavo C. García, the young law student at the University of Texas who has stood out because of his intelligence and love of learning, will also speak.

Clearly, the literary-musical program scheduled for Sunday afternoon promises to be very interesting and instructive for the residents of Texas who have the blood of Hidalgo and Cuauhtémoc running through their veins.

The convention's singular and welcoming environment will offer an added attraction to our delegates. American citizens of Mexican origin should be proud that Laredo is one of the few cities where Mexicans, regardless of their citizenship, can feel at home. The Latin American element predominates in all facets of life. They have the opportunity to attain distinction and succeed in finance, politics, business and social pursuits. The racial prejudice that might otherwise prevent the progress of the Mexican or any other member of our race does not exist. Latin Americans from Laredo know perfectly well the bad treatment that our race faces in many counties throughout Texas and, despite this, do not harbor prejudice, nor do they seek vengeance or reprisals against anyone. In other words, Latin Americans from Webb County have shown that they are **good and genuine American** citizens with their views and behavior. If only this same fair and just spirit existed among all the inhabitants of the two hundred and forty counties of the Lone Star State. This would be good for the nation. The fair, fraternal and harmonious spirit that characterizes Latin Americans from Laredo was no doubt in the minds of Seguín, Navarro, Ruiz, Benavidez, Badillo, Esparza, Fuentes, Guerrero, Losoya, Nava and other racial brothers when they decided to lend their valuable support for democracy in Texas in 1836.[95] Long live Laredo! Long live LULAC!

San Antonio, Texas
June 2, 1936

The True Mission of Our League[96]

As is well known, LULAC is not a partisan political club but an organization that promotes the general progress of our race in the United States of America. We meet our purpose when a council creates its committees, meets regularly and sets out to work.

*Report on the Work of Council No. 16 of San Antonio,
June 1935 to June 1936*

The Education Committee, chaired by Alonso S. Perales, worked with school officials in re-opening night schools for adults and cooperated with state and federal school officials to inform the public about government help for studious youth seeking to complete secondary school and university studies. The Committee has also counseled studious Mexican youth who have sought help and guidance, offered presentations to parent-teacher associations and other groups, worked with the Association of the Mexican Library, and sought improved school facilities alongside the Association of Parents and Latin American Teachers from Ozona, Texas. Ozona offers inferior elementary school facilities to Mexican children compared to the ones provided Anglo American children. Because of this, our children are not receiving secondary schooling in Ozona. The Education Committee has also worked with the Health Committee of Council 16 and with the Anti-Tuberculosis Association of Texas and Bexar County in observance of the Latin American Pro-Health Week of San Antonio and other communities. The Education Committee has collaborated in all cultural activities in which fellow organizations have invited them to participate.

The School Facilities Committee, directed by Mr. Pablo A. Meza, with members Perales, Florencio R. Flores and Max García, has worked diligently to secure adequate school facilities for Mexican children on the west side of San Antonio. The Committee is glad to report that the School Board of San Antonio expressed an interest in serving our children at the same time that it initiated a construction project on the west side. The Board will spend a total of two hundred thousand dollars, with one hundred and thirty-eight thousand dollars reserved for improvements to Sidney Lanier School.

The Boy Scouts of America Committee, led by Mr. Matías C. Trub, has organized several troops on the west side of the city and has been taking a comprehensive approach to publicizing this work.

The Legal Assistance Committee, chaired by Attorney Pablo G. Gonzales with attorney Isidoro R. Flores as a member, has extended important help to needy and deserving persons who were about to lose their homes.

The Health Committee, headed by Dr. Hesiquio N. Gonzalez with Drs. Rodolfo O. Monsalvo and Orlando F. Gerodetti as members, has been exemplary in promoting the Latin American Pro-Health Week during 1934, 1935 and 1936. The Committee does this in association with the Anti-Tuberculosis Association of Texas and Bexar County. During the Latin American Pro-Health Week, the committee makes the necessary arrangements for conferences and film screenings on health and hygiene in schools, churches, etc. Thousands participate in these meetings. The committee has also collaborated with charitable organizations that request its assistance.

Council 16 is pleased to announce that its repeated initiatives in favor of adequate drainage services on the west side are finally producing results. City officials have been installing approximately twenty miles of drainage pipes in that part of the city.

The Anti-Red Districts Committee, chaired by Mr. Florencio R. Flores, including Mr. Pablo A. Meza, Mr. Max García and Perales as members, has continued to work with tenacity and passion to close the brothels and cribs located along streets that school children take on the way to school. The committee is pleased to announce that its efforts have met with success. This year, the committee has expanded its sphere of activity by calling for the closing of ALL brothels and cribs established on the west side against the wishes of the Mexican community. The houses are a blight and an affront to the general community, aside from contributing to the spread of diseases and all kinds of vices. The committee expects that city, county and state officials will close the houses in accordance with our laws, as a statement of fairness to the Mexican people of San Antonio and for the good of the entire community.

The Residential Homes Committee, presided by Mr. Jorge D. Vann, with Perales, Mr. Florencio R. Flores, and Mr. Pablo A. Meza as members, has worked with Reverend C. Tranchese, Rector of Guadalupe Church, to replace the unhygienic *corrales* and *jacales* on the west side of the city with hygienic and habitable homes.

The Recreational Centers Committee, headed by Mr. Pablo A. Meza, and made up of Lieutenant Colonel Francisco L. Chapa, Perales, Mr. Florencio R. Flores and Mr. Max García, has collaborated with the Civic Club of Latin American Ladies to convince city officials to construct adequate recreational centers for children on the west side. Its efforts have not been in vain. Reliable sources have informed the committee that the City of San Antonio bought a plot of land in a good location. It will be **fully accessible** to a large number of children on the west side.

The Committee for the Poll Tax, chaired by Mr. Carlos Albidress, with Perales as member, has urged Latin American voters from Bexar County to pay the Poll Tax before the first day of February of 1935. The committee, with the help of several members of Council 16, printed and distributed ten thousand issues of *Actualidad*, the annual publication of the Committee.

The Latin American Cadets Committee, led by the Lieutenant Colonel Francisco L. Chapa, is organizing a group of Latin American cadets at Sidney Lanier School.

The Justice Committee, led by Alonso S. Perales and made up of attorneys Isidoro R. Flores and Pablo G. González, continues to fight racial prejudice against our race. When necessary, the Committee has reminded government officials on the provisions of the Constitution that guarantee everyone equal rights, equal protection under the law and equal opportunities and privileges. Recently, the committee pointed out to the organizations responsible for the city's centennial ceremonies that when they sought to honor the memory of everyone who took part in the fight for the independence of Texas, they should have noted the Tejano heroes. The organizations disregarded them completely like this past March during the commemoration of the fall of the Alamo.

The Committee Pro-Plaza Típica Mexicana. Perales presided over the committee, while Mr. Florencio R. Flores, Mr. Pablo A. Meza, Mr. Max García and Lieutenant Colonel Francisco L. Chapa served as members. They sought to persuade the Centenary Committee of San Antonio to spend seventy-five thousand dollars to construct a typical Mexican plaza like the ones in the Republic of Mexico. It could become a major city attraction, especially with the tourists. The committee was not successful since the Centenary Committee decided to spend the money on a stadium and other things. At any rate, the LULAC proposal left a deep and long-lasting impression.

The Home Beautification Committee. Mr. Carlos Albidress chairs the committee. The members include Mr. Florencio R Flores, Mr. Homero Whitt, Mr. Matías C. Trub, Perales, Mr. Jorge D. Vann, Mr. Agustín A. González, Lieutenant Colonel Francisco L. Chapa, Mr. José C. Ramírez, Mr. Max García, Mr. E. F. Gariel, Mr. Manuel D. Imperial,

Mr. Wenceslao Martínez, Attorney Pablo G. González, Mr. Manuel Maese, Mr. Pablo A. Meza, Mr. Mauro M. Machado, Mr. Eleuterio Hernández, Mr. Ernesto Vidales, Mr. Alex Reyes, Mr. Gregorio R. Salinas, and Dr. Rodolfo O. Monsalvo. The committee is participating in a home beautification contest on the west side. It works with the Real Estate Board and the Federation of Women's Clubs from San Antonio. The group will give prizes at the end of the contest on July 1, 1936. Its members believe that the committee has an excellent opportunity to demonstrate to our Anglo American friends and fellow citizens that Latin Americans will cooperate in any civic activity to improve, dignify, and beautify our communities.

The Entertainment Committee. Mr. Manuel Maese chairs the committee, which includes Mr. Max García, Mr. Florencio R. Flores, Mr. José Ramírez, Mr. Eleuterio Hernández and Mr. Rodolfo Ramirez. The committee has prepared various programs for the enjoyment of Council No. 16 members and their friends.

The Committee for the Observance of Music Week, chaired by Mr. Jorge D. Vann, includes the following members: Lieutenant Colonel Francisco L. Chapa, Mr. E. F. Gariel, Mr. Homero Whitt, Matías C. Trub, Mr. Florencio R. Flores, Mr. Carlos Albidress, Mr. Manuel Maese, Mr. Ernesto Vidales and Perales. The Committee led the participation of Council No. 16 in this year's National Week of Music. Mrs. Eli Hertzberg, National Representative, and Mrs. Ester Pérez Carvajal, General President of the National Association for the Observance of Music Week in San Antonio, invited the Committee to participate.

The Child Protective Committee, presided by Mr. Keno Guerrero, with the support of Mr. Alex Reyes and José M. Rodríguez, has been doing a wonderful job with delinquent Mexican youth. The committee, in cooperation with county officials, has established a system whereby businesspersons and professionals counsel youth who face problems for the first time on how to become **good** citizens.

The Forthcoming Elections and the Future of Our Children[97]

This month, intelligent and socially aware Mexican Americans from Texas can take a decisive step in supporting Mexican youth in our schools by endorsing the resolution adopted by LULAC in their Laredo convention on June 6 and 7. The resolution recommends that Latin American voters support candidates to the Texas Legislature that, once elected, will approve a law that gives the Superintendent of Public Education the authority to deny funding to any common or independent school district that does not provide **all** the children the school facilities that the Constitution and laws of Texas guarantees them. The State of Texas pays each district an annual sum of seventeen dollars and fifty cents (the amount will be twenty dollars next year) for the education of each child registered in the previous school census. Obviously, apart from the money that the state provides each district, local officials assess property values and collect taxes and in that way assign additional funds to the schools. The amount that the state grants to the districts is considerable. It is also common knowledge that many Texas school districts assign Mexican children to schools that are in the poorest conditions. They are mostly educated in run-down shacks while the Anglo American children receive instruction in modern and magnificent brick buildings. In some districts, like in Ozona, school officials do not allow Mexican children to attend their high school. Anyone who is interested in learning about this can read *The Education of Mexican and Spanish-Speaking Children in Texas*, the masterful work of Dr. Herschel T. Manuel, Professor of Psychology at the University of Texas, or they can inspect any school to see that our race does not receive justice. Some could ask why this occurs if the Constitution and the laws of Texas call for

equal school facilities for **all** the children. This is the answer: it happens because of the arbitrary actions of unjust school boards that spend a small part of their money on our children and the rest on the Anglo American youth. The members of the school boards are not entirely to blame for the problem. The voters who elected them are also responsible when they insist on spending most of the money on the Anglo American children. At the same time, no one can dispute that the boards have absolute control over school matters. It follows that if they wanted, they could do what is right, even if the people who elected them contracted cholera in the process. The result of this deplorable situation is that the Anglo-American children are educated in palaces, ours in huts and shacks.

It is true that the parents of the Mexican children can, if they vote, select school board candidates that will be fair to our children. In the majority of cases, however, Latin American voters are a minority and almost all the Saxons believe that the Mexican should not be educated, that it is useless. It is also obvious that the aggrieved can appeal before the tribunals of justice to demand that the school boards observe the law. Unfortunately, this is not effective. First, the general environment in which the proceedings occur is unfriendly to our race. Secondly, we need money in order to file a case, and we have none. The best alternative is what LULAC recently suggested at its Laredo convention. It would be a cause for celebration if intelligent and conscientious Latin American voters agreed with us and insisted that candidates to the Texas Legislature who seek their vote on June 25 support a bill that we proposed. The bill would give the Superintendent for Public Instruction the authority to deny funding to school districts that do not provide to **all** the children the **equal** school facilities they are entitled according to the Constitution and our laws.

San Antonio, Texas
July 1936

The Next Elections and the Future of Our Raza[98]

We all know that ours is a representative republic. That is, we live in a republic and the men that we select govern us with that in mind. Our country—the United States of America—undoubtedly comes close to being a true democracy. Speaking in general terms, its citizens can express with greater freedom their preference at the ballot box. They can vote for anyone they wish without fear of retaliations or vengeful actions. Citizens know that officials count their votes fairly.

Of course, exceptions exist. In some counties, criminals have unjustly and needlessly denied peaceful citizens their lives and authorities have not punished them. In these places, the sheriff is like a king that can trample an individual's rights at will. All kinds of shenanigans occur during elections when circumstances dash away the hopes of free and honest citizens. These abuses, however, are due to apathy and indifference and, often, to the lack of civic courage among the people. If we reflect for a moment, these abusive officials are obviously the servants of the people and the people can overthrow them with a majority vote whenever they wish. Mexican-American voters of Texas should always remember that our progress and well-being largely depend on how we act politically. We have to be intelligent and conscientious voters and must elect able, righteous and honest persons.

Everyone knows that Texas has counties where Mexicans suffer the unspeakable partly because of racial prejudice and because of the despotism of the officials who govern in them. In Wharton County, for example, Mexican Americans cannot vote in the primary elections, supposedly because they do not belong to the white race.

In Raymondville, Willacy County, the same kind of officials and a sheriff took a group of Mexicans out of jail and into the brush in 1926, and killed them like dogs. Even today, an Anglo Saxon can treat a citizen of Mexican origin in the most villainous and cowardly manner with impunity.

In Ozona, Crockett County, school officials do not allow our youth to attend high school simply because they are Mexicans.

In Crystal City and La Pryor, Zavalla County, Mexicans suffer all kinds of abuses at the hands of well-known officials and their friends who never pay for their crimes. These are typical cases occurring in many Texas counties.

It is an irrefutable fact that, given the form of government that we have, one of the best ways to correct this situation is for the Mexican-American voter to decide to act intelligently and conscientiously during election time. For instance, on the twenty-fifth of this month, we will elect everyone, from the governor of the state to the constable in our precinct. This is the moment to approach all the candidates, especially persons seeking to be judges, attorney general, legislators and sheriffs. We need to tell them that we are tired of the abuses against our race and that we are now giving our vote to competent and honest persons. Above all, we will vote for persons that will respect and protect Mexicans in accordance with their constitutional rights and regardless of their citizenship. It is time that Mexican Americans vote for their own good, namely, to secure the justice that they deserve and to which they are entitled according to our Constitution and our laws, and in that way assure a future for our race in the Lone Star State.

San Antonio, Texas
July 1936

The Mexican American and the Recent Elections[99]

Mexican Americans, like myself, who have long observed the political behavior of Mexican Americans in South Texas, should feel very gratified, because the recent elections have placed a bright horizon before our race in the Lone Star State. Simply put, we can see that Mexican Americans have begun to vote **intelligently and conscientiously** and they reject the usual practice by political bosses who take groups to the ballot boxes, well coached on how and for whom to vote. In other words, Mexican Americans, fortunately for our nation and our race, have started **to think for themselves**, and to elect able, righteous and honest persons that are clearly determined to help us solve civic-social problems that affect the progress and well-being of our Raza.

This trend is very beneficial and honors any republic. Intelligent citizens are clearly necessary if a government is to exist of the people, by the people and for the people.

Indeed, public officials are in a position to realize works that can bring great benefit to the community. For instance, officials could insure that districts provide all children good schools and competent teachers, that grocery stores practice the highest form of hygiene and that the **entire** community enjoy a good drainage system. Local government could build parks for the enjoyment of **all** inhabitants, clean and pave the streets or at least maintain them in good condition and free the public of criminals, smugglers and vice-ridden elements who do harm. Residents, regardless of race, color or political and religious creed, could observe city, state and federal laws and courts could render justice to everyone. Lastly, city, county and state governments could promote measures that benefit everyone, at least the majority, and, depending on the case, insure that no one directs unfavorable distinctions at a minority simply because of their race, color or creed. Public officials that are interested in these things and that truly seek to do **everything** related to progress and the well-being of the people are good public servants and represent the ideal that the people should insist to have in power at all times. They deserve the admiration, support and votes of all good citizens.

With respect to Mexican-American citizens, we have problems of vital importance to our progress and well-being that must be resolved. For instance, Mexican-origin persons face the unspeakable in almost all cities and counties. I will be more explicit. Authorities do not provide our children adequate school facilities, public officials neglect our housing areas, including the streets, drainage and general hygiene issues and officials and others assault, abuse and humiliate our people in controversies between Mexicans and Anglo Americans. Mexicans always end up losing. This means that in some places public officials do not care about Mexicans and, therefore, fail in their duties. It means that they are **not good public officials** as far as the residents of Mexican origin are concerned.

I repeat what I have always said: the solution is to some extent in the hands of the Mexican-American voters. Mexican Americans have to tell the candidates with all frankness that the voters of today are not like the ones from yesterday. Politicians can no long take Mexican Americans to the ballot box like uninformed persons or automatons. They do not sell their votes, not for a beer or for any amount of money. The modern Mexican Americans are intelligent and conscientious and only vote for **good officials,** for able, righteous, just and honest candidates who are sincere in helping us solve our civic-social problems. In other words, the Mexican Americans of today want and **insist on** public officials who will be fair with our Raza.

The Mexican American and the Recent Elections II[100]

We, the Mexican Americans from San Antonio, have been working for years to solve important problems that are before us. We have called for adequate school facilities for our children, the installation of drainage amenities and the construction of hygienic and habitable homes in areas where none exist so that we can more effectively fight tuberculosis and other diseases that ravage our poor. We have sought to close the red light district for the protection of our children and for the good of our entire community, to establish recreational centers that are adequate for the children of the west side and, last but not least, we have fought for better Latin American representation in our city and county. Because of this, we have been more careful lately to vote for candidates that promise to work with us in making our wishes a reality. Our firm objective took palpable form in the recent county election. During scheduled meetings, Latin American orators underscored the absolute need to elect candidates willing to work with us in resolving our numerous civic-social problems and, although our victory was not complete, we are convinced that Mexican American voters are advancing slowly but surely. Even more, it seems that politicians can no longer buy the majority of the Mexican American voters of Bexar County with a beer, a pat on the back or money. On the contrary, they are intelligent, fully conscious of their rights and obligations and they give their votes to able, righteous and honest candidates. They are also fully determined to provide our communities the schools, hygienic and habitable homes, drainage and other facilities that are essential to our progress and advancement as citizens.

It is clear that some persons have once again denied us the hope for adequate Latin American representation in local government but, even under these circumstances, we see a great improvement. In the election for County Commissioner place one, 10,331 citizens registered to vote and 4,492 of them voted for our Latin American candidate. The majority of the 5,839 votes given to the other candidate are understandable if we take into account the following problems. FIRST, the Anglo American citizen is not inclined to vote for a Mexican-American candidate. SECOND, public employees instruct the large group of Mexican Americans that work with the city and the county on how to vote. THIRD, the insufficiently informed Mexican Americans who lack social awareness and do not care about the advancement of our race or our community are only interested in selling their votes to the numerous racketeers that, unfortunately, are ready to pay. If we add to these issues that our candidate ran as an independent, that is, without the backing of any political organization, we can well explain our defeat in seeking adequate representation for Latin Americans in county government.

We are generally optimistic, however, and should be satisfied since the results demonstrate beyond any doubt that the number of self-respecting and intelligent Mexican-American citizens is growing in Bexar County while the unprepared and contemptible citizens are fewer day by day. Moreover, the masterly work of Dr. O. Douglas Weeks, *The Texas Mexican and the Politics of South Texas*, gives prophetic voice to our situation. After noting the various methods that the political bosses use to trick the Mexican-American voter, he notes:

> Regardless of such practices, there is indication of something different for the future. In the urban communities, in particular, "the younger generation," as one Mexican American expresses it, "though still timid, are the products of a better education—they are beginning to think for themselves and the time will inevitably come when newcomers, dissenters now in the old regime and enlightened Mexican Americans may rise to establish themselves.[101]

San Antonio, Texas
August 1936

[Published in *La Prensa*, August 4 and 5, 1936.]

How to Request School Facilities for Our Children[102]

According to the Constitution and laws of Texas, youth has a right to **equal school facilities**. As is well known, our Mexican youth enjoys facilities that are inferior to the ones assigned to Anglo American children in almost the entire State of Texas. In places like Ozona and Hondo, Latin American leaders are energetically struggling to secure justice for our children. Now then, the courts have decided on repeated occasions that before they can render a judgment to require the school boards to comply with the law and make available adequate school facilities for **all** the youth, the parties involved have to exhaust all possible remedies at the district level. Sometimes they arrive at good results without turning to the courts. In order to encourage the effective work of our leaders on behalf of our children, I take the liberty of suggesting the following:

We must first organize ourselves. All the mutual aid societies should join this cause. In other words, it is necessary to show that the Mexican-origin community, regardless of citizenship, supports our social movement.

Let us suppose that a common school district does not allow our children to attend their high school and maintains elementary school children in shacks at the same time that they teach Anglo Americans in splendid brick buildings. Well then, you send a petition to the school board in English, more or less as follows:

How to Request School Facilities for our Children[103]

_____, Texas
_____, 1936

Honorable Board of Trustees
_____, Common School District
_____, Texas

Gentlemen:

We, the undersigned taxpaying American citizens of Mexican or Spanish extraction, of _____, _____ County, Texas, being desirous in developing within the members of our race, the best, purest and most perfect kind of a true and loyal citizen of the United States of America, and to eradicate from our body politic all intents and tendencies to establish discrimination among our fellow citizens on account of race, religion or social position as being contrary to the true spirit of Democracy, our Constitution and Laws, respectfully make the following requests:

1. That children of Mexican or Spanish extraction be provided with school facilities equal to those furnished children of Anglo-American descent. We mean school buildings, equipment and recreational grounds as good as those provided for Anglo-American children. Furthermore, we request that competent teachers teach our children in the same proportion that they are provided for Anglo-American children.
2. That school officials allow children of Mexican or Spanish descent who have graduated from Grammar School to attend the High School available to other children in the _____ School District.

We base our requests upon the following constitutional and statutory provisions, which we are quoting. We are not saying that we consider ourselves colored, but remind you that under our Constitution and laws **all children** are entitled to equal school facilities, regardless of race, color or creed:

"Separate schools shall be provided for the white and colored children and impartial provision shall be made for both." (Constitution of Texas, Article VII, Section I).

"All available public school funds of this State shall be appropriated in each county for the education alike of white and colored children, and impartial provisions shall be made for both races. No white children shall attend schools supported for colored children, nor shall colored children attend schools supported for white children. The terms "colored race" and "colored children," as used in this title, include all persons of mixed blood descended from Negro ancestry. (Article 2900, Vernon's Annotated Texas Statutes, Volume 8).

"All children, without regard to color, over six years of age and under eighteen years of age at the beginning of any scholastic year, shall be included in the scholastic census and shall be entitled to the benefit of the public school fund for that year. The board of school trustees of any city or town, or independent or common school district, shall admit to the benefits of the public schools any person over six, and not over twenty-one years old at the beginning of the scholastic year, if such person or his parents or legal guardian reside within said city, town or district." (Article 2902, Vernon's Annotated Texas Statues, Volume 8).

"All person born or naturalized in the United States, and subject to the jurisdiction thereof, are citizens of the United States and of the state wherein they reside. **No state shall make or enforce any law which shall abridge the privileges or immunities of citizens of the United States; nor shall any state deprive any person of life, liberty or property, without due process of law; nor deny to any person within its jurisdiction the equal protection of the laws.**" (Article XIV, Section I, Constitution of the United States of America).

"**No citizen of this state shall be deprived of life, liberty, property, privileges or immunities, or in any manner disfranchised, except by the due course of the law of the land.**" (Article I, Section 19, Constitution of Texas).

We would especially invite your attention to the underscored portion of the preceding quotations from the Constitution of the United States of America and the Constitution of the State of Texas. Referring especially to the first constitutional provision above quoted, if the State of Texas cannot make or enforce any law which shall abridge the privileges or immunities of citizens of the United States, it follows that a school board, which is merely a creature of the Legislature of the State of Texas, cannot do so either.

In view of the foregoing, we are certain the Honorable Board of Trustees of the _____ Common School District will agree with us that to deny to us taxpaying citizens equal school facilities and the right to send our children to the high school now available for the children of this community is to deprive us of our rights under the Constitution of Texas and the laws of this state.

In asking you to respect our rights as citizens of the United State of America, we would remind you that we are now celebrating the one hundredth anniversary of Texas Independence, and that many a Texas Mexican fought side by side with their Anglo-American brethren, that Texas might come into being and that liberty, justice and democracy might be more firmly established. Never for a moment, we are certain, did those great and valiant Texas-Mexican and Anglo-American heroes imagine that the day would come when the descendants of those Texas-Mexican heroes might be deprived of their constitutional rights and privileges by their Anglo American brethren of Texas.

Gentlemen: we appeal to your sense of justice and fair play.

Respectfully submitted,
(Signatures here)

* * *

The largest number possible of presidents of societies should sign the petition, the original and four copies should be prepared. Next, prepare a letter for the president of the school board, more or less with the following language, and attach the original of the signed petition. The letter should be sent with the petition by certified mail, along with a request for an acknowledgment of receipt. In other words, write outside the envelope "Return Receipt Requested." This way, the president cannot say that he did not receive the letter.

* * *

_____, Texas
_____, 1936

Honorable _____
President, Board of Trustees
_____Common School District
_____Texas

Dear Sir:

    We are enclosing herewith a petition signed by taxpaying citizens of _____ County, Texas, respectfully requesting equal school facilities for children of Mexican or Spanish descent.

    We shall appreciate a reply, in writing, from your Honorable School Board not later than _____, 1936. If we do not hear from you by that date we shall assume that you refuse to grant our request and we shall govern ourselves accordingly.

    Please direct your reply to us to _____

Respectfully yours,

(One or two presidents can sign this letter, or everyone can do it if so desired).

    If the time period set by you is exceeded (it can be from fifteen to thirty days) and you have not received a response, send a letter that is more or less the same and also by certified mail, to Dr. L. A. Woods, State Superintendent of Public Instruction, Austin, Texas with a copy of the petition. You would report that neither the school board of the local district nor the County responded.

    If, after taking all these steps, you do not receive a response or you do not obtain satisfactory results, you can register a suit at the District Court to force the local school board to comply with the law over education.

    It would be convenient if you keep copies of the petition and the correspondence, as well as post office receipts, to use them in court if it becomes necessary.

When the issue emerges in an independent school district, you proceed in the same way, except when it is not necessary to write to the county's school board.

This author sincerely calls for the use of votes so that his racial brothers can secure school facilities for our children without having to turn to the courts.

San Antonio, Texas
September 1926

The Education of the Youth Is Obligatory: Chapter 18 Civil Statutes of Texas Compulsory Education[104]

Article 2892. Attendance Requirements. Every child in the State who is over seven years and not more than sixteen years of age shall be required to attend the public schools in the district of its residence, or in some other district to which it may be transferred as provided by law, for a period of not less than one hundred and twenty days. The period of compulsory school attendance at each school shall begin at the opening of the school term unless otherwise authorized by the district school trustees and notice given by the trustees prior to the beginning of such school term; provided that no child shall be required to attend school for a longer period than the maximum term of the public school in the district where such child resides.[105]

Article 2892a. Child attendance between seven and fifteen. Provided, however, that every child in counties in no less than three hundred and twenty-five thousand (325,000) population according to the preceding Census, who is seven years and no more than fifteen years old shall be required to attend the public school in the district of its residence or some other district to which it may be transferred, as provided by law, for the entire school term of the district in which said child attends school.

Article 2893. Exemptions. The following classes of children are exempt from the requirements of this law:

1. Any child in attendance in a private or parochial school which shall include in its course of study of good citizenship, and

shall make the English language the basis of instruction in all its subjects.
2. Any child whose bodily or mental condition is such as to render attendance inadvisable, and who holds definite certificate of a reputable physician specifying this condition and covering the period of absence.
3. Any child who is blind, deaf, dumb, or feeble-minded for the instruction of whom no adequate provision has been made by the school district.
4. Any child living more than two and one-half miles by direct and traveled road from the nearest public school provided for the children of the same race and color of such child and with no free transportation provided.
5. Any child more than twelve years of age who has successfully completed the work of the seventh grade of a standard elementary school of seven grades, and whose services are needed in support of a parent or other person standing in parental relation to the child, may, on presentation of proper evidence to the county superintendent, be exempted from further attendance at school.

Article 2894. Excuses for absences. Any child not so exempt may be excused for temporary absence due to personal sickness, sickness or death in the family, quarantine, severe storm which has destroyed bridges, and made the regular means of travel dangerous or for unusual causes acceptable to the teacher, principal or superintendent of the school in which the said child is enrolled; provided that the excuses are in writing and signed by the parent or guardian of the child. Any case so excused may be investigated by the authorities discharging the duties of attendance officer for the school from which school the child is so excused.

Article 2895. Attendance officer. The country trustee of any county having a scholastic population of more than three thousand may elect a school attendance officer for said county upon petition of at least fifty resident freeholders of said county setting forth good reasons why said county should have an attendance officer. A public hearing should be had on said petition after due notice thereof given by publication in a newspaper published at the county seat for three consecutive weeks, or if there be no such newspaper, then by printing public notices in two public places within the county and one at the courthouse door of said county. If, after such hearing, said trustees believe that a school attendance officer is necessary to the proper enforcement of the provisions of this law, and that the schools of said county will be benefitted by having said attendance officer, the said board may elect such officer as herein provided.

The board of trustees of any independent district that has a school population having more than two thousand may in like manner elect an attendance officer for said district.

Said attendance officer may have his salary paid from the available school funds belonging to said county or district, not exceeding two dollars per day for the time actually employed in discharging his duty. In any county or independent district where such attendance officer is not so elected, the duties of said attendance officer shall devolve upon the school superintendents and peace officers of such county or district who shall perform the same without additional pay. Counties or independent school districts which may avail themselves of the option to elect school attendance officers may elect the probation officer or some officer or officers of the juvenile court of said county to serve as such attendance officer.

Article 2896. Powers and duties. The attendance officer shall have power to investigate all cases of unexcused absences from school, to administer oaths and to serve legal process, to enforce the provisions of this law, to keep records of all cases of any kind investigated by him in the discharge of his duties, and to make reports of his work as the State Superintendent may require. Nothing in this law shall be construed to authorize any attendance officer to invade or enter without permission of the owner or tenant thereof, or the head of any family residing therein, any private home, or private residence, or any room or apartment thereof, except to serve lawful process upon any parent, guardian or other person standing in parental relation to any child affected by this law, or to forcibly take corporal custody of any child anywhere without permission of the parent or guardian thereof, or with the compulsory attendance law, and said list shall be furnished to the attendance officer. All notices, forms and blanks to be used by any of the superintendents, principals or officials of any school be prescribed by the State Superintendent. Any teacher giving instruction to any child within compulsory attendance age shall promptly report any unexcused absences to the attendance officer.

Article 2897. Superintendent shall furnish list, etc. The county superintendent shall furnish to the superintendent of schools of each school district in the county, and to the principal of the school in case there be no superintendent, a complete list of all children of scholastic age belonging in said district, as shown by the last scholastic census and the record of transfers to and from said district. The superintendents and principals of the various schools of said county shall report to said county superintendent the names of all children subject to the provisions of this law who have not enrolled in said school, and the superintendent, principal or other official of private, denominational or parochial schools shall furnish to said county superintendent a list of all children of scholastic age enrolled in the school presided over by said official and the district in which said child was enumerated in the public school census. From such reports the county superintendent shall make up a complete list of all children within scholastic age enrolled in the various districts of said county who have not enrolled in some school and are not complying with the compulsory attendance law, and said list shall be furnished to the attendance officer. All notices, forms and blanks to be used by any of the superintendents, principals of officials of any school shall be prescribed by the State Superintendent. Any teacher giving instruction to any child within compulsory attendance age shall promptly report any excused absences to the attendance officer.

Article 2898. Parole of pupil. Any child within the compulsory school attendance age who shall be insubordinate, disorderly, vicious or immoral in conduct, or who persistently violates the reasonable rules and regulations of the school which he attends, or who otherwise persistently misbehaves therein so as to render himself an incorrigible, shall be reported to the attendance officer who shall proceed against such child in the juvenile court. If such child is found guilty in said court the judge shall have the power to parole said child, after requiring the parent or other person standing in parental relation, to execute a bond in the sum of no less than ten dollars, conditioned that said child shall attend school regularly and comply with all the rules and regulations of said school. If the superintendent or principal of any school shall report to the attendance officer for said school that said child has violated the conditions of his parole, said attendance officer shall proceed against such child before the judge of the juvenile court, and if such child shall be found guilty of violating the conditions of said parole, the bond shall forthwith be declared forfeited and shall be collected in the same manner as other forfeited bonds under the general laws of this State, and the proceeds of same shall be paid into the available school fund of the common or independent school district. The judge of said court may, after a fair and impartial hearing given to said child, again parole said child, requiring such bond as he may deem prudent, and require said child to again enter school. If said child shall violate the conditions of the second parole and shall be convicted of same, he shall be committed to a suitable training school as may be agreed upon by the parent of the child and the judge of the juvenile court in which the child is convicted.

Mexicans: Educate Your Children[106]

On previous occasions, I have pointed out the injustices that often victimize us. I will now give focus to a serious injury that we have inflicted on ourselves for a long time: the failure to educate our children.

History tells us that humanity has always organized itself into social classes and that a determining factor in life is the economic standing of the individual. We know that, except for rare instances, the economic standing of a person determines how their intelligence is used. All human beings are born endowed with intelligence, some more, some less. Some have the opportunity to develop their intelligence and they take advantage of this. Regrettably, almost all of us find that some Mexicans frequently fail to make use of the opportunity to educate themselves. I refer to the Mexicans living in this country. Let us be frank: our social and economic standing is due more to our ignorance than any other factor. It is time, therefore, that we awaken from our lethargy, end our deplorable situation and prevent it from affecting future generations.

We have the custom of sending children to school until they reach the age when they can work. As soon as the opportunity to earn a dollar arrives, we put them to work and they never return to school. Consequently, we become a part of the laboring class in the states bordering Mexico and always find ourselves obligated to do the work that the educated classes disparage and reject. In sum, we adopt the lowest social class in this country. This represents an injustice that we commit on ourselves, and a calamity that we bring on our race. If we seek a better life, if we wish to advance, we must educate ourselves.

Observe the Anglo Saxons and follow their example. The American child remains in public school until their schooling ends. Their children use this instruction to face their challenges in life, to find a job, to shape their future and to begin their professional studies. Mexican youth have the same opportunity. Why do we not use this opportunity? Why do we make slaves to ignorance of our children? Our responsibility, Gentlemen, is to educate our Mexican children so that they can become our leaders in the near future, well prepared to work towards the development of our race.

Alonso S. Perales, Member
Secretariat of the Inter-American High Commission

Washington, DC
May 1923

VOLUME II

In Defense of My People

Commentary on Volume I, *In Defense of My People*
Profesor Manuel A. Urbina[1]

The appropriately titled *En Defensa de mi Raza* has left a deep impression on my soul. Its author has moved me with his just ideas and international approach (related to the good understanding that should exist between the American and Mexican communities in Texas), and his clarity, frankness, sincerity and loyalty to his people and his Raza.

We must admire the author for appearing before Boards of Education demanding school facilities for our Mexican children that are equal to the ones provided for the Americans, and insisting that these same schools help with the schooling of our adults. Alonso S. Perales has also gone before real estate companies and lashed out against them with his spirited complaints against their unjustified refusal to sell lots and homes to Mexicans. We have seen him on more than one occasion going before internationalist-minded organizations and presenting a full view of the repulsive crimes that Saxons commit against our racial brothers. Perales has raised his courageous voice in front of mayors, courts and governors demanding equality for the people of Mexican origin. His loud protests for justice have reached the Supreme Legislative Body of the Nation and his strong and powerful voice has resonated in the White House, and he has done this solely **because of his love for his people and his raza**. This is why the book title could *not* be more appropriate, giving Dr. Carlos E. Castañeda ample reason to say in the prologue, "We are not exaggerating when we say that Attorney Alonso S. Perales can very well call himself the defender of ***nuestra raza***."

Conditions will change in the Imperial state when a significant number of Mexicans carry themselves without an exaggerated sense of self. They should also have a deep understanding of history, sociology, economics, law, etc. and, above all, a genuine love for our racial brothers. Then and only then will we achieve social vindication and witness the aurora of our well-being and that of our children. As is well known, we have witnessed numerous instances in which many evil and ignorant Saxons have blatantly trampled into oblivion the rights of Mexican immigrants as well as American citizens of Mexican origin. With this behavior, they are slowly instilling into the hearts and minds of thousands of people the idea of future world wars that bring destruction, ruin and the death of entire nations.

The great George Washington made use of his brilliant knowledge and his genuine humanistic understanding when he declared the following ethical-sociological truth: "The culture of a nation is measured by the treatment it extends to foreigners."[2]

So, if we were to set out to measure the cultural level of Americans from Texas based on how they treat our Mexican brothers, we would conclude that their culture is questionable. Everyone should know that our criteria is fair and recognized as an inviolable principle that the Great Father of the Nation affirmed. This logically means that malicious Saxons who behave badly towards our Mexican brothers can choose to be whatever they want to be and adopt whatever names they may fancy, but they are not the genuine sons of the noble Washington. They make up a kingdom of vanity, hate and racial prejudice deserving the prophetic words that Daniel directed at the prideful, conceited and blasphemous Belshazzar, ". . . you have been weighed on the scales and found wanting."[3]

Can moral ideals lead to full social fusion while Saxons consistently treat Mexicans the same or worse than they do Blacks? A recent case from El Paso is suggestive. Blinded by an ignorance of ethnology and a prejudice without precedent in the history of the world, Alex Powell, the city's registrar, tried to classify Mexicans alongside Blacks.[4]

While Mexicans are courteous, friendly and hospitable towards Americans who cross the Rio Grande, Anglo Saxons from Texas frequently treat Mexicans with distrust, cruelty and disdain, and they offend and humiliate them.

Vigorous and dignified action,
    Righteous and inspiring,
Selfless and relevant,
    Stands out as redemptive gain:
    All of this envelops
    EN DEFENSA DE MI RAZA

San Antonio, Texas
October 12, 1936

En Defensa de Mi Raza: My Opinion on the First Volume and its Author[5]
Profesor José de la Luz Sáenz

Alonso S. Perales has titled his collection of articles and letters published in the English and Spanish-language press *En Defensa De Mi Raza*. A photograph and short biographical sketches grace the book. Although people know the author, his likeness and accounts of his life are indispensable to a youth that is enthusiastically stepping up to relieve us in the pro-Raza struggle.

We have trusted this man's abilities since his early years such that we believe he is just beginning to blossom as a writer. Perales will leave his people and his country a legacy of experiences, thoughts and hopes that will set the standard for our race in the future. "A broach is enough to make the point."[6] In this simple, but concrete manner, people who know him place all their hopes in this young man of sensible and just ambitions. He is true to our stoic, racial tradition that prefers that we burn in low flame than to bow submissively to pressure.

You will find in his articles and letters many ideas emerging out of the different moments that pressing circumstances have dictated to him. Read them. Perales speaks to us with an open heart that is free of all the subtleties of a Lucifer.

The world now and then takes pleasure upon seeing such persons stand out among the masses. Everyone knows that they are not out to seek wealth. People are glad or happy when history treats the poor and unwanted classes well, when society grants them justice along with a few victories in life.

Note the obstacles that he has faced. It has always been like this and continuous to be, that is how we want it. They have motivated him to no end. His contemporaries have been as envious as if someone had placed a ladder at his feet and suddenly told him to climb it, and there he goes!

Read him, young people. Adopt his life as a standard and adjust it to your needs. Surpass it; that is your right. This is your time. The future well-being of the Raza Americana of the New World proclaims it for you.

McAllen, Texas
October 1936

A Brief Statement on the High Purpose of *En Defensa de Mi Raza*
Profesor Juan Sauceda[7]

You have a true apostle of human rights before you.

Alonso S. Perales, a man of virile soul and renowned patriotism, offers his book as the tribute of the good son to his homeland, and although it is his first, *En Defensa de Mi Raza* achieves greatness. He is frank and unapologetic, and clear in his intention to redeem his people.

Perales casts aside ambiguous words and offers **Truths** embellished with simple and unmistakably clear descriptions of the real actions that the youth of today will find easy to replicate. This is what he has in mind. With each clever defense that he commits to paper, we witness a shining and inviting path brimming with intelligence. Our youth should follow his example. The longing to be useful to the nation and our Raza lives within them as well.

When reason beams its righteous rays over the multitude of pessimists and reclaims denied rights, even gold loses its brightness and luster. Its brilliant glow has never distorted the straight and narrow path of the tillers who pursue the good for its own sake.

His highest goal is to see that justice triumphs. His ambition is to affirm justice, the right that the divine has granted to adults and children, to the strong and the weak.

En Defensa de Mi Raza seeks to help the youth live their lives well, not to secure accolades for the author. He asks for your approval by doing as he does, not by admiring him. You can only repay the sleeplessness and hardships that he endured in defense of his Raza by imitating him in whatever sphere of action that you choose. The sincere interest that you express in improving your immediate social condition will serve as the best and most welcomed crown of recognition that you will be extending to the work of the descendant of Ilhuicamina, Cuauhtémoc and Juárez.[8]

Youth of America, read the grand fruit of his labor. Perales has seasoned *En Defensa de Mi Raza* with the sweet delight of his intense suffering, with the free-flowing tears born of scorn and sacrifice.

If you were fortunate to have tasted the succulent fruit that is his book, take good care of the gift that you have received because it will become the fortifying foundation of wise counsel for the struggles to come. The laurels of the victors will crown you as the self-conscious citizens who serve their nation and humanity well.

Benavides, Texas
November 26, 1936

A Protest in Support of a Mexican-American Legionnaire[9]

Managua, Nicaragua
August 14, 1928

American Legion
Falfurrias, Texas

Sirs:

I just read in a Texas newspaper that on July 4 the Falfurrias Post of the American Legion refused to allow Mr. Maximiliano Hinojosa, an American citizen and World War veteran, to participate in a celebration in his hometown because "Mexicans" were not allowed. This occurred even though Mr. Hinojosa was wearing the American Legion's emblem on his lapel.[10]

On August 14, 1927, the writer, a US-born American citizen, assisted in organizing in Texas the League of United Latin American Citizens, and on January 1, 1928, Mr. J.T. Canales, an attorney from Brownsville, Texas, succeeded him as President General of said league. For your information, I am enclosing herewith a complete statement of the aims and purposes of our organization.

Lacking the details of the Falfurrias incident, I shall confine myself to your policy of discrimination. If your policy accords that kind of treatment to American veterans of Mexican extraction merely because of their racial origin, you are very discouraging to those of us who are trying to develop within the members of our race, the best, purest and most perfect type of true and loyal citizen of the United States of America.

If you have any statement to make on the subject, I shall be pleased to hear from you.

I am, Gentlemen, yours for better American citizens.

Alonso S. Perales
c/o American Legation

* * *

Managua, Nicaraga[11]
August 14, 1928

Mr. John T. Winterich, Editor
The Americana Legion Monthly
Indianapolis, Indiana

My Dear Sir:

For your information, I am enclosing herewith copies of communications and two enclosures that I just sent to the Falfurrias Post of the American Legion.

I believe it would be a great help to the American Legion, to the League of Latin American Citizens and a great service to our country if you would be good enough to occasionally write an article in *The American Legion Monthly* discouraging racial discrimination in your organization,.

Thanking you in advance, I am yours truly.

Alonso S. Perales

Managua, Nicaragua
August 10, 1928[12]

Mr. Maximiliano Hinojosa
Falfurrias, Texas

My Dear Sir:

I have received an issue of *Diógenes* from McAllen dated July 14, 1928, that includes commentary by Mr. Rodolfo Uranga, a writer with *La Prensa*, regarding an incident said to have taken place in Falfurrias on July 4. He states the following:

> The indignation expressed by citizens who are like our brothers—due to a shared language, religion, etc.—at times erupts in loud protests, like in Falfurrias in July. When someone told Mr. Hinojosa that Mexicans could not join the American Legion festivities, he responded with the same fury that he showed in the trenches when he took the American Legion emblem from his lapel and threw it violently on the floor, and stomped on it in front of the Anglo Saxons who were there.

Mr. Hinojosa, I would appreciate it if you could send me everything that the press has written on the incident, including the names of the Anglo Saxons responsible for it.

I take this opportunity to congratulate you for your strong and appropriate response. Awaiting your reply, I remain your loyal friend and servant.

Alonso S. Perales

Issues Facing Our Race in the United States, I[13]

Although I am far away from my racial brothers and my work in Nicaragua takes up much of my time, I continue to think about the serious problems that we face in the United States during my moments of rest. This is why I once again write and remind my racial brothers—and American citizens as well as Mexican citizens in the United States—that modern, civilized humanity expects us to make a greater effort to advance in our intellectual, economic and social evolution.

I have always maintained that the evolution of American citizens of Mexican origin depends on education, organization and the intelligent and conscious exercise of their voting rights, and that the future of Mexican citizens living in the United States is based on education and organization. Today, I will speak to the obstacles to our progress that we must address immediately. Mexican-Americans and Mexican citizens lack well-trained persons to lead us. Few exist and, unfortunately, most of them suffer from one or all the unnatural ailments that afflict humanity and obstruct its continued development. These conditions are laziness, timidity, selfishness and envy. The ones who lack initiative are poor in civic courage or spend their time scheming and obstructing the good works of others.

When I returned to Texas in June 1927, I was determined to establish or collaborate in the formation of a determined group of American citizens of Mexican origin that would seek to hasten our general development. With this in mind, I worked with others to organize the League of United Latin American Citizens. I was greatly disappointed to see that some persons were not enthusiastic while others opposed the effort and sought to destroy the organization, as if that would weaken us and deny our community. Ultimately, the ship's pilots saved it from the storm. When I left for Cuba in January, it was well on its way, if not with great speed, at least with a clear destination. If the opposition has been unable to sink it and its pilots have avoided a shipwreck, I assume that it continues on the sea route mapped out at its launching.

In June, Profesor José de la Luz Sáenz, a well-known teacher and mentor of our Mexican youth in Texas and a veteran of the Great World War, initiated the just project to erect a monument in San Antonio. It would honor the Mexican-American and Mexican heroes who gave their lives in European battlefields for the stars and stripes and showed the courage and stoicism of the bronze-like Raza. What a beautiful and sublime task. Although many of my racial brothers and even persons of other races warmly embraced the idea and cooperated with *Profesor* Sáenz, others refused to give the moral and material support that the project deserved, and they were determined to undermine its success.

Managua, Nicaragua
July 26, 1928

Issues Facing Our Race in the United States, II[14]

The opposition is on the right path when justified by powerful motivations like scorn against persons of reprehensible or questionable character, but as I noted in my previous article, yours truly was responsible for the first organizing initiative and Profesor Sáenz for the second. I should not be the one to attest to my own character, but no one can say that I have in any way exploited our race. Regarding Sáenz, he is one of the few active leaders who is firm, sincere and honest in matters related to our race in the United States and is genuinely interested in the well-being and the future of the descendants of Hidalgo and Cuauhtémoc, especially in Texas. How can we then explain the opposition towards us?

Latinos in the United States, regardless of citizenship, have the obvious moral responsibility—if we really have a drop of self-respect—to use all acceptable and lawful means within our reach to adapt to our situation. We live among people that have become the most progressive in the civilized world due to their intelligence, morale, enthusiasm and devotion to honest work. To live among them, and not march with them on the path of progress due to our laziness and other failings is embarrassing. The descendants of Hidalgo and Cuahutémoc living in the United States should imitate and second everything that the Anglo Saxon does. We do not have to travel to England, France, Germany, Italy or Spain to seek examples of human progress. We have the models here.

In my travels throughout Latin America, I have observed that many countries lack evidence of progress. They are almost in the same condition as when Christopher Columbus discovered America. Ignorance and poverty, and dirty, unhygienic, unhealthy and backward towns and cities predominate. Even though I felt inclined—not unlike my fellow Anglo Saxon citizens that visit these countries—to critique these backward places, upon reflection I have decided otherwise because our lamentable intellectual, economic and social conditions in the United States do not allow me to do this. On the contrary, I maintain that our fault is almost unexplainable, because although we live in the United States (many of us were born and raised here), the first among nations, and under the influence of the American people, we have not followed the good and convincing example of the active, ambitious, industrious and progressive Anglo Saxons. If I was to criticize Latin Americans for their lack of progress, someone would no doubt ask me, "And what about the Mexican neighborhoods of San Antonio, Houston, Dallas and other cities and towns in the United States? Are you not also backwards?" I would have to agree since the facts speak for themselves. And so, we must ask, how do we remedy the situation? Are we to continue in our backward state? Are we going to follow the example of the progressive Anglo Saxon? I offer these questions for the consideration of our Spanish-speaking readers in the United States, especially the organizations, leagues and societies of Texas that claim to have the well-being and future of our race in mind.

Managua, Nicaragua
July 27, 1928

[*Diógenes*, McAllen, TX, August 25, 1928.]

Issues Facing Our Race in the United States, III[15]

Unquestionably, the moment has arrived for Mexican Americans and Mexicans living in the United States to wake up from our lethargy and seek redemption. Latinos are called an inferior race. Anglo Saxons say that we are inferior because we do not progress and are content with our backward state. Because of this, we must decide to rise up to the same level as the Anglo Saxons. This is how we will demonstrate that although we have not yet shown our progressive nature, we are not inferior. When we dedicate ourselves to seeking progress, Anglo Saxons will not be helping us. They seem to be so repelled with our backward condition that they are indifferent towards any effort to improve our situation. With this in mind, a daily from San Antonio says the following regarding Mexicans from San Antonio in its December 15, 1927, issue:

> Dr. Max Handman, Chairman of the Department of Sociology at the University of Texas stated in a talk delivered before the Interdenominational Council on Spanish-Speaking Work, at the Methodist Church of Travis Park, that the social and economic condition of Mexicans from San Antonio was difficult and required radical changes.[16]
>
> Dr. Handman conducted a recent study based on 1,500 Mexicans from San Antonio. He found that their problem was more of a racial nature than environmental. The Mexican mutual aid societies often come into conflict with Anglo Saxons when they come into contact, noted Dr. Handman.

Mexican Americans and Mexicans should proceed steadfast towards our redemption, and if we meet opposition—regardless of where it originates—we will vanquish it and continue on our way. Note what Colonel L. M. Maus said in 1921, after conducting a study of the intellectual, economic and social situation of Mexican Americans and Mexicans in Texas, New Mexico, Arizona and California:

> The American public generally looks upon the Mexicans as only a partially developed race of people, still in the springtide of civilization, and lacking many fundamental qualities so essential to good citizenship and stable government.[17]
>
> Lightly spoken of as "greasers" and regarded as bandits and professional revolutionaries, you will rarely find an American who is willing to give them credit even for a few of the many good qualities they possess and, hence, the Mexican people have suffered greatly in the public sentiment of our country.

To underscore that the Anglo Saxon considers the Latin race an inferior race, I now turn to Harry L. Foster's observations in his book, *Mañana-Land*.

> Like most persons with the inferiority complex, the Latin American is extremely sensitive. He resents, even more than the humiliation of *gringo* assistance, the assumption of loftier worth attributed to the Anglo Saxon.[18]
>
> The charming woman writer in particular—who makes a brief trip to the more modern cities of Chile and Argentina, meets only the aristocracy, and completes her book as a bread-and-butter letter to the delightful people who fed her tea and cakes—is inclined nowadays, . . . to picture all the Latin Americans as infinitely superior to our own crude selves.[19]
>
> All of us, even though we may have come to have a genuine affection for our friends to the South, we still do not con-

sider ourselves their equals. We know that all *gringos* are not superior to every Latin American, but we are confident that man for man, lawyer for lawyer, doctor for doctor, soldier for soldier and farmer for farmer, the Anglo Saxon usually surpasses his counterpart in physique, intelligence, education, ability and character, if not in refinement. Latin Americans are aware of the contrast and sometimes admit it voluntarily. They are naturally a trifle resentful when the *gringo*, by word or action, reminds him of it.[20]

Such is Mr. Foster's conclusion regarding Latin Americans after visiting all their republics.

Raising the intellectual, economic and social level of the Mexican American and Mexican would not only assure our well-being but it would place us in a favorable position to gain respect from Anglo Saxons. This is all that we would need to justify any effort or sacrifice to advance as a people. I hope that if my racial brothers who live in the United States adopt the self-esteem and pride that they should have, they will accept my suggestion.

Mexican people do not belong to a **naturally** inferior race. The history of our race unequivocally supports this view. A few days ago, a friend commented on this very subject:

> I find your conclusions somewhat pessimistic, Mr. Perales, since Dolores Del Río, Lupe Vélez, Raquel Torres, Captain Emilio Carranza, Ramón Navarro and the well-known caricaturist Miguel Cobarrubias have recently been raising the name of your race high.[21]

I agree, of course. I also believe that these persons, as well as others who lived before them, have absolutely demonstrated the latent capacity of our Raza. That is to say, they have shown what the Mexicans can do when they set out to succeed in life. Even more, we have to agree that while some Mexicans bring honor to our Raza, others discredit it a thousand ways. Mexican Americans and Mexicans in the United States bring no honor to our race in the face of the unacceptable position that we are in and next to the well-recognized and respectable place that the progressive Anglo Saxons occupy. In other words, we need to develop persons like Captain Carranza and reduce the size of the overwhelming majority that is satisfied with living poorly and does not care to engage their reality.

In my forthcoming article, I will suggest actions that if adopted would greatly contribute to our social redemption in the United States.

Managua, Nicaragua
July 30, 1928

[*Diógenes*, McAllen, TX, September 1, 1928.]

Issues Facing Our Race in the United States, IV[22]

In my opinion, the development of Mexican Americans depends on their education, organization and the intelligent and conscious exercise of our voting rights. Mexican citizens in the United States need to obtain an education and pursue self-organization.

On other occasions, I have addressed the issue broadly, which is why I now limit myself to a brief statement. Education is the most important challenge because all human progress depends on it. It increases our capacity to earn dollars, and this obviously allows us to raise our socio-economic standing, known in English as the "Standard of Living." It naturally follows that if we are to match Anglo Saxons, we must educate ourselves. This aspect of development is slow but its results are certain. We should not falter but must redouble our efforts and continue moving forward.

Organization is also important because in unity there is strength. Unfortunately, our Raza is not united. The organization of our race in this country will occur when we can count on a larger number of active, determined, intelligent, interested, sincere and honest leaders, and when lethargy (the lack of initiative and civic courage), egoism, envy and hypocrisy disappear from our politics.

Voting rights are also important but they will do us more harm than good until we learn how to use them. Suffrage will be useful when we vote intelligently for candidates that are the true friends of our Raza. Once in power, they will want to grant us justice when we deserve it and not deny it to us simply because we are Mexican.

Once we educate ourselves and our organization is in place, we can take a determined step towards our social redemption with a hygiene campaign. In order to match Anglo Saxons, it is necessary that the descendants of Hidalgo and Cuahutémoc act decisively to keep their homes and yards clean. They should also be hygienic with their persons since Anglo Saxons are very clean and they loathe, not without reason, persons who are not. This is one reason why they consider themselves superior to the Latino. Let us change this so that Anglo Saxons can only say that we are poor, but not dirty. On the way to New Orleans by train this year, I heard an Anglo Saxon say to another:

> During my stay in San Antonio, I visited the Mexican barrio, *Mexiquito*, to satisfy my curiosity. I found it interesting, but I could not help but notice the lack of cleanliness among those people.

Let us discourage this kind of observation.

Of course, we can also practice saving. We should not spend everything that we earn unless it is necessary. Frugality has contributed significantly to Anglo Saxon progress and well-being. Savings would allow many Mexican Americans and Mexicans to establish fully modern neighborhoods with paved streets like the ones that our Anglo Saxon neighbors build. In order to establish modern and attractive residential areas it would be necessary to restrict the sale of these lots to persons able to build a home valued at three-thousand dollars or more. Allowing for the construction of a home worth five-hundred dollars next to another that has a value of three-thousand dollars or more would not result in neighborhoods as modern as theirs. If we could do this, we could respond to our Anglo neighbors who wish to know where and how we live by showing them our modern neighborhoods, and tell them, "Here they are, Gentlemen, the modern neighborhoods of progressive-minded Mexicans that are equal to yours." Without a doubt, this would represent a clear step towards social redemption. By the way, no one should interpret this as a malicious form of segregation since any Mexicans that had the means to build a house worth three-thousand dollars or more would have the complete liberty to do so. This system has brought magnificent results to Anglo Saxons. We should follow their example.

I conclude by saying that my only motivation for writing on this subject is the hope of seeing my race progress and reclaim their honor. I also hope that Mexican Americans and Mexican citizens do everything within their means to secure our redemption as quickly as possible

Managua, Nicaragua
August 2, 1928

[*Diógenes*, McAllen, TX, September 8, 1928.]

A Letter Praising Dr. Herschel T. Manuel[23]

Rio Grande City, Texas
December 18, 1930

Dr. Herschel T. Manuel
Professor of Educational Psychology
University of Texas

My Dear Sir:

I have just finished reading your excellent book entitled *The Education of Mexican and Spanish-Speaking Children in Texas* and hasten to offer you my sincere congratulations. The book is an exceptional presentation of the facts and it will no doubt be very useful to anyone who is interested in understanding a problem that demands resolution. I am sure that everyone of Mexican or Spanish origin in Texas will also appreciate the fair and impartial manner with which you have examined the subject.

I have always been interested in the advancement and well-being of my people in Texas, and have consistently preached the gospel of education because I believe that this is the solution to the problem. Your book, which addresses various aspects of the issue, touches me deeply.

Regarding the segregation of our children in the first three grades, it is a purely racial practice, and as much as school officials may try to convince us that it is due to pedagogical considerations, they will not succeed. We know that segregation is racial and illegal and that school officials always find ways of avoiding the spirit if not the letter of the law. Just like school officials in some places are determined to violate the spirit of the law, we the American citizens of Mexican and Spanish origin are resolute in opposing their unjust actions and tactics. As the General President of the League of United Latin American Citizens, I can assure you that our society will not stop until we put an end to segregation. Our league's principal goal is the development of first class, loyal citizens, and it is obvious that we cannot succeed if school officials insist on segregating our children. This is not the way to produce loyal citizens. School officials who are segregating our children are contemptible and anti-American. The work of LULAC conserves the Republic of Texas. The school officials that segregate our youth tend to destroy it.

Yours,
Alonso S. Perales
General President,
LULAC

[*Diógenes*, McAllen, TX, December 20, 1930]

Presentation by Alonso S. Perales on the Radio Program "La Voz de La Raza," June 8, 1932

Honorable listeners: I dedicate this talk to the studious Latin American youth.

I wish to extend my sincere congratulations to all the young Mexican men and women who graduated this year from high schools and colleges in the United States. Seeing our youth complete their education has always been a source of pride and satisfaction for me. There are two powerful reasons why we should all be pleased when our young graduate. First, the advancement of our race in this country largely depends on their education. We cannot expect rapid progress if our Mexican students drop out of school by the time they reach the third or fourth grade, or before they finish the secondary grades. Clearly, if we set out to see our students complete their studies with all that the schools offer them, we would have more professionals, merchants and skilled workers and less drivers, waiters and laborers. Demanding and difficult work is not shameful when honest labor is involved. However, if society is to judge our people by their intelligence and abilities, our race should maintain the same intellectual level as the most advanced races. If we wish to rid ourselves of the bad impression that some people have of us, we must quickly increase our educated and well-prepared ranks. As long as people can admonish us for being largely uneducated, we will have a hard time rejecting the persistent view that we are inferior. When we are able to say that the uneducated among us is a minority, our situation will change completely.

Young people who graduate from high school should continue studying even at the cost of major sacrifice. In our country, you only need to have the desire to educate yourself. Students who have to work during the day can find excellent colleges with night classes that can help them develop a professional career. San Antonio, for example, has three law schools and a liberal arts college with night classes. Latin American youth should not overlook these opportunities. I have observed that only nine Spanish-surnamed students were among the three hundred and fifty students enrolled in college last year.

The second reason to celebrate the graduation of our students is that with each case we gain one more leader for our race. Latinos from Texas need effective leaders interested in the advancement of our race. That is to say, we need more men and women to resolve the educational, economic, political and social problems that we face.

My hope is that Mexican students will continue to graduate from high schools and colleges that are of the highest caliber, for the sake and pleasure of our Raza.

San Antonio, TX
June 8, 1932

Societies as a Means for Progress[24]

I was very pleased to read a letter from Mrs. Beatriz Blanco de Allen Hinojosa, director of the journal *Album De La Raza*, to the Mexican societies of San Antonio, as follows:

> Knowing that the progress of a people largely depends on the united effort of its members, we seek to establish a periodical that can serve as the mouthpiece for societies with Raza membership. With this purpose in mind, we ask that as soon as possible you please send us a statement of your organization's goals as well as a description of its activities since its founding.

The Madam Director of the *Album De La Raza* is quite right in believing that the progress of a people mostly depends on the work of its organizations. World history demonstrates this. People who do not have cultural, commercial, civic and social organizations, but that depend on the government for its development are usually the most backward. The countries with governments that receive the support of societies in all progressive spheres of activities are the most fortunate.

Your citizenship definitively does not matter if we are talking about the progress of all Mexicans living in the United States. It is necessary that we join dedicated and effective societies. We must understand our individual obligations to society. It is exactly because a great number of residents from San Antonio and other localities are aware of this that we have several societies that constantly fight for their communities. We have organizations that include Chambers of Commerce, Rotary Clubs, Kiwanis Clubs, Conopus Clubs, the Boy

Scouts of America, the League of United Latin American Citizens, Parent-Teacher Associations, the Anti-Tuberculosis Association, women's organizations and mutual aid and philanthropic societies.

It is an unimpeachable fact that the development of San Antonio and other cities is due largely to the work of the previously noted organizations. It is also true that the success of these societies is due principally to each one of their members—or at least the majority of them—who are perfectly clear about their obligations to their communities.

We, the descendants of Cuauhtémoc and Hidalgo who live in the Alamo city and other places in Texas, are important to the cities and towns where we reside, and we cannot avoid our responsibilities. We are duty bound to work diligently and purposefully towards the development of our cities. Since the majority of the Mexicans find themselves mostly in *barrios*, we should all work for the progress of those neighborhoods and their residents. Seeking such change is like fighting for the advancement of our cities and towns. At the same time, we have many opportunities for effective social work among our people. Mexicans in the United States must make haste in progressing intellectually, economically, socially and civically. I take this opportunity to emphasize that Mexican leaders, regardless of citizenship, are responsible for the future of our Raza.

We already have the organizations necessary for this work. They are already fighting for the development of the cities and towns where they reside, as well as for the progress and well-being of our race. We can count on LULAC, chambers of commerce, cultural and social clubs, mutual aid societies, philanthropic organizations and other such organizations. We need our members to continue working and a public that provides greater encouragement and support. An organization that is useful and indispensable to the progress of a group deserves our encouragement and support.

We should familiarize ourselves with the basic principles of the organizations where we live and select the ones that best reflect our individual views and interests in the civic-social struggles. Once the selection is made, we should support the organizations faithfully and enthusiastically because they are a very important in the progress of a people.

Cooperation[25]

On the subject of cooperation, I think it is necessary to point out why we often fail to support good and effective societies. Some of us are too egotistical and do not worry about the well-being of the group so long as we are able to satisfy our own individual needs and desires. Some may ask, "Why should we worry about others, if we have everything that we need?" This attitude has been disastrous around the world because it has retarded progress. When society categorizes groups as retrograde and inferior, it is because they include persons who have disregarded the well-being of their own. We can change our name, but we cannot deny our blood.

Others do not cooperate because they do not have a clear idea about these organizations. They know even less about the benefits that the organizations can bring to the group because they do not understand the responsibilities that the societies assume on behalf of their communities. Dr. Rudolph M. Binder, Sociology Professor from the University of New York, says that people belong to one of five groups in the more advanced societies. Some persons are apparently content with living and nothing more, while others make up the indigent and criminal populations. Still others take good care of their children, but their concern does not go any further than that. The fourth group includes individuals who long for power to lord over others. Members of the fifth group are ready and able to find the means to carry out a more productive life, that is, within what the groups will allow. Dr. Binder adds that socially aware persons who stand out because of their progressive outlook take initiatives. At the same time, Dr. Binder reminds us that these leaders have always lacked sufficient cooperative support, the great obstacle that we all face. He states:

Men who have always been satisfied with the current state of things, however, are included in all social classes. In some cases, this has been due to an unwillingness to seek progress. In other cases, they have been unable to understand and appreciate progressive measures, and this situation continues today. The problems for the reformers start here and will follow them as they continue their work. The leader seeks progress for all humankind. He believes to have found the means that are necessary to accomplish this. Persons who do not wish or cannot advance to higher levels undermine his efforts. More than ever, the leader needs the support of everyone who works for the group because he knows his limitations. Everyone has talents, however small they may be. Society must develop these talents if it is to continue growing, and leaders must receive the satisfaction that they seek. The leader is encouraged only when those that surround him also evolve. The leaders insist and should continue insisting on the progress of everyone for their own good and the good of others.[26]

The Importance that We Give the Adult Schools[27]

We are encouraged by the enthusiasm with which Latin Americans from Texas have responded to the call from the government of the United States to attend the schools for adults. The reports that we have received from McAllen, Del Rio, Alice and other places are heartening. In San Antonio alone, approximately 1,400 students—all Spanish-speaking—have enrolled at Sydney-Lanier High School. This marks a new phase in the evolution of Latin Americans in this city and the state. Clearly, schooling for adults is the key to the quick resolution of our civic-social problems. Our fellow adult citizens will be better prepared to participate with confidence and intelligence in organizations that seek to move our community forward because of the schooling they are receiving. I am referring to the League of United Latin American Citizens, the Parent-Teacher Association, the Anti-Tuberculosis Society of Texas and Bexar County and the Boy Scouts of America. Mexicans, regardless of citizenship, should join these kinds of organizations because in cooperating with them, we will definitively speed the progress of our Raza in Texas.

In order to be effective in areas of social service, we must have some preparation. One of the major purposes of an education, as Dr. Albert Einstein once said, is to awaken the civic consciousness and a sense of social responsibility among citizens. An individual cannot cooperate well if he does not awaken to this consciousness and responsibility. In other words, in order to win over individuals to the world of public service it is necessary to familiarize them on the nature of the organizations noted above. We need to talk to them about the organizations and their activities. They need to know that we urgently need them to be more active and take greater interest in issues that affect us so that we may progress more rapidly.

The opening of the schools for adults fills me with optimism and I am confident that we will soon be able to count on hundreds of leaders and followers, both men and women, to advance our cause for social redemption with enthusiasm, devotion and intelligence. We will soon see Latin Americans seeking better school facilities for our youth, improved health conditions and upstanding character traits among our youth in the Young Explorers of America. They will also encourage a sense of civic duty among our compatriots through conferences that inform them about the function of government and their rights and obligations as citizens. All of this will soon become a reality, thanks to the schools for adults.

Impressions of a Trip to Mexico[28]

Mr. Perales shared the following impressions after a trip to Mexico:

My wife and I are so pleased with our trip to Monterrey and Saltillo. During our stay at the capital of the republic last year, we concluded that Mexico is not only a rich and beautiful country, but it should be called a nation of art, as much for its natural beauty as for the fact that every one of its sons and daughters are artists.

Now that we have visited Monterrey with greater calm, we have returned very impressed with its industrial progress as well as with their recent engineering projects. The road to Chipinque is without a doubt a masterpiece. To travel by car to a mountain peak at one thousand five hundred meters in distance is a great feat. Every Mexican is proud to know that Mexico has engineers as good as any that you can find anywhere else in the world. These public works clearly demonstrate the potential of our race.

We were also impressed to see Mexicans working in the factories of Monterrey and assuming positions of responsibility in glass works, foundries and steel factories. It brings great joy to see our brothers working as directors, managers and office personnel, and not as street cleaners, or even as mechanic helpers, as we are accustomed to seeing in this country, especially in Texas. Mexicans in Mexico are able to develop their intelligence without having to face the obstacle of racial prejudice. Mexico has always produced professionals and officials that are as competent as the best that you can find anywhere else. If Mexicans do not reach the same level of development in Texas, it is because Anglo Saxons will not allow it, all along boasting of their supremacy. I wish that everyone who has Mexican blood but has not visited important Mexican cities had the opportunity so that they can see how beautiful and grand Mexico is and, above all, so that they can erase from their minds the racial inferiority complex that the Anglo Saxon has sought to impose on us.

The Formal Petition for the Construction of a Distinctly Mexican Square, Presented by Representatives of LULAC at the Last Meeting of the Centenary Commission[29]

The Centenary Commission ended its public hearings on Tuesday afternoon with the recommendation to spend four hundred thousand dollars that the federal government provided for the centenary celebration of Texas in San Antonio.

Attorney Sidney J. Brooks, Vice President of the Commission, chaired the meeting since General Claude V. Birkhead, President of the Commission, was away from the city. Numerous delegations presented their final arguments in support of their respective projects. The Society of the Descendants of the Immigrants from the Canary Islands and LULAC were among them.

Ms. Ester Pérez Carvajal represented the first group. She proposed the purchase of the property on the north side of the Spanish Governor's Palace to honor the memory of the "pilgrim fathers of Texas." Mrs. Carvajal added that in the event that the federal government cannot spend the apportioned amount on permanent structures, her organization proposed an archive with letters and other documents under the expert supervision of the University of Texas. The collection would highlight the colonial history of Texas.

Attorney Alonso Perales, Pablo A. Meza, Max García, Lieutenant Colonel Francisco L. Chapa and Reverend John Bruce Dalton, Rector of the Christian Church in Downtown San Antonio, represented LULAC. As the representative for the Centenary Committee of his organization, Perales reportedly said the following:

My friends and I represent the League of United Latin American Citizens, a civic organization with numerous councils in Texas that include American citizens of Mexican origin. We respectfully propose that the Honorable Centenary Commission spend the sum of seventy-five thousand dollars to construct a traditional Mexican square on the west side of the city with a beautiful kiosk, a majestic fountain, trees, etc. encircled by typical Mexican businesses in appearance. We believe that such a square would be a beautiful initiative for the following reasons:

First, we would be extending friendship to the peoples of Latin America—especially the Mexicans—when we build a traditional site on the Mexican west side that is beautiful and useful and that we can proudly put on display when the tourists come to San Antonio asking to see the Mexican community that they call "Little Mexico." Aside from its residents, what do we have in the Mexican neighborhood that is truly representative of Mexico? I think that you will agree with me when I respond by saying NOTHING. It is true that we have a square that regularly sells tamales, enchiladas and menudo, but the city only decorates it on special occasions for the pleasure of visitors—like last year, when the Kiwanis held their convention here. Why have city officials not built a traditional and permanent Mexican square? It is true that some businesses on the west side sell Mexican curios, but it is also the case that once the tourists walk out of these establishments, they face businesses of ill repute.

What impression will the tourists take away regarding the Mexicans and the Anglo Americans? It will surely be unfavorable.

Second, such a square would no doubt attract tourists in greater numbers than ever because of the forthcoming celebration of the centenary and the completion of the Pan American Highway.

Third, it would do justice to the American citizens of Mexican origin and the people of San Antonio, since, as you know, we have been working diligently and enthusiastically for years to clean, dignify and beautify certain parts of the west side of the city. Along these lines, we plead for the destruction of the *jacales,* the homes of our poor Mexican brothers, and the construction of hygienic and comfortable homes in their place. We also want city officials to close the houses of ill repute known as the "Red Light District." The district is located on the west side of town, against the wishes of its Mexican residents. If the honorable Centenary Commission accepts our proposal, your good help would definitely help us reach our objective.

In summary, the construction of a beautiful and traditional Mexican square on the west side of the city would be a lovely gesture of friendship towards the Mexican community and our race as it would be typically Mexican. It would attract tourists who will not only spend their money but also receive a favorable impression of San Antonio's two great peoples— the Mexican and the Anglo Saxon. Lastly, the Anglo American people of San Antonio would be saying that it is ready to extend to the American citizens of Mexican origin the justice that it claims.

Mrs. Frank W. Sorrell, President of the Society for the Beautification of the City of San Antonio followed by warmly recommending the proposal presented by the Centenary Committee of LULAC.

LULAC Protests an Incident, Mexican Texans Forced to Pull a Car with Ropes. The Complainants Claim that the Detectives Exceeded their Authority[30]

Three young men of Mexican origin were indignant because two well-known San Antonio detectives arrested them on January 24, 1836, tied them with ropes and made them pull a car for ten miles until they reached the courthouse. The detectives explained that the youth had stolen the car. According to our sources, the Pro-Justice Committee of Council 16 of the LULAC—made up of Attorney Alonso S. Perales, Attorney Pablo G. González, Attorney Isidoro R. Flores, Pablo A. Meza, Florencio R. Flores and Gregorio R. Salinas—immediately submitted a complaint with the Civil Service Commission of Police Officers and Firemen.

> We, the members of Council 16 of the LULAC are not against punishing delinquents of Mexican origin. On the contrary, we believe that it is in the best interest of society that all delinquents be duly punished. However, we insist that delinquents be disciplined according to the dictates of the law and not by arbitrary methods. The detectives exceeded their authority and committed a crime when they tied them with ropes and forced them to pull a car for ten miles. The young men may not have been guilty of the crime that is alleged. Actually, the detectives acted against the dignity of our people. Therefore we issue a vigorous protest.

Perales Congratulates Calleros and His Colleagues[31]

San Antonio, Texas
October 10, 1936

Mr. Cleofas Calleros
El Paso, Texas

Dear Mr. Calleros,

In reference to reports that the El Paso City Registrar attempted to classify Spanish-speaking persons as colored, I extend my congratulations to you and all your associates for your courageous stand. I stand by you with heart and soul and am ready to assist you in any way I can. San Antonio uses three official classifications, namely White, Mexican and Colored. We have never registered a formal protest because we, as persons of Mexican descent and regardless of citizenship, are very proud of our racial extraction and do not wish to convey the impression that we are ashamed of being Mexicans.

We have always resented the inference that we are not Whites but realize that racial classifications may be necessary for statistical purposes. We understand that it may be necessary to use racial classifications for statistical gathering purposes and have often suggested to public officials that it is in the interest of **the true American and improved international relations** to adopt the convenient statistical categories that we use, namely Anglo American, Mexican or Latin American and people of color. I completely agree that **we continually and forcefully** challenge all attempts to belittle our Raza. This is what I have sought to do for the last seventeen years, as is evident in my first volume of *En Defensa de Mi Raza*.

I send you my warmest greetings and wish you success in everything that you do.

Sincerely yours,
Alonso S. Perales

Attorney Valls Stands Up for the Mexican People, the Strong and Noble Attitude of the District Attorney, His Heart Swells with Resentment Towards the Reproach from El Paso, "We Don't Ask for Privileges, But Equal Rights before the Law"[32]

While visiting San Antonio after a stay at Hebbronville where he has been holding court hearings, District Attorney John A. Valls commented to a representative of *La Prensa* on the issue that surfaced in El Paso on whether to classify Mexicans as a "colored race."

Without hesitation, District Attorney Valls shared the following comments on the case before his return to Hebbronville:

> I am glad and excited that the Latino people from El Paso have responded firmly and vigorously against certain officials who have classified the Mexican people as a colored race.
>
> This audacious act of discrimination, the product of ignorance and prejudice, has obviously injured the sublime pride of the Mexican people who have immediately responded by defending their great racial qualities and purity of blood.
>
> The mere thought of this cruel reproach and affront makes my blood boil with indignation, and the patriotic feelings in my heart surge with resentment and shame.
>
> The Mexican race are a sensitive and noble people. They have rejected life itself when their liberty and rights have been threatened, and they have found inspiration in the highest ideals, their devotion to honor and their contempt for insolence.

A people who believe in God, the dictates of conscience and the rights of man embodies the true American spirit whether they originate in the states of Maine or Texas, or they are puritans or Mexicans.

I do not wish to speak in vindictive or unyielding terms, but I do invoke the spirit of justice among fellow citizens that demand respect and trust, along with an affection for the people of Mexico.

The people of Mexico have a legendary and a righteous reputation of romance and nobility. Their pages of history speak of epic achievements, and our generous hearts are pleased to remember them fondly.

The deserving and highly patriotic people that they are, Mexicans are indignant before such an attempt to classify their race as a people of color.

A magnificent and vigorous blood, as good as any beating heart can host, runs through their veins.

We hold the Constitution of our nation in one hand and the bible of our God in the other, without regretting anything in our past and gratified with our present. With the greatest trust in the future, we of Latin blood stand firm before the whole world with as much pride and patriotism as the greatest sons of this nation.[33]

We do not ask for special privileges or any advantage. We only ask for equal rights before the law. We will build our future with accomplishments and courage.

* * *

San Antonio, Texas[34]
October 15, 1936

Honorable P. G. Lucas, President
Anti-Tuberculosis Association of Bexar County

Dear Mr. President:

I have long wanted to ask that our association classify Mexicans as Whites when compiling its statistics. I had not submitted an official request because we are very proud of our racial extraction and I did not want to convey the impression that we are ashamed of being Mexicans. However, the recent actions by the El Paso City Registrar brought to our attention the advisability and importance of settling this matter for good. This occurred when the registrar submitted his vital statistics reports to the Bureau of the Census of the US Department of Commerce. Naturally, my people registered a vigorous protest.

I am enclosing copies of two telegrams that speak for themselves. You will notice that in his reply to US Congressman Maury Maverick, the Director of the US Census Bureau states that the objectionable classification is due to an error made by the Division of Vital Statistics of the Bureau of the Census and that this will not occur again.[35] Federal and state agencies will now use the following classifications: Whites (including Mexicans), Negroes, and all others.

This is to advise you that I will appreciate it very much if our association will now use an identical classification regarding us, that is (1) Whites, including Mexicans.

Thanking you, I remain, Sincerely Yours,

Alonso S. Perales

Explanatory Note: Prior to Attorney Perales' letter, the Anti-Tuberculosis Association of Bexar County used the following classification system: Whites, Mexicans, and Colored. Council No. 16 of LULAC endorsed the statement. Perales sent similar letters to Charles K. Quin, Mayor of San Antonio and Dr. John W. Brown, State Health Officer of Texas as the President of the Justice Committee of Council 16.[36]

Mayor Quin Responds to a Letter from Perales[37]

Attorney Charles K. Quin, Mayor of the City of San Antonio, answered Perales' letter on December 2, 1936 and, among other things, said the following:

> I note that you request that the San Antonio Department of Health use the classification that the Department of Vital Statistics, Bureau of the Census, has recommended. This recommendation is accepted.
>
> For your information, I have just called the Health Department to inquire whether our local Vital Statistics has classified Mexicans as colored. They have advised me that they have never used that classification.

To All the Councils of the League of United Latin American Citizens[38]

El Paso, Texas
October 8, 1936

Recently, the Local Registrar of Statistics of El Paso attempted to classify the members of our Spanish-speaking race as Colored in his annual report to the Bureau of the Census, US Department of Commerce.

Vigorous protests and demonstrations followed immediately and we secured an injunction to prevent the registrar from classifying us as colored people for the purpose of registering vital statistics records for the Census. The registrar responded that the census directed him to prepare his annual report to Washington in that manner, but that he would classify the local Spanish-speaking community as White.

There is no question that the Census has insulted our race by classifying us as Colored in its reports. It is about time that each council of LULAC do something to correct this error.

Therefore, I suggest that we petition our respective congressman to call on the proper officials of the Census to classify us as Whites and not Colored.

This issue is of vital importance to the members of the League and I ask that you extend your wholehearted cooperation which I am sure each of you will be glad to render.

With kindest personal regards to each and all of you, I remain,

Yours fraternally,
Frank J. Galván, Jr.
President, LULAC

Mexicans Are Not to Be Classified as Colored in Texas; an Objection by Maverick and LULAC Members

The letter was sent by a Representative of the Federal Congress and the Census Representative responded indicating that the issue occurred due to an error.

Yesterday, Attorney Maury Maverick received an official delegation, consisting of Alonso S. Perales, Carlos Albidress, Carlos A. Ramírez and Florencio R. Flores, representing LULAC Councils 16 and 2 of San Antonio. The delegation delivered a resolution proposed by Perales and adopted on October 14 by Council 16 and seconded by Council 2.

The resolution, related to the protest against classifying Mexicans as Colored, includes the following:

> WHEREAS, we have received a missive from Attorney Francisco J. Galván Jr., General President of our League, to the effect that the Director of the Civil Registry of El Paso recently attempted to classify the members of our Spanish-speaking race as Colored when he presented his annual report to the Bureau of the Census;

> WHEREAS, in response to demonstrations, vigorous protests and a subsequent court decision, the registrar announced that the Census asked him to prepare the annual reports in this manner;

WHEREAS, Council 16 of LULAC, a civic organization composed of American citizens of Latino origin, RESOLVES in their meeting of October 14, 1936, to issue the most robust protest against such an insult by the Census; and

RESOLVES, that we establish a commission to present to Attorney Maury Maverick, US Representative of the Twentieth District, an appeal that he raise this issue immediately with the census so that the agency clearly and permanently classifies persons of Mexican or Spanish origin as Whites and not as Colored.

(signed)
Carlos Albidress, President
Council 16 of San Antonio, TX

Council 2 of San Antonio wholeheartedly endorses and adopts the resolution.

(signed)
Carlos A. Ramírez
Council 2 of San Antonio, TX

Once Attorney Maverick read the resolution, he sent a telegram to the Bureau of the Census protesting the issue and asking for an explanation. He received the following:

Honorable Maury Maverick, Representative[39]
Congress of the United States of America
San Antonio, Texas

The classification that you question in your telegram of October 15 is due to an error that the Division of Vital Statistics made in not following classifications established by the Bureau of the Census. The Census has not classified Mexicans as Colored in its population, agriculture and business reports. An error occurred in the classification of Mexicans as Colored in reports on vital statistics. We assure you that this will not occur again. The government will use the following classifications: White, including Mexicans, Negros, and all others. Thank you for your interest in looking over the well-being of our citizens.

(signed)
William L. Austin
Director of the Census

The Issue Has Ended[40]

US Representative Maverick immediately sent a message to Attorney Perales, in his capacity as the head of the committee that presented the protest.

With the statement that the head of the Bureau of the Census sent Representative Maverick, the action taken and announced at El Paso, Texas, which led to the protests by Mexicans in El Paso and San Antonio, and Attorney John A. Valls, District Attorney in Laredo, is in effect nullified.

San Antonio, Texas
October 15, 1936

Honorable William L. Austin
Director of the Bureau of the Census
Commerce Department
Washington, DC

Telegram

Dear Mr. Austin:

I wired you the following paragraph today:

I understand that your agency classified Americans of Mexican or Spanish origin as "People of Color." They and the inhabitants of the states of the Southwest take this as a very serious insult and, on their behalf, I protest such insult, if true. Please telegraph me if this is true so that I can engage the issue in a more detailed and complete manner. I appreciate your immediate response regarding the correction of such declarations.

The classification is also not accurate from an ethnological point of view. The popular use of the word "Colored" in the entire United States means African origin, and the Mexican or Spanish people are clearly not of African origin and, as such, the "Colored" designation is inaccurate.

Mexicans have been citizens in Texas for one hundred years, they have attended our schools, speak English as well as any other person and are no more different than, for example, the Italians, Romanians or Dutch that live in Oshkosh, Wisconsin, or in the City of New York. Neither the Italians from New York nor the other races are classified "Colored." Consequently, from the legal and common-sense perspective and the ordinary sense of justice and usual racial classification practices, the designation is unfair to the persons who live in the Southwest who are American citizens and happen to be of Mexican or Spanish origin.

Again, I protest on their behalf and suggest that the classification change. There is no reason to believe that a racial classification is necessary. If you think it is necessary to give Mexicans a racial classification, I see no reason for it. Having classified certain groups as "Whites" does not mean that we would now classify Mexicans or Spanish as "Other Whites," as you suggest. To classify these people as "Colored" is to mix them with the Negroes, which they are not. It also triggers extreme emotions. You should respect the sensibilities of the group. I ask that you give this issue immediate attention and correct the error.

I would be deeply grateful if you gave this matter your quick attention and advise me on what can be done.

Your attentive and faithful servant.

Maury Maverick, Member
US Congress

Mr. Cleofas Calleros in San Antonio[41]

Mr. Cleofas Calleros, representative of the Department of Immigration of the National Catholic Welfare Council of El Paso, arrived in San Antonio on Saturday to clarify the issue of the classification of Mexicans as a "Colored Race" in the birth and death records of San Antonio, Houston, Dallas and Fort Worth.[42]

Mr. Calleros led the first protest in response to the attempt by Alex Powell, the Secretary of the Civil Registry of El Paso, to classify the newly born of Mexican origin as a "Colored" race. The protest resulted in Dr. J. T. McCamant, Head of the Health Department of El Paso, to declare "that they had not intended to adopt this classification and that they would not do it."

As if to justify what they had announced to do in El Paso, Mr. McCamant also said that other Texas cities were using the classifications of "Whites" and "Negroes," and including Mexicans in the latter group. He noted San Antonio, Houston, Dallas and Fort Worth as examples. This is what motivated Mr. Calleros to come here. He sought to clarify if San Antonio officials were classifying Mexicans as "Colored" and, if so, to register a complaint.

Mr. Calleros visited *La Prensa* and personally shared the facts that we now provide to our readers.

When the Department of Health of El Paso tried to classify Mexicans as a "Colored Race" on October 5, LULAC and the Veterans of the World War petitioned for an injunction against such action before the District Court. Dr. McCamant responded to the court that he wanted to go through with his decision in El Paso because San Antonio and other cities in Texas were using the classification in question. In his response to the court filing, he stated that he wanted to proceed with his plans because San Antonio and other cities in Texas were using the same designation or classification for Mexicans. Dr. McCamant presented the report that San Antonio officials sent the week ending on October 3. He entered the report as evidence that San Antonio uses the designation in question.

The Case was Resolved in Washington

Mr. Callejos submitted a protest before the National Catholic Council in Washington and its director was able to obtain a re-designation of Mexicans as a "White Race."

"But there is still the local problem in each community," Mr. Callejos told us "and each place must launch a campaign to abolish the designation."

On Saturday evening, Mr. Callejos met with Maury Maverick, US Congressman, Alonso S. Perales, Florencio R. Flores and Carlos Albidress. They decided to meet today at 10 a.m. with Mayor Charles K. Quin to protest the humiliating process and to ensure that the city will now classify the births and deaths of Mexicans with the "White Race" designation.

According to the statements by Dr. McCamant, San Antonio officials are submitting reports to Washington that classify Mexicans as "Colored." This information originated with L. P. Bishop, administrator for the Health Department and Dr. W. A. King, medical doctor from San Antonio.

Our Nation Will Protest the Classification of Mexicans, the Mexican Chamber of Deputies Will Prepare It[43]

ASSOCIATED PRESS

Mexico DF, October 19. Deputy César A. Lara announced this afternoon that he is waiting for official confirmation appearing in newspapers that the State of Texas classifies Mexicans as Negroes before he proposes a statement of protest in the Chamber of Deputies.

Other deputies declared that they are approaching President Lázaro Cárdenas to request that he submit a formal statement through diplomatic channels against any instance in which the US government classifies Mexicans as an "inferior race."

The local newspapers have already noted that several Mexican organizations from El Paso have protested the practice of classifying Mexicans as "Negroes" in the city's birth and death data.

Maury Maverick, US Congressman, Alonso S. Perales, Carlos Albidress, Attorney Carlos A. Ramírez and Jacobo I. Rodríguez, representatives of LULAC Council 16, met yesterday with Mayor Quin on the classification of our people by government offices.

Perales reported to us that Mayor Quin said the following:

> Regarding the instructions attributed to the federal census on the classification of Mexicans, the Health Department of San Antonio has been registering Mexicans since June of this year as colored people in its reports to the office of the census.

Mr. Quin added that such a classification has occurred in response to instructions from the census offices, but that the Health Department of San Antonio locally registers them as Mexicans and that, in accordance to the laws of the state of Texas, Mexicans are Whites.

Actions by Mayor Quin

Perales also informed us that Mayor Quin read copies of several letters that he recently sent to Senators Morris Sheppard and Thomas Connally in which he pleads that they intervene to insure that the census modifies its method of classification so that officials do not classify Mexicans as colored people.

Maverick's Letter

After the previously noted meeting, the mayor and Perales visited the office of Representative Maverick. He dictated a letter to William L. Austin, Director of the Bureau of the Census. Representative Maverick pleaded that Mr. Austin immediately send instructions with the correction that he promised in his telegram of the fifteenth of this month so that the error not be repeated by the Division of Vital Statistics in Washington and that, in the future, three classifications are to be used: Whites, including Mexicans; Negroes and other races.

Representative Maverick also requested that Austin make the correction retroactive and that he send copies of the instructions in question to him and LULAC.

More Actions in Support of Mexicans[44]

Representative Maverick proposes a way to avoid new incidents

Attorney Perales, along with Carlos Albidress, Attorney Carlos A. Ramírez and Jacobo I. Rodríguez, visited Mayor Quin to affirm the terms of the classification of Mexicans in the demographic records of San Antonio. Perales has continued to leave no doubt about how government officials classify persons of Latin American background—in observance of the law.

Perales provided us with copies of the correspondence from Representative Maverick to the Director of the Bureau of the Census in Washington, dated October 15, 1936.

Perales also informs us that he and his colleagues will continue to insist that the government use the categories of Whites and Colored without a separate one for Mexicans to designate members of the Latin American race. They are doing this to avoid misunderstandings and incidents like the one that recently occurred in El Paso.

The petition is in accord with the laws of Texas that identify the inhabitants of Mexican origin as members of the White race.

* * *

San Antonio, TX
October 15, 1936

Honorable William L. Austin
Director, US Bureau of the Census
Washington, DC

    I understand that Americans of Mexican or Spanish descent are classified as people of color. They, as well as residents from the Southwest states, in general, consider this to be a great insult, and in order to support them, I am protesting against this. Please send me a telegram to confirm if this is true in order for me to discuss the issue with you in a detailed and extensive manner. I will appreciate an immediate response to correct the aforementioned statements.

Maury Mauverick, Representative
US Congress
Washington, DC
October 15, 1936

* * *

Honorable Maury Maverick
US Congress Representative
San Antonio, TX

    The contested classification in your telegram from October 15, 1936 is a result of a mistake made by the division of vital statistics when it did not follow the classifications established by the Director of the US Bureau of the Census. The Census Director has not classified Mexicans as people of color in his vital statistics reports on population, agriculture and business. The promise is that the mistake will not be repeated. We will use three classifications, white, including Mexicans; Black and everything else. I appreciate your interest in watching over the wellbeing of your citizens.

William L. Austin, Director
US Bureau of the Census

The Bureau of the Census Declares Mexicans as Whites

The director of the Bureau of the Census has just sent Representative Maverick a long letter that explains with great clarity and care the case of the classification of Mexicans as Colored. He states that this is a Texas issue, that his office did not send instructions to San Antonio to use such a classification, but that the HEALTH DEPARTMENT requested its use.

The letters between Representative Maverick and the director of Bureau of the Census appear below:

San Antonio, Texas
October 19, 1936

Honorable William L. Austin[45]
Director, Bureau of the Census
Department of Commerce
Washington, DC

Regarding the Classification of the people of Mexican Extraction

Dear Mr. Austin:

I telegraphed you on October 15 regarding the classification of people of Mexican extraction and you in effect responded that your agency would only use three classifications: Whites, including Mexicans, Negroes and everyone else.

We called on the Mayor of San Antonio today and he stated that the classification of "Colored" was in pursuance of instructions from the Bureau of the Census in June of this year.

I, therefore, am very anxious that you do two things:

FIRST: instruct the various cities of Texas to change the classification as set out in your telegram to me.

SECOND: that a retroactive reclassification be made of people of Mexican extraction to "Whites, including Mexicans," and in that way correct the situation and everyone will be satisfied.

This is extremely important to these people in view of the fact that possibly thirty or fifty years from now the Census could use the records to prove that someone is "Colored." In the next few years, many of our people will migrate to other states in the union. Let us suppose that one of these people migrated to Mississippi or Alabama. Some officious clerk might examine the records and find the registry, and this would be very distressing and humiliating. As far as that is concerned, Mississippi and Alabama would not be the only places where this would be humiliating and embarrassing. This would also be the case in northern and western states.

I shall appreciate it if you will make every possible effort to make this reclassification retroactive. I am sure that this would not require more than some possible indexes and a few headings. If this is acceptable—and I am sure that it would not be expensive—I would very much appreciate if you would use a rubber stamp with the words printed somewhat as follows: "Erroneously listed as Colored. The classification should be Whites, including Mexicans."

If you use such a rubber stamp in the original documents, the situation will be such that if someone asks the census for copies, the error will be evident in the copied documents.

It may not appear to be a very important or serious matter from where you sit, but I assure you that it is very serious, not only for the people of Mexican extraction but for the old American stock as well.

I want you to send copies of your instructions to the cities and your subordinates so that Latin American newspapers can publish them. The request for these documents should not interfere with the conduct of your affairs. It will simply assure the hundreds of thousands of people who have Spanish names.

Yours very truly,
(signed)
Maury Maverick, Representative
US Congress

* * *

Washington, DC[46]
October 26, 1936

Honorable Maury Maverick
San Antonio, Texas

Dear Mr. Maverick:

I have received your letter dated October 19. Clearly, you as well as the Mayor of San Antonio have bad intelligence regarding the collection and preparation of vital statistics by the US Bureau of the Census.

The recorder of vital statistics gathers the original records of births and deaths for the state in Austin, Texas. The census receives copies of these records and pays for them. Each state in the union has its own laws over vital statistics and conducts its own collection. The Census, by federal law, secures copies of those records and prepares the birth and death records for the United States.

The federal government has spent more than thirty years carrying out this cooperative arrangement and in preparing the birth and death records, responsibilities that currently includes every state in the union. The state of Texas was the last to join in this recording procedure. This occurred in 1933.

A combination of state and federal laws governs the collection of statistics of births and deaths. The steps that the census can take to change the racial classifications will be clear once I explain the relation between the census and the health offices in cities and states.

Acting under the Texas Law of Vital Statistics the local enumerators—of which there are one thousand three hundred and eighty-four of them—collect birth and death certificates. The Office of the Texas Health Department archives and stores these certificates. By state law, these certificates require racial information.

The Census received from Texas offices—like from other states—a non-official but complete and accurate copy of the records. The census pays the state for these copies.

The Census uses these copies in its compilation of birth and death statistics and destroys them after the tables are constructed. As such, the census does not have an archive of the individual birth and death records. Since federal law required that the census reports remain confidential, no one can obtain copies of these unofficial copies. Officials use the reports to prepare the statistics.

Consequently, whatever change is sought should be proposed to the Office of Vital Statistics of Texas where the original and official records are archived. Nevertheless, the original records do not generally include the word "Colored." The records contain specific information regarding racial origin, such as Negro, Indian, Mexican, and White.

Given the cost of tabulating large numbers of statistics, the census cannot provide separate tables for all the racial groups. This is why we compiled tables with summaries of figures related to Whites and All Others. The group identified as All Others is known as "Colored" because it includes mostly Negroes, although Indians, Chinese, and others are also incorporated. The Mexican category was included in this heterogeneous group under the antiquated classification. From now on, the classification will appear as follows:

1. Whites, including Mexicans
2. Negroes
3. Other Races

The current relationship between the Census and the individual cities from Texas is somewhat different. Five cities (Dallas, El Paso, Fort Worth, Houston and San Antonio) send a weekly report to the census. These reports only provide the number of deaths, but not personal information on each of the departed. For the sake of brevity, local officials provide reports on the deaths of whites and "all the others."

The Census did not send instructions to the city of San Antonio regarding the reports, but the city's health office requested on July 29, 1936, that its information be classified in that manner in the Weekly Health Index.

The Census has requested that each city that previously used a racial classification in its weekly reports adjust their telegraphic submissions with the new classifications. I am attaching a sample of the new form.

Since the Census does not have the original records and the Office of Vital Statistics of the state archives them in Austin, we use the copies that we obtain for statistical purposes and in accordance with the law. It was most unfortunate that our division of vital statistics committed an error upon classifying Mexicans as "Colored." Obviously, this will not occur again in any public information produced by the Census. **The government will classify Mexicans as "Whites."**

Sincerely, your servant
(signed)
William L. Austin, Director
US Bureau of the Census

Several Clubs Discuss the Case of the Shanties and Sheds in San Antonio[47]

The clubs Zonta, Altrusa and two groups representing the Women's Business and Professional Club met on Wednesday at midday. The organizations received the following guests: N. Straus Nayfach and Jesse N. Fletcher of the Junior Chamber of Commerce, the Reverend Carmen Tranchese, rector of Our Lady of Guadalupe Church and Vice President of the Anti-Tuberculosis Society of Bexar County. Alonso S. Perales, Florencio R. Flores and Pablo A. Meza also participated as LULAC representatives, while Mrs. E. T. Cornelius, representing the Mexican Christian Institute, and Mr. Arthur Biard, prominent real estate figure and civic leader of San Antonio also participated.

After lunch, the participants promptly entered a discussion on the war against sheds and unhygienic neighborhoods.

Mr. Fletcher, President of the Junior Chamber of Commerce, stated that he has two reasons for supporting the campaign. He is concerned that the neighborhoods are dilapidated and unhealthy and the shanties are major causes for the spread of diseases. Humanitarian concerns have also prompted him to act. After the presentation, the participants viewed a film of selected parts of the city to draw a clear contrast between the districts where the shanties abound and the places that have hygienic and habitable residences. Mr. Nayfach narrated the film.

The Rev. Tranchese Speaks

Soon thereafter, the Rev. Tranchese spoke. He said that the war against the shanties is well justified under all circumstances, even from the economic point of view. The current situation has caused many diseases, especially tuberculosis among the poor. This requires that the public hospitals and welfare agencies treat them, meaning that the public ends up paying the costs. He also referred to juvenile delinquency and the criminalization of the adults, which also represents a cost to the people of San Antonio. Lastly, he referred to the fact that this city spends thousands of dollars advertising the climate and other attractive features offered by this community, but that it was ineffective when people from other places in the union read that San Antonio has the highest mortality rate from tuberculosis than any other American city. Rev. Tranchese finished by stating, "Let us convert San Antonio into a truly healthy metropolis."

They Should Pay Better Wages

Mrs. E. T. Cornelius followed by saying "The dust and dirt in the shanties and huts are not typical of the Mexican people who live in conditions that are being remedied." Necessity forces those unfortunate persons to live like that." She pointed out that one of the ways to correct the situation is to pay poor people a higher wage for their work. "I have observed," added Mrs. Cornelius, "that as soon as the heads of household are able to move, they leave the shanties for hygienic and habitable places.

Perales, General Inspector of LULAC and President of the Commissions of Education and Justice of Council 16 followed by introducing his fellow members, Mr. Pablo A. Meza and Mr. Florencio R. Flores. He added, "We have just heard from the representatives of the Junior Chamber of Commerce, Our Lady of Guadalupe Church and the Mexican Christian Institute. Now you are going to hear the Mexican-American point of view."

The Animated Words of Attorney Perales

My companions and I are representing LULAC, a civic organization with numerous councils in Texas that seek to produce first class citizens of Latino origin. As such, we are very interested in acquiring the necessary means for the completion of our project. Clearly, we see the war against the *corrales* and shanties with profound concern. We fear diseases on our persons and families and, as the speakers that preceded me stated, we are very interested in the development of good and progressive citizens of Mexican origin in the Lone Star state and long for their progress in this city, our state and our nation. However, our experiences in our civic struggles have led us to conclude that this progress is impossible when the citizens of a country place an unfortunate minority in a corner of a city and tell them: 'Yes, we acknowledge that you are American citizens, but we do not want you to progress. We will not allow you to educate yourselves well, nor are we going to pay you a wage that will allow you to live in a hygienic and habitable house. We only want you to sweep our streets and be our domestic servants. This attitude is an injustice to them and does serious harm to the nation because instead of preparing them to contribute to the progress and development of the nation, they do the opposite. Someone will inevitably complain that we Mexicans are a burden to the community where we live. The members of LULAC have found that the general tendency among our fellow Anglo American citizens is to educate the Mexican youth in shanties and huts while they construct magnificent brick buildings for the Anglo American children. Some communities in Texas do not allow our Mexican youth to attend their high schools because officials do not permit it. We have also discovered that our fellow Anglo American citizens—we speak in general terms—do not care if we live in unhygienic corrals or shanties, nor are they inclined to pay Mexican workers a wage that could help them progress and be content, regardless how intelligent or capable they may be.

We Must Seek Social Justice for the Mexican

Ladies and Gentlemen, there is no doubt that the best that we can do in San Antonio and in the entire state of Texas is to give the inhabitants of Mexican origin all that is necessary for them to develop as educated and progressive citizens, like the members of the most advanced races in our cosmopolitan nation. This is the just and humane action to take, the very thing that serves the best interests of the Republic of Texas. If we do this, we will produce excellent citizens and will develop a broad mutual understanding between the two great races of the Western hemisphere and, even more, we will enjoy a more authentic and effective form of international cooperation. On the issue of Mexico-US relations, we Tejanos believe that you can secure this cooperation when you entertain leading Mexican officials who occasionally visit and, during after-dinner conversations, make speeches on goodwill and international solidarity. You do this without understanding that we can only win the hearts of the people of Mexico **by granting social justice to Mexicans in Texas**, not with banquets or superficial gestures of goodwill.

The business and industrial leaders of Texas, our orator continued, should not lose sight of the fact that if the people of Texas win over Mexico's frank and sincere friendship, they will also attract their dollars, since it is an undeniable fact that the best foreign business partner that Texas can have is the Mexican Republic.

According to official statistics for 1935, the United States imported goods worth $42,326,000 dollars and exported an amount equivalent to $65,567,000. This gives us an idea of the importance of our trade relations with Mexico. Like good businesspeople, **we must treat Mexicans well in Texas so that we can win over our friends and brothers on the other side of the Rio Bravo.**

The citizens and inhabitants of Mexican origin in the Alamo City are very pleased to see that so many Anglo American citizens are daily joining the movement that seeks social justice for our Raza in this city.

Wonderful! This is a solid indication of better days for our community and our state. All of you can forever rest assured that we appreciate your friendly and Christian posture and your valuable and constructive cooperation. Pray to heaven, Ladies and Gentlemen, that we continue cooperating to solve our shared problems and that the day is not far when we will finally see **a genuine Americanism** and **a lasting and true international friendship**.

Mr. Biard followed by approving the project presented by the orators.

Again, the Classification of Mexicans, It Appears in the Social Security Form[48]

Perales, the Inspector General of LULAC and President of the Pro-Justice Commission of Council 16, received a telegram yesterday from Mr. Cleofas Calleros, from El Paso, Texas, also a member of LULAC. The letter reads as follows:

> Contact Attorney Maury Maverick immediately and implore that he protests Social Security Form SS-5 that the Post Office is distributing. Item 12 on the first page re-classifies Mexicans as **not White race**. Ask that he telegraph the Department of the Treasury and the vice president and plead that they stop circulating the forms or that they remove the word "Mexican."

Perales met with Attorney Maury Maverick, US Congressman, who quickly sent several telegrams protesting the classification. Maverick and Perales then met with Attorney Oscar Powell, the district's representative with the Social Security Administration. Attorney Powell immediately asked one of his secretaries to bring him a copy of Form SS-5 of the Social Security Administration, and found that Item 12 in the second page read as follows:

> If you are White or Negro, place a mark (x) in the corresponding space. If you are not White or Negro, write in the appropriate space your color or race. Typical examples of classifications for other colored persons are: Mexicans, Chinese, Japanese, Indians, Filipinos, etc.

Attorney Powell responded to Perales:

> You are right in protesting. I will take immediate action on the matter. However, I should warn you that about fifty million forms have been distributed in the United States and, therefore, it will be difficult to resolve the problem.

Congressman Maverick and Perales, however, are determined not to waste one single second to see that the problem is resolved in a manner that is satisfactory to the Mexican people of the United States of America. Attorney Perales said the following when *La Prensa* asked him for a statement:

> Congressman Maury Maverick, Mr. Cleofas Calleros and I are working hard and fast to avoid another injustice on ***Nuestra Raza***. If the laws of the United States of America recognize us as Whites, and given that the US Bureau of the Census has resolved the issue and ordered that in the future we are to be classified as Whites, the Department of the Treasury has mistakenly classified us as **Not a White Race**. On behalf of Attorney Francisco J. Galván, Inspector General of LULAC, I protest vehemently against this injustice and urge **all** the presidents of the councils of LULAC as well as the presidents of all the other Mexican-American and Mexican societies from this country, that they do the same. The presidents of Mexican-American societies should **immediately telegraph** their US Representatives to protest and to urge them to present their formal protest before the Department of the Treasury and before his Excellency John N. Garner, Vice President of the United States of America. He is currently in Uvalde, his home. **We must act immediately. There is no time to lose.**
>
> Another thing: I advise **all** the employees of Mexican origin who receive Form SS-5 to be careful in classifying yourselves as **Whites**. In other words, place a mark (x) immediately after the word White. This way, in the process of protesting and abiding by the laws of our country, and in

accordance with the Resolution of the Bureau of the Census, we will classify ourselves as **Whites**. When we do this, **we do not violate any law of the nation. The only thing that we do not obey is the arbitrary and mistaken instruction from the Department of the Treasury. This is why we should not have any fear whatsoever. When we classify ourselves as Whites, we do nothing more than to obey the laws of our nation.** Obviously, in order for the correction to be complete we should contact our congressional representatives, pleading that they in turn and on our behalf ask the Department of the Treasury to make the correction.

The Classification of Mexicans as Whites[49]

Many individuals have asked me how persons of Mexican origin in the United States should identify themselves when they fill out Form SS-5 from the Social Security Administration. My response has been and will always be the following: We should identify ourselves as WHITES. That is, we should mark (x) immediately next to the word White, this way: White (x). I base my view on the following reasons.

Article 2900 of the Civil Code of Texas identifies colored races as follows:

The words "colored races" and "colored children," as used in this title, include all persons of mixed blood that are of Negro lineage.[50]

Article 493 of the Penal Code defines the White race as follows:

The term "Negro" also includes all person of mixed blood descended from Negro ancestry since the third generation inclusive, though one ancestor of each generation may have been a white person. **Any person that is not included in the foregoing definition is deemed a White person within the meaning of the law.**[51]

Article 1659, second section, notes as follows:

The definition of the word Negro. **The term Negro, as used herein includes every person of African descent as defined by the statutes of this state.**[52]

In the July 25, 1934, opinion of Attorney James V. Allred and now governor of our state, requested by Bryan Blalock, Travis County District Attorney, he stated:

Moreover, the common usage of the words "White Persons," as it is generally understood by the people of this state includes persons who are commonly designated "Mexicans." The whole course of racial legislation in this state is predicated upon that proposition. See, for example, INDEPENDENT SCHOOL DISTRICT VERSUS SALVATIERRA, 35 S. W. (2) 790.[53]

As used in this opinion, the term "Mexican" is intended to include those persons of Caucasian descent or of mixed Caucasian and American Indian blood. So understood, it is my opinion that "Mexicans" must be considered "White citizens" within the meaning of the above quoted resolution of the Democratic Convention.

We have carefully examined the cases of *Takad Ozawa v. United States*, 260 US 178, 43 Supplement, Ct. 65, and United States versus Vhagat Singh Thind, 261 US 604, 43 Supplement, Ct. 338. Neither of the cases cited hold that Mexicans are not to be considered "White persons;" those cases decided that within the meaning of the naturalization laws the term "White persons" means persons of Caucasian descent. On the other hand, it has been expressly decided that under the foregoing statute Mexicans are eligible to naturalize. **In Re Rodriguez, 81 Fed. 337.**

It is therefore my opinion, and you are respectfully advised that, in light of common understanding of the terms, and in view of the practical construction of the same, Mexicans are to be considered "White citizens" within the meaning of the resolution adopted by the

State Convention of the Democratic Party on May 24, 1932, and hence that if those persons are otherwise qualified to vote, they are entitled to participate in the democratic primary election to be held on July 28, 1934.

(signed)
James V. Allred, Attorney General
State of Texas

The director of the Census confirmed his explanation and resolved the matter in a letter to Congressman Maury Maverick on October 26, 1936.[54]

Thus, the laws of our nation recognize us as **Whites**, and we should obey these laws by classifying ourselves as **Whites** in Form SS-5 of the Social Security Administration. As is evident, our racial dignity and our obligation to obey the laws of our country places on us the essential obligation to classify ourselves as **Whites**.

The Government of the United States Corroborates the Opinion of Attorney Perales

In a telegram to Congressman Maverick, Guy T. Helvering, Commissioner of Internal Revenue, Treasury Department, states the following:

> Regarding your telegram addressed to the Secretary of the Treasury on the classification of Mexicans on Form SS-5. The Bureau of the Census decision was not made until October 29, 1936. On that date approximately forty million forms had been printed. You will of course realize that it would have been impossible to reprint these forms. **Notwithstanding the instructions on item twelve, Mexicans should be classified as Whites.**[55]

The previous telegram of November 23, 1936, is a response to a message from US Congressman Maverick that Perales had suggested. The telegram read as follows:

> Honorable Henry Morgenthau
> Treasury Secretary
> Washington, DC
>
> I protest the classification of Mexicans as **Not White Race** in Form SS-5, item 12 of the Department of the Treasury. The Bureau of the Census has adopted the following classification: **Whites, including Mexicans, Negroes, and all others**. All the official classifications should be the same.
>
> (signed)
> Maury Maverick
> Member of Congress

After receiving the telegram from Helvering, US Congressman Maverick assured Perales he would contact the Department of the Treasury requesting general instructions to the entire country that Mexicans should be classified **White**.

[Taken from *La Prensa*, San Antonio, TX, November 26, 1936.]

Telegram[56]

Mission, Texas
December 10, 1937

Alonso S. Perales
614 Gunter Building
San Antonio, Texas

Advise outcome of the representations made by the US Treasury regarding Security Act cards. Having difficulties with the Post Office regarding the classifications. We will hold on to the cards. Answer immediately.

Adolfo de la Garza, President
Council 5, Mission

Telegraphic Response to Mr. de la Garza

Frank Bane, Executive Director of the Social Security Administration, telegraphed US Representative Maverick on November 27 with the following:

> Regarding your telegram, as official response to Form SS-5, question and instructions on item twelve, the Internal Revenue Service says that, notwithstanding instructions, the government should classify Mexicans as Whites. We understand that the Bureau of the Census did not make its decision until October 29, 1936. By then, the agency had printed approximately forty million forms. Of course, you can understand that it would have been impossible to reprint the forms. The

United States Postal Service sent an official response to El Paso and Laredo. Considering covering more territory through Postmasters and publicity.

If the Postmaster from Mission refused to classify Mexicans as Whites, I suggest that you immediately notify the Department of the Treasury, Frank Bane and your US Representative.

The following persons also contacted Perales on the classification issue and received responses:

Mrs. F. I. Montemayor, Secretary of Women's Council 15, Laredo, TX, LULAC
Mr. A. C. Fernández, President of Council 14, Poteet, TX, LULAC
Mr. Eligio Marín, Freeport, TX
Mr. Pedro Fernández, Victoria, TX

The Words of Alonso S. Perales through KMAC Station on the Occasion of an Artistic Contest

Miss Luz González, President, Club Copelia:

I very much appreciate the kindness of the CLUB COPELIA in honoring me the way you do this evening. I will never forget the honor that you bestow on me tonight.

I accepted your invitation immediately and now gladly address the Mexican people of San Antonio. I applaud the idea of a contest sponsored by Bell Furniture with the collaboration of local clubs to show the public of San Antonio the artistic talent that exists among the Mexicans. Wonderful! I am delighted to see that organizations are giving our people the opportunity to display their talents and in that way demonstrate the latent capacity of our Raza.

I celebrate with great enthusiasm the interest that the Mexican clubs of San Antonio have in the artistic side of our evolution. It is an unmistakable indication of our progress. It is good to see that some persons really care and work for the well-being of our people. Blessed is our race for having sincere, active and enthusiastic persons who work earnestly for the progress of our people.

Mexicans would do right by adopting the following motto: FOR THE PROGRESS OF MY RAZA. Every day, we should dedicate some of our time to something that contributes to this idea. We are well aware that society grants races, like individuals, the recognition and respect they have earned with their capacities, attributes and virtues.

The work of our leaders has been doubly difficult and trying. They have faced obstacles caused by racial prejudice and the apathy of some people. Allport, the sociologist, has stated that since the beginning of time some persons have been content with the way things are. According to him, in some cases this has been due to the lack of a will to take the necessary steps to progress and, in other cases, the inability to understand and appreciate progressive actions.

We must keep in mind that the progress of our Raza requires two things. Leaders should be ready to devote the necessary time to guide and orient our people and the community should be prepared to progress. Nothing discourages the leader more than the apathy or indifference of a people regarding the actions necessary to benefit them. Binder comments on this:

> Leaders seek to develop all of their kind. They think that they have discovered the necessary actions, but persons that do not want or cannot raise themselves to higher levels frustrate their efforts. Even more, leaders need the group to work alongside him, since he recognizes his limitations. Everyone has a talent, however small it may be. They must develop it if society is to advance.[57]

Let us continue with our struggle.

November 1936

The Poll Tax or Voting Tax[58]

What is the Poll Tax or Voting Tax?
According to the laws of Texas, every **American citizen** must pay in order to vote.

How much do we have to pay in Bexar County?
One dollar and fifty cents. A state law allows counties to charge an additional amount of twenty-five cents, more or less, for its own use. This is why some counties require one dollar and seventy-five cents.

What happens to the money?
One dollar is for the public schools and fifty cents is for the general revenue of the county.

Is every **citizen** required to pay the electoral tax?
Definitely yes. Otherwise, they will neither have a voice nor a vote in government. That is, citizens will not be able to express their will regarding the persons that should fill elected positions or the problems that government should resolve. In other words, citizens that do not pay the electoral tax in Texas are inconsequential to our nation's government.

Is the vote the most powerful weapon that citizens can use to throw out bad officials?
Absolutely. The people elect them and the people are the ones that can throw them out **by voting against them if they are incompetent, dishonest, unjust, good for nothing officials**.

The founders of this republic intended that the people rule and the public officials act as their servants. In order for this to happen, however, the citizens need to be **free** and **intelligent** and pay the Poll Tax, or the Voting Tax, so that they can vote.

Who has to pay the Voting Tax in order to vote?
Persons between the ages of twenty-one and sixty years who have lived in the state since January 1 of every year should pay it.

Do persons under twenty-one years have the right to vote?
No.

Who can vote without having to pay the electoral tax?
1. Persons over sixty years of age.
2. The blind.
3. The deaf and mute.
4. Persons with a permanent physical disability.
5. Those who have lost a hand or a foot.

These persons, however, need to secure a certificate before the election from the county's tax collector that notes such an exemption.

Can we pay the voting tax at any time?
No. Government officials collect the tax in October, November, December and January. The last day when citizens can pay it and ensure their right to vote is January 31.

What does the payment of the poll tax have to do with our progress and well-being?
A great deal. If you do not pay the Poll Tax, you cannot vote, and if you do not vote, you cannot remove from power the city, country, state or federal officials, and members of the school board that do not treat our Raza well. For instance, a county sheriff who tolerates or defends his deputies who

unfairly arrest and at times deny peaceful and honest citizens or residents their lives; or

Criminal prosecutors (whether a county or district attorney) who do not pursue with diligence and determination persons who abuse honest and peaceful persons and become defenders of the delinquents; or

A mayor and commissioners who only care to pave, clean and beautify the communities where Anglo Americans live and do not concern themselves one bit with the well-being and progress of Mexicans; or

A mayor and commissioners who classify our own as a colored race; or

Judges who always rule in favor of Anglo Americans even though the Mexicans are not guilty; or

School boards that construct impressive brick buildings for the education of Anglo American youth, while they require that ours receive instructions in huts and shacks and deny them the right to attend high school. There is no better solution than the ballot box. We should not forget that in our state no citizen cannot do this without paying the Poll Tax, the Voting Tax.

Do women also have to pay the Poll Tax?
Yes, since they have the right to vote. In our country, women have the same civic and moral obligation as men—to elect **competent, fair and honest** persons to public office.

Do Mexican citizens that pay the Poll Tax have the right to vote?
No. The right to vote is only available to the citizens of the United States of America.

How does one acquire citizenship in this country?
According to the first clause of the fourteenth amendment of the federal constitution, anyone born or naturalized within the jurisdiction of the United States are citizens of the United States and the state he or she inhabits.

At the start of your questions and responses, you say that in order to ensure that public officials are loyal servants to the people, as intended by the founders of this republic, it is necessary that the citizens are **free** and **informed**. Could you explain what you mean with the words "free" and "informed"?

Citizens should study the qualifications and views of the candidates for public office, as well as the policy issues that are to be resolved in the ballot box (the issuance of bonds and constitutional amendments, for example) and then vote as their conscience dictates. Your vote should express your **personal opinion** and not someone else's. In other words, we should try to vote independently for whatever we wish and not according to what someone tells us or suggests that we do. Obviously, in order to develop our own sense of things, we should listen and read the arguments in favor and against candidates and related policy issues. This is very different from voting blindly—without studying or even thinking about the issue—only because so-and-so tells us to vote for this or that candidate.

Concerning this, I will take the liberty of making a very special recommendation. Everyone should receive some civic instruction to carry out their role as citizens. With this purpose in mind, I recommend that all civic organizations purchase the following pamphlet. It sells for ten cents each:

"The Civic Catechism on the Rights and Obligations
of American Citizens"

English-Spanish Edition, published by the National
Catholic Welfare Council
1213 Massachusetts Ave., NW,
Washington, DC

Another useful work that I also recommend, and it DOES NOT COST ANYTHING, is the following:

"US MANUAL OF INFORMATION FOR
IMMIGRANTS AND FOREIGNERS"
Published by The National Society, Daughters
of the American Revolution
Memorial Continental Hall
Washington, DC

This pamphlet is available in English, Spanish and several other languages. When requesting it, you should specify the language. Both works are very useful for all the citizens or residents of this country. Every president of civic organizations would do well in ordering as soon as possible a copy for each member.

San Antonio, Texas
December 1, 1936

A Letter from San Antonio Councils 16, 12 and 2 of the League of United Latin American Citizens to Manufacturers and Businessmen and other Persons from San Antonio Requesting a Higher Daily Wage for Mexican Workers

Dear Sirs:

The undersigned, members of LULAC, a national civic society made up of American citizens of Latin origin, request your help in solving a serious problem affecting the progress and well-being of this community.

We are very interested in producing first-class citizens of Latino origin as well as in working for the progress and advancement of our communities. Because of this, we actively and enthusiastically participate in almost all the civic activities of this city. At the present, for example, we are cooperating with the local Junior Chamber of Commerce in its campaign against the *corrales* and shanties to lower the high mortality rate caused by tuberculosis and other illnesses. We are attaching a pamphlet so that you can see that in San Antonio more people die from tuberculosis than in any other city in the United States.

We believe that if clean and habitable homes replaced such *corrales* and shanties, we would not only be doing justice to the persons who live there, but would be making our city one of the healthiest, progressive and attractive in the country.

We, along with many leaders and civic organizations of San Antonio, are convinced that the basic problem is an economic one. In other words, in order for Mexicans to educate themselves and their children and to live in clean and habitable homes, it is necessary that they receive a daily wage that will allow them to maintain a normal human existence. We honestly and firmly believe that if manufacturers, executives and other persons that hire Mexican workers would raise their wages, they would not only act at a high humanitarian level, but their actions would bring economic benefits to the entire community. Clearly, the recipients of the raises would have more money to spend on rent, food, clothing and other indispensable items in the normal life of a citizen.

Can we count on your cooperation?

We thank you in advance for your consideration of this important issue, and await your response, sincerely yours,

LEAGUE OF UNITED LATIN AMERICAN CITIZENS

Atty. Alonso s. Perales
Inspector General and President
Committee in Favor of a Daily Wage

Carlos Albidress, President
Council No. 16

Mrs. Amelia P. de Ramírez, President
Ladies Council No. 12

Atty. Carlos A. Ramírez, President
Council No. 2

Florencio R. Flores
District Governor

Committee Members

Jorge D. Vann
Dr. Hesiquio N. González
Wenceslao Martínez
Juan Esquivel
Eugenio A. Hernández
Agustín A. González

Atty. Pablo G. González
M. C. Trub
Gregorio R. Salinas
Eleuterio Hernández
Ernesto Vidales

San Antonio, Texas
December 5, 1936

Mexican Visitors Bring Much Benefit[59]

The Mexican team of polo players that visited our city left a very good impression. General Jesús Jaime Quiñones heads the team, and it includes Major Antonio Nava, Major Manuel Ruanova and Captain Vicente Fonseca. They came in response to a special invitation by the San Antonio Chamber of Commerce to participate in an international polo tournament that took place on December 30 and 31, and January 2 and 3.

On December 29, the Mexican polo players played against a team from Austin that included George Miller, J. B. Gilmore, Cecil Smith and Rube Williams, the last two being of world stature. The next day, they competed against a San Antonio team that included Jack Lapham, Rube Goodnight, Roy Berry and Semp Russ. On January 1, they played against a local American military team and on the second, they once again played against the Austin team. The Mexican team lost the first two games and won the last two, which were really the most important ones in the series.

The Mexican polo players play well and are excellent riders. Besides this, they are educated, very affable and modest. This is why they have left a great impression among the Anglo American and Mexican people of San Antonio. The Anglo American people knew how to observe and judge the Mexican polo players with impartiality, and today they appreciate, respect and admire them. We, the Mexicans from San Antonio, not only appreciate, respect and care for these special racial brothers, but we are very proud of them as much for their brilliant performance as polo players as for their upstanding and courteous behavior.

Mexican artists of importance as well as the best musical bands and orchestras from Mexico have occasionally visited us and received well-deserved honors. Recently, a group of motorcyclists and pistol shooting champions, and members of the federal highway police, performed very dangerous acts in a public exhibition that amazed thousands of admiring viewers. They also left a significant impression and received the most favorable accolades.

This is exactly the kind of effort that we need to ensure that a sincere and genuine friendship reigns over our great peoples of America since it is an indisputable fact that esteem and respect can only be secured with mutual dealings and understanding.

The Mexican-origin inhabitants of Texas, irrespective of citizenship, face very important civic-social problems that we need to resolve. We are determined to secure adequate educational facilities for our youth, hygienic and habitable homes for poor people and a reasonable and decent daily wage for our workers. In sum, we are resolute and seriously interested in speeding up our progress and development as integral members of this community. We do not always secure **all** that we need and are entitled to have because of the prejudice that exists against our Raza. This author believes that now, as always, and given the racial situation that we face, we have no other practical option but to change public opinion. That is, we must build a consciousness of caring in the minds and hearts of our fellow Anglo American citizens and friends towards the Mexican from Texas. This is precisely why educated and creditable persons from the Mexican Republic who have distinguished themselves in the arts, sciences and athletics can help us. They are the ones who can help us build that mutual understanding that we so very much need to secure the social justice that we long to have.

I hope that Mexico will continue to send to our country, especially Texas, ambassadors of goodwill like General Quiñones, his companions and everyone else that we have mentioned. This is for the good of our people and for the pride and satisfaction of the citizens of this country who are very proud that the noble, glorious and heroic blood of Hidalgo and Cuauhtémoc flows through our veins.

Perales Congratulates the Junior Chamber of San Diego, Texas

San Antonio, Texas
February 16, 1937

Dr. A. Durán y Carbajal, Editor[60]
El Demócrata
Post Office Number 269
San Diego, Texas

My good and distinguished friend:

I write to extend my affectionate greetings to you as well as to my other good and prominent friends from your city. At the same time, I offer my sincere and warm congratulations for your beautiful campaign for progress that the Junior Chamber of Commerce has initiated. Magnificent! This is how I like to see our Mexican-American leaders, working in earnest, with faith and enthusiasm for the progress and well-being of our people and our communities. Your last article has touched me deeply.

This is exactly what we need in order to reach the level of our fellow Anglo American citizens and neighbors. We must have self-esteem and civic pride in our cities, communities and neighborhoods that depend on Mexican-American leadership for their progress. Our Raza must not appear in an unfavorable light next to the Anglo American cities, communities and neighborhoods. We accept that many Anglo Americans, by virtue of their better financial situation, can live luxurious and elegant lives that are beyond the reach of our people. This does not mean that our Mexican-American leaders should not do what is within their means to clean, beautify, modernize and advance our progress and well-being. However, to do this we must emulate some of our LULAC councils. Council 16 from San Antonio and the Junior Chamber of Commerce from San Diego are examples. In short, we must work if we are to be progressive citizens. We will never see the progress and well-being that we envision for our communities if we remain inactive and indifferent towards everything that promises the advancement and dignity of our Raza.

As Mexican Americans from San Antonio and other places, we rejoice and feel pride upon seeing our fellow Mexican-American citizens from Duval, Webb, Zapata and Starr guide their communities towards the future. We are pleased and delighted that circumstances in those counties can make Mexican Americans, our Raza and, really, the entire world, feel at home. That is, in such places where the honorable descendants of Hidalgo and Cuauhtémoc, as well as the no less worthy descendants of Washington and Lincoln, advance in all fields of activity. These places are totally devoid of racial prejudice and symbolize the ideal circumstance that no doubt existed in the minds, souls and hearts of Antonio Navarro and Francisco Ruiz, signers of the Texas Declaration of Independence. Antonio Menchaca, Juan N. Seguín and other Tejano patriots of Hispanic lineage who lent their support for liberty and democracy in Texas also must have dreamed of this. We enthusiastically and sincerely applaud every step that you take to place the counties and communities that you lead and govern at the same level of public spirit and progress found in the counties and communities that our fellow Anglo American citizens govern.

Long live the Counties of Duval, Webb, Zapata and Starr, the last bastion of true liberty and democracy for the Mexican American from Texas! Long live these four bulwarks of true Americanism, pride of the Mexican American from the Lone Star State! Long live our nation and long live our Raza!

Yours truly, who cares for you,
Alonso S. Perales

The Insult against Mexicans Is Repeated in San Angelo[61]

Some businesses misread the good taste of the people of San Angelo by sponsoring a theatrical function that included an exhibition of a few dogs. The event was a disaster because the people obviously had little interest in dogs.

The remarkable thing is not the bad taste of the businesses, but the lack of tact and intelligence when their leaflets announced that the event would take place in the Municipal Auditorium and that the gallery was reserved for Mexicans and Negros. In other words, they once again insulted Mexicans.

Mr. Enrique M. Johnston, editor of the weekly *El Latino* recommended, as he has done on previous occasions, that the organizations and the community refuse to do business with persons that treat our people badly.[62] The editor did not make his protest in the newspaper nor did he recommend to the Mexican public that they not dignify the dog show with their presence. Instead, he immediately wrote to the Mexican Consul in Del Rio, Mr. Guillermo L. Robinson, and to Alonso S. Perales from San Antonio, who is a true champion of the Mexicans in this country.

Consul Robinson responded to Mr. Johnston, thanking him for informing him about the incident and noting that he intended to visit with the appropriate San Angelo authorities to resolve the case.

Mr. Perales, the engaging person that he is and wanting to act promptly, sent a letter in English to the mayor of San Angelo, translated as follows:

Protesting against the Segregation of Our Race in San Angelo

San Antonio, Texas
April 30, 1937

Honorable Mayor of the City of San Angelo
San Angelo, Texas

My Dear Sir:

I have before me a handbill announcing a show that is to take place in the Municipal Auditorium of San Angelo on May 1, 1937. I notice that the following statement appears in parenthesis at the foot of the handbill: "Gallery Reserved for Mexicans and Colored People." I am writing to voice my emphatic protest against this insult upon my worthy Mexican race, and to solicit your assistance in preventing a repetition of these humiliations. It is within your power to deny the use of the Municipal Auditorium to prejudiced, ignorant, narrow-minded individuals like the ones responsible for the affront I am pointing out.

The writer, an American citizen of Mexican extraction who is just as proud of his racial origin as of his citizenship, is an active member and one of the founders of the League of United Latin American Citizens, a national civic and patriotic organization seeking to produce first-class American citizens of Mexican descent. I am also deeply and actively interested in President Roosevelt's Good Neighbor Policy that seeks strong ties of friendship between our two great races of the western hemisphere. I can readily see where President Roosevelt and his allies as well as our League of United Latin American Citizens are going to fail in our endeavors unless we receive the cooperation of every American citizen, particularly persons like yourself who are in a position to render valuable assistance in this connection.

Assuring you that the inhabitants of Mexican descent of San Angelo and the entire state of Texas will be truly grateful if you prevent a recurrence of these unfortunate and disagreeable incidents, I remain sincerely yours for better American citizens and a more genuine Pan-Americanism.[63]

Alonso S. Perales
(Taken from *Las Noticias*, Del Río, TX)

Summary of Resolutions by Atty. Alonso Perales, Delegate of Council 16 During the Ninth Annual Convention of the League of United Latin American Citizens, Houston, Texas, June 5 and 6, 1937[64]

Resolution 1. At the opening of the first session of the convention, the congregation unanimously approved a motion by delegate Alonso S. Perales. In response to the motion, the Supreme Council and the rest of the members and other persons who were present in the General Assembly rose to pray for the repose of the late Ben Garza, the first General President of LULAC, who passed away recently.

Resolution 2. Approval of the Black-Connery Bill pending before the US Congress, which seeks to establish a minimum wage, a maximum hour of work and the prohibition of child labor.[65]

Resolution 3. The proposed change to the US Constitution allowing Congress to limit, regulate and prohibit work to person under eighteen years of age is approved.[66]

Resolution 4. We energetically protest the position of the school officials from Hondo to deny adequate school facilities to Mexican youth from said district.

Resolution 5. We propose that the soon-to-be-published work by the historian Frederick C. Chabot, titled *With the Makers of San Antonio*, include the biographies and photographs of Antonio Navarro and

Francisco Ruiz, signers of the Texas Declaration of Independence, and of Texas patriots Antonio Menchaca and Juan N. Seguín.[67]

Resolution 6. Resolved to approve the Wagner-Steagall bill pending before the US Congress intended to provide clean and habitable houses to the poorest people of this country.[68]

Resolution 7. Resolved to approve the bill pending before the US Congress intended to punish any person that tries to overthrow the government by force or violence and also resolved to continue warning the Latin American people about the evil results that communism, fascism and other "isms" can bring to the American form of government and its institutions.[69]

Comments. As is evident, resolutions 2, 3, 4, 5, 6 and 7 seek to benefit our race and nation. The assembly passed the resolutions unanimously. Attorney Manuel C. González, the legal consul to the Mexican Consulate General of San Antonio, was the only person who opposed them and asked for the microphone to voice his opposition from the floor.

Echoes from the Grand General Convention Celebrated in Houston, Texas[70]

La Prensa spoke in due time about the LULAC convention held on June 5 and 6.

Readers would be rightfully bored to hear what someone with greater ability has already written on the subject. But since we felt it necessary to share pertinent information with our good members from Kingsville, we are taking the opportunity offered by the local newspaper *Las Novedades*.

The League is advancing every day in the intellectual and political arenas. Like an evening in Spain, its stars brighten with the bright and calming rays of a young and virile spirit. We are engaging in one of LULAC's most sacred responsibilities, to prepare the comforting home for the young ones of tomorrow who must also struggle for the rights that we seek. The leaders that were present re-affirmed their pledge to stand firm and left as the committed apostles of the cause that they are. The delegates of Council 24 from Kingsville once again remind us that although the spirit of the last supper of the Nazareth is replayed in these conventions and Judas will always be present, in the not-too-distant future, many false prophets will claim to be redeemers of La Raza but we will point them out as the worst of their tormentors.

Alonso Perales, our well-known leader, proposed the resolution of most importance because we seek to improve the social condition of our own. He recommended support for the Black-Connery and the Wagner bills.[71] Perales also asked that LULAC pay for the biographies of our historical figures that participated in the War for Independence and the Alamo in a book that will be published soon. The educated and honorable attorney made several motions, and a number of adversaries who want to hold back his brilliant work confronted him. We hope that venomous reactions do not change our men of bronze and that someday our people will accept the League's work as the best way to advance our cause.

Notes on the Immigration Laws of the United States of America[72]

Persons who have resided in the United States since before July 1, 1908, and who entered illegally can legalize their residency by submitting affidavits signed by American citizens. The US Government cannot deport them, nor do they need a passport unless they have plans to visit Mexico or travel in the United States.

Persons who entered the United States illegally between July 1, 1908, and June 3, 1921, and have lived here continuously can legalize their residency by applying for a passport without asking for it from an American consulate office in Mexico. Applicants can submit three copies of their request in writing to the closest US Immigration Office. Such persons are not deportable, but if they visit Mexico, they cannot return without securing a visa from the nearest American Consulate office. The applicants must pay ten dollars and a head tax of eight dollars.

The US Government cannot deport persons who entered the United States illegally between June 3, 1921, and July 1, 1924, and who have lived continuously in this country simply because they entered illegally. On the other hand, these persons cannot secure a passport while they are in the United States. Such individuals are here illegally because they crossed the border without paying the head tax. They can remain here without fear of deportation, but they must have letters that affirm that they have lived continuously in the United States during the period noted above. The best letters or records of proof can include statements from persons who have hired you, the owners of the establishments where you have worked and the owners of the homes where you have lived. Rental receipts, letters from school officials noting the time that your children have attended school, receipts for water, gas and light payments, as well as proof of contributions to community causes can support claims of residence in this country. You can travel to any part of the United States with these documents.

People who enter the United States illegally after July 1, 1924 will be deported once they are located.

Speech on Behalf of the Mexican Community of San Antonio Upon Accepting a Community Center Constructed by the City[73]

Honorable Mayor and Council Members, Ladies and Gentlemen:

I feel highly honored to represent the inhabitants of the western section of the city on this occasion. In the fulfillment of my mission, permit me to express on their behalf and in the name of all other persons of Mexican or Latin descent who are interested in the western section of the city, our deep and sincere appreciation for your fine gesture. You have provided the children of this section of the city with a recreation center worthy of our community. It is a place where our children might, during their spare time, indulge in wholesome diversion, develop physically, mentally and morally and eventually become the best, purest and most perfect kind of true and loyal citizens of the United States of America.

Definitely and firmly consecrated to this high ideal, the modern and progressive Latin American leadership of San Antonio has been endeavoring, actively and persistently, for several years, to secure adequate school and recreational facilities for the youth of our community. We have also sought better housing, sanitation and other facilities designed to promote the progress and welfare of all the inhabitants of the western section of San Antonio. We have worked for facilities to make the western section as healthy, dignified and respectable as the other sections of our metropolis and the most fertile ground for the production of good citizens found anywhere in the city.

When, as is the case at this present instance, we receive the wholehearted cooperation of our municipal government in the furtherance of our lofty aims, the leaders of our community who have been striving unceasingly for the obtainment of these facilities raise their heads with profound civic ecstasy. We join with the legion of friends and followers smiling, rejoicing and taking the hands of their honorable mayor and city council members to say, "Well done, and many thanks."

San Antonio, TX
March 6, 1937

Congressman John N. Garner (Now Vice President) before the Immigration Committee of the US Congress, Advocating against Restricting the Entry of Mexicans into this Country[74]

Regarding LULAC, founded on the initiative of the author of this book, in Harlingen, Texas, on August 14, 1927, Dr. O. Douglas Weeks states in his article, "The League of United Latin American Citizens, a Texas-Mexican Civic Organization," the following:

The organization selected Mr. Alonso S. Perales, an attorney in Brownsville in 1927, and since employed in various capacities by the Department of State, Washington, DC, to be president. Mr. José T. Canales, a prominent Brownsville attorney and former member of the Texas State Legislature, inherited the position when the former went to Washington.

Congressman John N. Garner referred to this organization and its leaders as follows: There has been organized in this country what is known as American Mexican Citizens Association or some such name and that association numbers among its membership very many people of the very highest type. For instance, Mr. Canales, a member of the Legislature, is the president of the organization. President Coolidge has appointed Perales to supervise the forthcoming election of Nicaragua. The Gentleman is an outstanding American citizen. He is a man of high character and superior ability.

Office of the Minority Leader of the US House of Representatives[75]

Washington, DC
May 31, 1929

Mr. Ben Garza, General President
League of United Latin American Citizens
Corpus Christi, Texas

My Dear Mr. Garza:

I received your letter dated May 27 regarding Attorney Alonso S. Perales. I wish to say that our relations have been very cordial, and I will work with him to the extent that I can to remedy the situation at the border, including the recent immigration law.

I see that you have designated Attorney Perales Honorary President of your organization, a well-deserved honor. I know his work in South Texas alongside you, Attorney José T. Canales from Brownsville and other leaders. Attorney Perales is setting an example in Washington with his work on behalf of the Mexican people, and the spirit and purpose of your organization.

I consider it a privilege to have the opportunity to work with a man with such impressive capabilities and high purposes as Attorney Perales. Your society has demonstrated excellent standards in selecting him as your official representative in Washington. No other man is possibly as well prepared and familiar with the many problems that your organization wishes to resolve.

In appreciation of your letter, and once again praising the service that your organization is doing for the good of the people from the border, I remain yours truly,

John N. Garner

Defending La Raza before the Immigration Committee of the US Congress[76]

2121 New York Avenue, N.W.
Washington, DC
June 21, 1930

Mr. Manuel C. Gonzales
303 Houston Building
San Antonio, Texas

My Dear Sir:

This is in reference to the telegram that you and Mr. Clemente N. Idar sent to the Immigration Committee on January 30 that neither Mr. J. T. Canales nor I represent the League of United Latin American Citizens in Washington.

This is to inform you that neither Mr. Canales nor I made such a declaration. Mr. Canales clearly stated that he was representing certain interests from the Valley and never mentioned LULAC. I appeared to defend my Raza, and not to represent LULAC. The records from the hearings support what I said. Nevertheless, if I had wanted to appear as a representative of LULAC, I had the perfect right to do it, since on May 28, 1929, Mr. Ben Garza, General President of our league wrote Congressman John N. Garner with the following:

> The Executive Committee also decided to name Attorney Perales an official representative of our organization in Washington.

On several occasions, persons have testified that our Raza is inferior and degenerate, and I believe that it is our responsibility to refute this unjust and false assertion. These are the only reasons that I went before the committee. Of course, I understand that Mr. Idar, General Organizer for the American Federation of Labor, opposes our defense of Mexicans in this case. What I do not understand is why a man like you, employed as an attorney by the Mexican government for the purpose of defending Mexican citizens in Texas, would have tried to discredit me before the committee.

It is obvious that the position taken by you and Mr. Idar was shameful and inappropriate. You have not harmed Mr. Canales or me at all, but you have certainly ridiculed our League and have interfered in our defense of the Mexican people. **I was acting free of charge because of the affection that I have for my Raza. You, on the other hand, received pay from the Mexican government to defend Mexican citizens, and tried to undermine my efforts.**

Make sure that you know what you are saying next time that you and Mr. Idar might want to send telegrams to committees in Washington. You have made yourselves look like perfect asses on this occasion. Men of your age who claim to be honorable and sincere leaders of our Raza in this country should know how to behave.

Alonso S. Perales

* * *

2121 New York Avenue, N.W.
Washington, DC
January 31, 1930

Mr. Clemente N. Idar
219 Keller Street
San Antonio, Texas

My Dear Sir:

In response to your letter of January 27, allow me to assure you that neither Mr. Canales nor I appeared before the Committee as representatives of our League and very clearly stated that he was representing the Chamber of Commerce from the Valley. I went before the Committee to defend my Raza, and not as a representative of LULAC. The records from the hearings support what I say. I appeared as a private citizen and never said that I was representing the League. The records from the hearings support what I said. Nevertheless, if I had wanted to appear as a representative of the League, I could have done it since Mr. Ben Garza designated me as such some time ago and wrote Mr. John N. Garner with this in mind.

Mr. Garza is here, he has appeared before the Committee. When officials asked me to appear before the Committee, I wrote to Mr. Garza and suggested that he come to Washington or that he send a representative. I also told him that some members of our League wanted to come to Washington to testify and that he tell them to come well prepared with **facts. As far as I was concerned, the issue was to defend the good name of our Raza. I assure you that I did not seek personal glory.** On several occasions, persons have testified that our Raza is inferior and degenerate, and I believe that it is our responsibility to refute these unjust assertions. The only thing that I lament is that in doing this, you and Mr. Manuel C. Gonzales (Attorney for the Consulate General of Mexico in San Antonio, Texas) have condemned me.

The position that you and Mr. Gonzales have taken is unjustified and, if you are Gentlemen, you should apologize immediately to Mr. Canales and me for the insult that you have directed against us.

Sincerely,
Alonso S. Perales

Postscript. Make sure that you know what you are saying next time that you and Mr. Gonzales might want to send telegrams to Committees in Washington. Do not make yourselves look like the perfect asses you have been this time. Men of your age who claim to be honorable and sincere leaders of our Raza should know how to behave better. You have ridiculed our League with your telegram.

Echoes of the Special LULAC Convention Held in Corpus Christi[77]

Corpus Christi, Texas, March 1934. The special LULAC convention has left a good impression, thanks to the tireless efforts of Mr. Ben Garza, Mr. Andrés de Luna and Mr. Luis Wilmot who did everything to ensure that the meeting was the most impressive possible. In addition to addressing a number of issues that are important to the League, they held a beautiful literary/musical program. Speakers included Mr. J. T. Wright, President of the Chamber of Commerce from Corpus Christi, Miss Elodia G. Uveda, a student from the College of Arts and Industries, Kingsville, and Mr. Gregorio R. Salinas, General Secretary of the League from San Antonio. Mr. Salinas replaced Alonso S. Perales who was busy at the time.

An interesting incident occurred during the morning business session that did not fail to draw attention. The delegates were discussing issues related to scholarships that the League has established for students of Latin origin. Manuel C. Gonzales, legal consul to the Consulate General of Mexico in San Antonio, emphatically opposed the idea of giving the scholarships to students who might be sons and daughters of Mexican citizens. Attorney José T. Canales immediately stood to protest, and asked the Legal Consultant of the Consulate General of Mexico: "Do you mean to say that we should not give scholarships to students who are sons and daughters of Mexican citizens even though the children were born in the United States? Do you want to tell me that a student born in the United States is not an American citizen?"

Gonzales responded: "The League is basically an American institution. We are trying to build on the basis of strict and purely American principles."

Canales stated that Gonzales was completely mistaken since the League's scholarships are for students of Mexican extraction, and the nativity of their parents does not matter. Perales, Delegate of Council 16 from San Antonio and Assistant to the Bexar County Attorney, decisively and enthusiastically backed Canales. The rest of the members of the League that were present also expressed support for Canales' statement with a booming ovation.

Attorney Pablo G. Gonzales from San Antonio and Mr. José L. Flores from Kingsville, candidates for the presidency and vice-presidency of the League, respectively, made a great impression among the members that were present with their abilities, talents and popularity. Undoubtedly, they will be the new leaders of this important organization that is growing day by day and becoming the best in pursuing the progress and well-being of the Latin Americans in the United States.

The League's annual convention will take place in Mission, Texas on May 5 and 6. Mr. Roberto E. Austin, president of the planning committee, has worked tirelessly to ensure that the convention will be a special civic and social event in the annals of the evolution of the Latin Americans in this country. They say that Dr. Carlos E. Castañeda and other distinguished professors from the University of Texas will be among the speakers.

A Letter from Dr. Herschel T. Manuel, Professor of Educational Psychology at the University of Texas[78]

Austin, Texas
May 18, 1937

Honorable Alonso S. Perales
Attorney-at-Law
Suite 614, Gunter Building
San Antonio, Texas

Dear Mr. Perales:

One thing after another has delayed my writing to express my appreciation for your great kindness in sending me a copy of your book entitled *En Defensa de Mi Raza*. To avoid further delay I am writing this informal note from home.

I want you to accept my deep and sincere appreciation. I also congratulate you on your great service to your people. As you know, I admire and value your work. You have been an able and vigorous leader. I am proud of my association with you in even a small part of this work.

With most hearty thanks and very best wishes, I am, cordially,

H. T. Manuel
San Antonio, Texas

* * *

July 5, 1937[79]

White Man's Union Association of Wharton County
Wharton, Texas

Sirs:

I have before me a copy of your Constitution and By-Laws, and I notice that the section regarding "Membership, Qualifications, etc." reads partly as follows:

> The term White Citizen, as provided herein, shall not include any Mexican who is not of full Spanish blood. Only persons who are White Citizens and who are otherwise qualified to vote under the Constitution and By-Laws of this Association shall be permitted to vote at any primary or other election held by this Association.

In this connection, I wish to invite your attention to the fact that under the date of July 24, 1934, at the request of the Honorable Bryan Blalock, County Attorney of Travis County, His Excellency James V. Allred, at the time Attorney General of Texas, rendered the following opinion:

> It is therefore my opinion and you are respectfully advised that, in light of common understanding of the terms, and in view of the practical construction of the same, Mexicans are to be considered "white citizens" within the meaning of the resolution adopted by the State Convention of the Democratic Party on May 24, 1932 and, hence, that if those persons are otherwise qualified to vote they are entitled to participate in the Democratic Primary election to be held on July 28, 1934.

I would like to remind you in a more detailed manner that Mexicans belong to the Caucasian Race. Under the Constitution of the United States and the Constitution and Laws of the State of Texas, all

Americans of Mexican extraction have the right to vote in all elections both primary and general if they have paid their poll tax and are otherwise qualified to vote. The fact that they have Mexican blood in their veins makes no difference whatsoever. I could quote you the decisions of the Federal and State Courts upon this point, but I believe I would be wasting my time, as I feel certain that you are as familiar with them as I am. However, I will pose a question. How would it suit you if the citizens of Web, Duval, Zapata and Starr Counties, the majority of whom are of Mexican extraction, were to form an Association similar to yours and have the following provision under the heading of "Membership"?

> The term "Mexican-American Citizen," as provided herein, shall not include any persons of Anglo-Saxon, Irish, Scotch and German blood. Only persons who are Mexican-American citizens as that term is used herein and who are otherwise qualified to vote, under the Constitution and By-Laws of this Association, shall be permitted to vote at any primary or other election held by this Association.

Would you like it at all?

Well, you need not fear that the Americans of Mexican descent of the counties I have mentioned will never do anything of the kind, even though it is well within their power to do so. They will not do it because they are honest-to-goodness Americans and harbor no racial prejudice in their hearts. They love our country, our flag and our institutions. They are exactly the type of citizen that Washington, Jefferson and their associates had in mind when they founded our great republic. They also measure up to the high caliber of men that Erasmo and Juan Seguín, Antonio Navarro, Francisco Ruiz, Antonio Menchaca, and other Texas patriots imagined when they cooperated so generously and wholeheartedly with their Anglo American brethren, that the Republic of Texas might come into being and that liberty, justice and democracy might be more firmly established. We are certain that those great and valiant Texas Mexican and Anglo American statesmen and heroes never imagined that the day would come when the descendants of those Texas Mexican statesmen and heroes might be deprived of their constitutional rights and privileges by their Anglo American brethren of Texas.

Assuring you that every Texas inhabitant of Mexican descent will appreciate it if you amended your Constitution and By-Laws to avoid the odious and unfair acts of discriminations against my people, I am yours for a greater America and better Americans.

Alonso S. Perales
San Antonio, Texas

* * *

July 6, 1937[80]

Miss Alberta Besch
The Palms, Our Lady of the Lake College
San Antonio, Texas

Dear Ms. Besch:

I have before me a copy of the magazine *The Palms* that includes an article entitled "Cosmopolitan *San Antonio.*" I noticed that you have prepared interesting paragraphs on Germans, French, Belgian, Irish, Italians, Polish, Czechoslovakians, Syrians, Chinese, Japanese, Jews, Greeks, and Blacks, but the material on the Mexican people is not as good as it should be. The first paragraph reads,

> The area south and west of the old Spanish Governor's Palace Old Mexico represents Old Mexico well. Inside nooks and on crowded thoroughfares, Mexican vendors sell candy, fruit, flowers of varied hues and freshly made tortillas. By day, Haymarket Plaza is a busy fruit and vegetable market where all classes of society mingle while doing their daily or weekly marketing. All during the day women with mantillas

drawn over their heads sit upon the pavement and puff leisurely at corn shuck rolled cigarettes while waiting for their customers. Outstanding among the Mexican customs of San Antonio are the chili stands that come out with the evening stars. From crude tables covered with oilcloth and presided over by typical Mexican women, they openly serve Mexican dishes such as chili con carne, chili and tamales. The odor of garlic and onion fill the air, while Mexican musicians sing their rhythmic tunes to the strum of sweet guitars. Stands on Washington Park specialize in all sorts of Mexican herbs, condiments, pottery, drawn work, hand-made furniture and baskets. The city has erected Cassiano Park on Zarzamora Street for the Mexican population of this city.[81]

The second and last paragraph noted the Cinco de Mayo celebration, a store of Mexican curios and several Mexican restaurants.

I can see from your references that you did not have good sources of information. No doubt, this is why you did not write something better about my people.

When you once again write about Mexicans in San Antonio, do me the favor of coming to see me and I will gladly provide you with the necessary information so that you can write, not an article, but a book. The Mexican colony of San Antonio is more forward-minded than twenty years ago. This is due to our modern, active and hard-working Latin American leadership in the civic arena. Thus, people do not treat us fairly when they say that the virtues and attractive features of the Mexican community are to be found in the sellers of candies, fruits, tortillas and chili stands. I once again say that I will be glad to offer primary and reliable information so that you can write an interesting and instructive article, and so that it does justice to the ninety thousand residents of Mexican origin in San Antonio.

Sincerely,
Alonso S. Perales

Protesting the Segregation of Our Raza in New Braunfels[82]

New Braunfels, Texas
July 8, 1937

Honorable Mayor and Commissioners
of the City of New Braunfels
New Braunfels, Texas

Gentlemen:

We, the undersigned taxpaying citizens of New Braunfels, hereby register our most vigorous protest against the segregation and eviction of persons of Mexican descent practiced at LANDA PARK. Likewise, we protest the signs at the Main Plaza where some benches are marked "For Whites," while others "For Mexicans." We protest for the following reasons:

First, both LANDA AND MAIN PLAZA are public properties and, as taxpaying citizens, we have as much of a right to use them without being subject to humiliations.

Second, as members of the League of United Latin American Citizens, a statewide civic and patriotic organization composed of American citizens of Mexican descent, we aim to develop within the members of our **Race**, the best, purest and perfect type of a true and loyal citizen of the United States of America.

Third, we know of President Roosevelt's Good Neighbor Policy, designed to strengthen the bonds of friendship between the two great Races of the Western Hemisphere.

However, it is obvious that we are going to fail in our endeavors unless we receive the cooperation of our fellow Americans, especially persons like you who are in a position to render a great service in this regard.

Assuring you that the inhabitants of Mexican descent of New Braunfels and the entire state would feel deeply grateful if you would avoid a repetition of these unfortunate and disagreeable incidents, we remain,

Respectfully yours,
THE LEAGUE OF UNITED LATIN AMERICAN CITIZENS,
LULAC, COUNCIL No. 70
Federico Luna, President
Jesús M. Treviño
Agustín Silva
Abundio González
Frank Morales

Perales Addresses the Mayor and the Commissioners of New Braunfels[83]

San Antonio, Texas
July 10, 1937

Honorable Mayor and Commissioners
of the City of New Braunfels
New Braunfels, Texas

Sirs:

Friends of mine from New Braunfels have informed me about the current disagreeable situation that resulted from your decision to mark benches in the Main Plaza that read, "For Whites," and others "For Mexicans," and to evict all persons of Mexican origin from Landa Park. This is not the first time that we hear that the German American people from New Braunfels treat persons of Mexican descent this way. If I remember correctly, this situation has existed for several years. Nonetheless, everything has its limits, and what occurred recently in that city has exhausted our patience.

I have frequently heard that Germans are most responsible for the prejudice in this country—especially in Texas—against persons of Mexican origin, but I have always refused to believe this because I have known many Germans in Latin American countries and have observed, with great satisfaction, their friendly and respectful regard for the native people of those republics. Many of them spend almost their entire lives in those countries, naturalize and become good citizens in their adopted countries. On the other hand, I have also noticed the friendly and hospitable attitude of the people of Mexico and other Latin American republics towards the German people who live in those countries. But now, given the situation in New Braunfels, I have no doubt in my mind that the German people in this city entertain prejudice against the Mexican people, and that they are not treating my Race with the respect and consideration that they have the right to expect.

A group of citizens in New Braunfels, known as Council No. 70 of the League of United Latin American Citizens, a civic and patriotic organization made up of American citizens of Mexican origin, is very interested in developing good citizens. The writer of this letter is proud to be the principal founder and active member of this organization.

As you can see from my biographical statement and service sheet, I am and have been for many years deeply interested in promoting friendly relations between the people of the United States and Latin America. Nevertheless, I am sure that you will agree with me that in order to succeed—in developing good American citizens as well as in strengthening ties of friendship with the people of Latin America—we will need the cooperation of all the other racial groups that make up our cosmopolitan nation, including the German people.

I plan to send a copy of this letter to His Excellency Franklin Delano Roosevelt so that he may know what some of us Texans are doing to promote his Good Neighbor Policy, and I also plan to publish this letter in the major newspapers of the United States and of Central and South America. Before I do this, I wish to receive a response from you to publish at the same time. It is best that we are frank and place our cards on the table. If we are to have a **legitimate Americanism** and a **true Pan-Americanism**, we must establish a better understanding among Latin Americans and other racial groups in the United States. We will never have understanding and goodwill with our Latin American neighbors to the South while maintaining poor understanding and goodwill among ourselves. We will not solve the problem with banquets and speeches. We must engage the issue thoroughly, and learn to respect and value each other.

Now then, we Americans of Mexican origin are sincerely and seriously interested in developing good American citizens and in strengthening our relations with the people of Latin America. Thus, the issue is this: Are you, the American citizens of German origin and everyone else who may be interested, willing to work with us in giving the Mexican race of this city the same respectful, civil and hospitable treatment that persons of German extraction receive from the people of Mexico and other peoples of the other Latin American Republics?

Awaiting your response, I remain yours, respectfully,

Alonso S. Perales

The True Origin of the League of the United Latin American Citizens[84]

The idea of establishing a strong organization to protect the interests of our Raza in Texas and to fight for its progress and well-being occurred to me in 1917, based on my observations and experiences in the state. Due to my young age and lack of preparation, the project remained a matter of conversation for years. I discussed the idea fully with my good friends and contemporaries, including Pablo González, son of Dr. Domingo González, and Filiberto Galván. They were both from San Antonio and my schoolmates.

I registered with the US military and in January 1920, left for Washington, DC, to study and prepare to return to solve the problems of our people in Texas. While in Washington, I continued to communicate with my friends González and Galván on the project. All of us thought and dreamed about becoming leaders of our people and contributing to the formation of an organization that would serve as a true bulwark for the protection of our racial brothers.

In Washington, I learned from the newspapers of Texas of the emergence of the *Orden Hijos de América* (Order of Sons of America) in 1921 and the *Orden Hijos de Texas* in 1922 (Order of Sons of Texas) from San Antonio. According to the newspapers, the organizations sought to work towards the good of our people. From afar, I applauded the establishment of these organizations because I longed for the existence of such organizations for the good of our people, and I did not care who founded them or what names they adopted.

I asked Galván and González that they apprise themselves of the organizations and their leaders and send me a full report. They did this. I came to San Antonio in June 1923 and personally investigated everything related to the organizations and their leaders, and to make sure of things, I quickly became a member of one of them. My distinguished, fine and highly esteemed *Profesor* José de la Luz Sáenz — one of the few Mexican-American leaders who is really concerned and fights selflessly for the progress and well-being of our Raza in Texas — accompanied me in my research. My friends González, Galván and Sáenz concluded that the organizations **DID NOT ALIGN,** in theory and in practice, **WITH THE IDEAL THAT WE HAD DEVELOPED**. In other words, we believed that although their principles were beautiful and fit with what we had in mind, in practice, the organizations did not follow them, and only served as instruments for the advancement of the political interests of their presidents. We wanted to see the emergence of a serious organization that would **TRULY WORK** for the progress and well-being of our Raza in Texas. We did not want an organization to prepare self-serving political types. We longed for an organization that would really **WORK** for the good of our people, and not one that would busy itself with **IMPRESSING** the political bosses and the public officials solely for the purpose of securing favors and positions in city government and the courts.

Sáenz and I decided in the summer of 1924 to tour several communities in Texas and offer conferences, or talks, on education, unity and constitutional rights, and to begin preparing the ground for a new organization. People received us well.

Another organization emerged in San Antonio in February 1927. It was composed of American citizens of Mexican origin and they called themselves the Order of Knights of America (not to be confused with the *Sociedad Caballeros de América*, founded on January 10, 1929, and that exists in San Antonio under the direction of Mr. Pedro B. Hernández and his wife Mrs. María L. de Hernández). I discovered that its members had belonged to the *Orden Hijos de América* and left it over some quarrels with its president. The service record of the Order of Knights of America convinced me that it was not what we needed. Also, the major leader of this organization, as well as the presidents of the other two *Ordenes* (the *Hijos de América* and the *Hijos de Texas*), had already revealed their interest in politics and did not have the abilities and qualities that in my view we needed in our leaders. Later developments have convinced me that I was not mistaken. As a result of this, I concluded that it was necessary to establish a new society that fit my ideal of the kind of organization that we needed and the quality and character of the leaders that should determine its destiny. Upon reaching the Lower Rio Grande Valley in July 1927, I made a declaration that appeared in *La Prensa* of San Antonio. The statement reads as follows:

> I plan to dedicate myself to the exercise of my profession in the Lower Rio Grande Valley and maintain my law office in McAllen and Rio Grande City by July 15 of this month, at the latest.
>
> I also plan to host some pro-Raza conferences in the near future. At the same time, I will be taking preliminary steps for the formation of a strong organization of American citizens of Mexican origin, first in the Valley and then in other Mexican communities. Its only objective will be to work in an honest manner in favor of the intellectual, economic, social and political betterment of Mexican Americans in particular, and the Mexican race as a whole. The success of such an organization will essentially depend on the kind of leaders that head it. They need to be honorable so that they do not mislead or exploit our unfortunate Raza from Texas. They should insure that our general progress comes quickly and they should be courageous so that they do not fear to seek justice when they see their rights as citizens of the United States of America violated. They also have to be intelligent so that they may be able to look over our destinies as citizens and as a race.
>
> I firmly believe that our Raza has a large number of leaders in Texas that bring together these qualities, and the day is not far when the organization of Mexican Americans will be a fact, and since this organization will be established over a solid base, its pro-Raza activities will be crowned with complete success in the state.

After holding several preliminary conferences and reunions with my friends from the Valley, I issued a call for a convention, which took place in Harlingen, Texas, on August 14, 1927. Delegates from numerous Mexican civic and fraternal organizations from throughout the state attended. Representatives of the *Orden Hijos de América* and the *Orden Caballeros de América* were among the delegates. The LEAGUE OF UNITED LATIN AMERICAN CITIZENS was born in this convention. Sáenz, Canales, Mr. Juan B. Lozano and other friends collaborated effectively with me in the formation of the league. The *Orden Hijos de América* and the *Orden Caballeros de América* refused to join the new organization. The General President of the *Orden Hijos de América* invited the LEAGUE OF UNITED LATIN AMERICAN CITIZENS to join his organization. We, the leaders of the new organization, responded that in order for us to join the *Orden Hijos de América* it would be indispensable to modify its constitution and bylaws in order to democratize the governance of the organization and insure its sound functioning. The President of the *Orden Hijos de América* conceded and its members appointed a committee to study the constitution and bylaws of the organization and to recommend the necessary reforms. One of the committee's recommendations was that the presidency rotate successively from one city to another so that all the members had the opportunity to fill the highest position in the organization and the organization would not become a tool in the hands of a president.

The General President of the *Orden Hijos de América* did not like the idea since he had been president of the organization since its beginning and wanted to continue filling the seat. Because of this attitude, the directors of the LEAGUE OF LATIN AMERICAN CITIZENS did not think it possible to continue entertaining the invitation from the president and, without losing time, continued moving forward with our league. The honor of being the first General President of the League of Latin American Citizens fell on yours truly. Sáenz, Don Deodoro Guerra from McAllen, Canales, other friends and I worked hard and enthusiastically. By January 1, 1927, we had Councils in Harlingen, Brownsville, Laredo, Peñitas, McAllen, La Grulla, Encino and Gulf, Texas.

After studying the issue closely, I decided to see how we could join our LEAGUE OF LATIN AMERICAN CITIZENS with the Corpus Christi Council of the *Orden Hijos de América* and the *Orden Caballeros de América* so that we could make the unification of Mexican Americans more effective in Texas. To be sure, our league had eight councils, the *Orden Hijos de América* noted three or four and the *Orden Caballeros de América* claimed only one. Before I left Washington for Nicaragua, I wrote about my fine and unforgettable friend Bernardo Garza of Corpus Christi, one of the best leaders that our Raza has ever had in the state of Texas. Ben (as his friends caringly call him) was the President of the Corpus Christi Council of the *Orden Hijos de América,* and ever since I met him in the summer of 1924 when his council invited me to make a presentation, he gave me the impression of being a socially engaged, sincere and honorable leader. He was precisely the kind of man that our Raza needed at the time and needs today to insure our progress and well-being in this country. Later, his deeds showed me that I had not been mistaken. This is the reason that when the Supreme Being called Ben, I did not hesitate to declare as I do again today with pleasure and for the sake of the coming generations:

> The passing of our distinguished and fine friend Mr. Bernardo Garza has saddened the souls and hearts of everyone (including me) who had the opportunity to engage and know him fully. He was one of our most sincere, honest, active and enthusiastic leaders and one of the hardest working in seeking the unification and progress of our Raza in the United States, especially in Texas. Mr. Garza was young and driven by the best desire to continue working for the good of our league and our Raza for as long as his health would allow it. His passing no doubt represents a loss that is so big that it is irreparable, not only for our league but for all our people.

In my letter to Ben prior to my departure for Nicaragua, during the early days of April 1928, I implored him to do everything possible to persuade the Council of the *Orden Hijos de América* from Corpus Christi and the *Caballeros de América* to join our LEAGUE OF LATIN AMERICAN CITIZENS. I also said that I would be very pleased if they elected him general president of our league at our following convention. I said this not to recruit him to work in favor of the merging, but so that his fellow members in the *Orden Hijos de América* and his friends in *La Orden Caballeros de América* could see the issue of the presidency in light of his role as the General President of the *Orden Hijos de América*. I received his response in Managua, Nicaragua in May 1928.

* * *

Tucson, Arizona[85]
April 21, 1928

Mr. Alonso S. Perales
Washington, DC

My dear friend:

The Post Office forwarded your letter of April 1 to me in Tucson, Arizona, where I am spending my vacation. I expect to be here until June 1 of this year. I am very glad to hear from you, as it has been a long time since I heard from you. I also can see by your letter that you are in Washington. I presume that you got through with your Pan-American Conference, and I hope that it was a success in every respect.

I want to take this opportunity to express my sincere thanks for the good words that you always have for our Corpus Christi Council. I am very happy to hear that your league is progressing rapidly, and there is no doubt in my mind that with all the well-intentioned men that you have at the head of your organization, nothing will keep you from having one of the greatest (if not the greatest) organization that God ever created.

I am very sorry to say that I am not in a position to do as per your good wishes. I am away from home for the time being. I give you my word of honor that just as soon as I am home, I will begin working on your case.[86] I know I can do this if God is willing.

I am glad to say that I have the full confidence of all the boys at home. Therefore, it will only be a matter of my getting back. Be assured that I will carry out your wishes.

I also want to take this opportunity to thank you for your high esteem and good wishes towards me, but I would rather see the high position of president general fall upon a more intelligent person like you, Idar, Canales or some other. My intentions are good, but I know that I lack the education to be at the front of such an organization. Nevertheless, I am always willing to put the shoulder to the wheel and see it go through.

Yours very truly,
Ben Garza

* * *

Managua, Nicaragua[87]
May 22, 1928

Mr. Ben Garza
c/o Metropolitan Café
Corpus Christi, Texas

My dear Friend:

I received your letter of April 21. I was very glad to hear from you.

Yes, I was successful in my assignment to the Sixth International Conference of American States, held in Havana the early part of this year. The conference itself was quite a success. I next took a post as Attorney for the Agency of the United States, General and Special Claims Commission, United States and Mexico. Government officials have now released me temporarily from the Nicaragua assignment as an attorney on General Frank R. McCoy's staff. As you know, General McCoy, President Coolidge's personal representative, will supervise the election for president of Nicaragua scheduled for next November. Upon the completion of my duties in Nicaragua, I intend to return to Washington by way of Texas. I shall make it a point to have a good chat with you then.

Mr. Garza, I want you to know that it makes me very happy to learn from your letter that you are willing to cooperate with the League of Latin American Citizens, and it would make me even happier to have you and the rest of my Corpus friends join our League, and to see you head our organization. It is entirely within the realm of possibility. You state that you do not consider yourself educated enough to be President General of the league. In this connection, allow me to state that in my humble opinion you are well qualified for the post because I firmly believe that you are intelligent, energetic, **HONEST** and **DEEPLY INTERESTED** in bringing about the evolution of our race in Texas. We need leaders who possess those qualities and qualifications, even if they are not highly educated. As far as our cause is concerned, we do not need educated politicians but sincere and honest men who will truly endeavor to improve the condition of our people in Texas. Those are the two qualities that our leaders must possess and which we must insist upon if we are to succeed in our noble and worthy endeavors. The League of Latin American Citizens is not a mere political club; at least it was not intended to be so when I joined and cooperated towards its organization, and I certainly do not believe it to be such today. However, should it at any time pursue such a course, you may rest assured that I shall have nothing to do with it. Of course, this does not mean that I do not believe that the members of the League should vote in election times. Quite the contrary, I hold that it is their duty to do so as good American citizens; but there is a great difference between intelligent and conscientious voting and unintelligent, corrupt mass voting. By voting intelligently and conscientiously for men who are true friends of our race, we can improve our political condition. However, if we all vote together and without thinking simply because some ambitious politician says, "Vote for so-and-so!"—as has been done in the past in Texas—we shall not improve our condition one iota. It might improve the condition of one or more members of our race, but it makes us a negligible factor in politics and good bating—a splendid instrument—to further the ends of ambitious, selfish politicians.

Please get in touch with Mr. Canales at once if you have not already done so. If possible, go to Brownsville and have a conference with him. You may show him my letters to you. Also, keep in touch with Prof. J. Luz Sáenz, of Peñitas, Hidalgo County, Texas. I recommend him to you as a sincere and honest leader of our people in Texas, and one in whom I have implicit confidence.

Sincerely Yours,
Alonso S. Perales

At the same time that I was corresponding with Ben, I maintained contact with Attorney José T. Canales and Profesor José de la Luz Sáenz. On June 9, 1928, I wrote Attorney Canales and said, among other things, the following:

> During the early part of April, I wrote to Mr. Ben Garza, President of the Corpus Christi Council of the Order of Sons of America and suggested that they get in touch with you at once with a view of joining forces with our League. I told him that if the Corpus Council would sever all connection with the San Antonio Council of the Order of Sons of America and join our league, they could retain their present name that would read Sons of America Council, League of Latin American Citizens. I also mentioned that he stood a good chance of becoming President General of the league at the next convention. He wrote me a very enthusiastic letter from Arizona, where he was spending his vacation, and promised to get in touch with you as soon as he returned to Corpus Christi, which he stated would be around the first of June. I hope he has already done so. Ben is a highly active young man and although he says he did not receive a particularly good education, I believe he would make a good president.

I sent the following letter to Profesor Sáenz on June 16, 1928, in which I stated,

> Did you get in touch with Ben Garza? If not, do so at once. I told you in my previous letter that he had replied to my letter of April 1. I suggested that the Corpus Christi Council of the Order of Sons of America join the League of Latin American Citizens. He favors the idea, and it seems to me that all he needs is a little encouragement from you and Canales. I believe Ben Garza would make a good President General of our league. He says that he does not consider himself educated enough to hold such a post. I replied that what we need is not highly educated politicians, but sincere, energetic, honest men who really mean what they say when they avow that they are deeply interested in the welfare and evolution of our race in Texas.

Ben wrote to me from Corpus Christi on August 22, 1928, with the following:

My dear friend Perales:

> It has been exactly two months since you wrote to me, but I did not care to answer until I had at least some good news for you. Therefore, I thought I would write to tell you that we are working slowly but surely to see what we should do to merge all of the three organizations.
> The hardest part is to merge the Sons of America without the consent of the president general. Of course, when it comes to Council No. 4, we could desert the order and join yours, but as we have already established such a good reputation in this town, we hate to lose what we have already accomplished. Besides, we would lose all the councils that we established. Now we are working on some scheme that will enable us to do all of these things so everybody will be satisfied at the same time.

We have a communication from the Order of Knights of America stating that they are coming to Corpus Christi in the next few days to have another conference with us about this matter. I hope we will come to some understanding at this conference on what we are going to do. I would like to hear from you by return mail; it may be that you will throw some light on how, in your opinion, we should go into this matter.

Ben wrote to me again on September 18, 1928, regarding the issue related to our League. He said the following:

We (the Local Council of the Order of Sons of America) were and are anxious to join something that perhaps would expand the activities of what you and I and many well-intentioned American citizens of Mexican blood have dreamed for some time. This is why we suggested that *El Paladín* from Corpus Christi start some propaganda to see if somebody really wanted to have an organization like the one mentioned above. We wanted to see if this would allow us to disband our local council and give those that were not satisfied with their organization a chance to start all over again. It may be that our experience allows us to make one solid organization regardless of the name. To my surprise, no one responded to our suggestions after I sent the newspaper to everyone that I thought would take part in the discussion.

Perales, as you know, we are helpless in Corpus when it comes to dictating what to do with the Sons of America. The only salvation that I can see is to have a mass meeting of all the organizations that have the same ideals and the same principles as ours. If the president general does not want to join with them, we can tell him to stay with his organization and we will join whatever we want. As far as we are concerned in Corpus Christi, we are still working—and working hard—but it is a shame that we are by ourselves, and that is why we are willing to join hands with everyone that wants our race to be in its rightful place.

I responded to Ben from Managua, Nicaragua, on September 13, 1928, and, among other things stated the following:

> Frankly speaking, I am somewhat disappointed to learn that the Corpus Christi Council of the Order of Sons of America and the Order of Knights of America have not yet joined the League of Latin American Citizens. You invite me to make suggestions. To me, that seems like a very simple problem. It is merely a matter of conferring with Mr. J. T. Canales, President General of the League of Latin American Citizens. You can discuss and decide the ways and means of joining the League at the conference. If you reach an agreement, go ahead and join the League. Later, delegates to a convention can elect general officers. I personally would recommend and support you for president general of the League because I consider you well qualified for the post. Members could revise the constitution of the League to insure its efficient and harmonious functioning. The League of Latin American Citizens has already given Mr. James Tafolla, Sr. many opportunities to do something to consolidate the three orders, as you doubtless saw from the communications that I sent you shortly before my departure from McAllen last January. Why he did not avail himself of the opportunity granted him, at his own request, I do not know.
>
> In order to accomplish the organization of American citizens of Latin descent in Texas it is necessary to have as president general of such an organization a man who is intelligent, honest, sincere, energetic and courageous, and who, furthermore, has the time to properly discharge his functions. He must be a man that will inspire full confidence. It is absurd to insist on having a leader who is not popular, since instead of facilitating the consolidation of our people, he will retard it.
>
> If the Corpus Christi Council of the Order of Sons of America and the Order of Knights of America believe that Mr. Tafolla possesses all the necessary qualities and qualifications and is, therefore, perfectly qualified to act as the

supreme leader of Americans of Latin descent in Texas, my advice is for both orders to unite under Mr. Tafolla's leadership. We can then enter negotiations with the president of the League of Latin American Citizens to further consolidation. In such an event, I consider it desirable that we ensure that all properly qualified members of the organization have a chance to be president of the organization. It is not fair for one man to monopolize the presidency forever. All good men should have an opportunity.

On the other hand, if you do not consider Mr. Tafolla qualified, and he refuses to permit someone who **IS** qualified to assume the office of president of the Order of Sons of America, then the Corpus Christi council has only one thing to do. The council could sever all connections with the Order of Sons of America and for both the council and the Order of Knights of America join the League of Latin American Citizens.

Latin Americans must organize, get out of the rut and forge ahead. Let us catch up with and keep abreast of our hard-driving fellow citizens of Anglo Saxon extraction. To accomplish this, no man should stand in our way. No man is big enough to block our progress. A whole is bigger than its fractions. For the sake of posterity and the good name of our Race, let us get together, my friends, and begin to solve our great problems. We can only do it through a well-disciplined, solid, powerful organization.

Mr. Ben Garza and other members of the Corpus Christi Council of the *Orden Hijos de América* approached Mr. Eulalio H. Marín, also a member of the council and director of the important weekly from Corpus Christi, *El Paladín*. They asked that he initiate a discussion on consolidation in preparation for the Convention of Mexican-American civic organizations. Mr. Marín agreed. I applauded the initiative, but I was really acknowledging **MY OWN INITIATIVE** regarding the merging of our League of Latin American Citizens, the Corpus Christi Council of the *Orden Hijos de América* and the *Orden*

Caballeros de América. I had taken the initiative, as I noted earlier, in the letter that I wrote to my friend Ben, from Washington, DC, during the early part of April 1928. Nevertheless, *El Paladín* has the distinction of being the first newspaper to publish the call. Regarding the published initiative of *El Paladín*, I wrote to the director of the newspaper from Managua, Nicaragua, on August 29, 1928, with the following:[89]

Dear Mr. Director:

I have just received the August 31, 1928, issue of *El Paladín* that places before the court of Mexican-American public opinion an **INITIATIVE** to establish an organization (not a new one) composed of all the organizations that now exist. It is to carry one name, have only one banner, and its program of activities will be far-reaching. The consolidated organization will establish councils in all communities that have people of *Nuestra Raza*. I applaud the **INITIATIVE** enthusiastically, and with pleasure I take the opportunity to declare that in order to organize Mexican Americans in the United States it is necessary that the leaders of the existing organizations unite and agree on the following:

I. That the leaders of the *orden* emerging from the proposal for the consolidation of Mexican-American societies be intelligent, active, sincere, honest men who have the civic courage that is necessary to act as our leaders, and that they may also be able to dedicate the necessary time to the work of the *orden*.

II. Local and general officers should be elected every year; all the members of the *orden* should have the full opportunity to be elected as officers at both levels; a majority of the votes by the delegates representing the different councils in a convention that is to be held annually shall elect the general officers.

III. That members share power in such a manner that no one person, member or officer of the *orden* will be able to use it as an instrument to draw benefit at the expense of our fellow citizens of Latin origin. Whosoever wishes to become a powerhouse should dedicate himself to it and take care to be fair, but that he not seek to advance his interests by masquerading as a leader who fights for our Raza. We must be honest.

IV. That once the *orden* is established, it actively addresses the issues that affect the interests of Mexican Americans and our Raza in the United States.

Deciding on the name of the *orden* is of secondary importance. We can consider three approaches:

a. Agreeing by majority vote on keeping the name of any of the existing organizations.
b. If a majority vote cannot resolve the issue, a drawing can settle it.
c. As a last resort, we can select an entirely different name.

I am sure that the **INITIATIVE** will succeed if the leaders of the organizations agree on the aforementioned, as I expect that they will if they are sincere when they say that they take to heart the interests and future of ***nuestra* Raza** in the United States. I am hopeful.

Fellow Mexican Americans: For the good of our Raza, let us unite. Let us emulate the example of our fellow Anglo Saxon citizens and we will develop rapidly. We cannot allow any man to impede our work. Let us unite and begin to solve the great problems that we have before us. We can only do this with strong, solid and well-disciplined organization.

On December 15, 1928, a member of the *Orden Caballeros de América* from San Antonio wrote to me at Washington, DC, noting the following:

Well, we are on the threshold of completing the consolidation started in Harlingen in August 1927. As I told you several times, this matter had to be handled in an easy manner until we could come to an agreement with those men who understood our aims and ideals clearly. Thanks to your advice, the progressive bunch of men headed by our old pal Ben Garza, took "the bridle by the teeth," came down here and told our friend the President General to resign or they would quit the order! You know how foxy an old . . . politician is, and the bunch of ifs and whys and alibis he can muster to his defense: he pleaded with the Corpus boys for one more chance, but they just simply "burned him up."

We finally agreed to call a convention at Corpus Christi, on the second Sunday in January. The Council of the Sons of America from here was to send a delegation of five men, we would send five also, five from Council No. 4 at Corpus and five from the League of Latin American Citizens. The twenty men were to form a Ways and Means Committee, and then and there consolidate into one solid organization. Now, we the Knights of America do not care under what name we work as long as we are doing our share in helping solve our problems in Texas, but we also have objections to consolidating with anything Jim Tafolla (James Tafolla, Sr.) may lead. It is now common knowledge that if the convention goes the other way, ninety percent of the many good men that in the past have belonged to the Sons of America are willing to come back and start all over again.

On December 24, 1928, the same member of the Orden Caballeros de América communicated with me once again and stated:

Glad you will try to attend the coming "get-together" convention. The boys here are very enthusiastic to hear of your coming, and all hope your presence will serve to pacify the now very turbulent waters that seem to divide our uncertain future.

* * *

As far as we can perceive, the only discontented element at the convention will be the President General of the Order of Sons of America (James Tafolla, Sr.) and his men, but we have made up our minds now, and nothing can hold us apart. So help us God.

I responded on January 4, 1929, as follows:

> Whether or not I shall be with you on January 13 will depend upon whether my duties permit me to leave Washington in time to arrive on that date. The probability of my being present would be greater if the date set were the third Sunday in January instead of the second. However, do not stop on my account. As I have noted before, no man is big enough to impede our progress or prevent our unification. A whole is bigger than its fractions. I will not stand in the way; on the contrary, I will do everything in my power to achieve those ends. Now, if every one of our leaders would assume this same attitude, I am certain that history will crown our labors with success.

While at Rio Grande City, I received the following from Attorney José T. Canales on February 8, 1929:

> I trust that you will make us a visit before you return to Washington. I did not have an opportunity to talk to you about various matters of interest and I would really like to get your opinion on some questions affecting the League of Latin American Citizens that you organized.

I responded to my friend Canales on February 9, 1929:

> I returned last night from a trip to Laredo, San Antonio, Corpus and Alice, and I have lots of news for you with reference to our organizational problem. The Order of Knights of America stands ready to consolidate with the others. On February 7, I conversed extensively with a group of Corpus Christi boys headed by Ben Garza (all members of the Order

of Sons of America), and they agreed to sever their connection with the Order of Sons of America. They said they were utterly disgusted with Mr. Tafolla (Mr. James Tafolla, Sr.) and would return the charter to him on the following day. They also decided to invite the League of Latin American Citizens and the Order of Knights of America to a conference in Corpus Christi, on Sunday, February 17. The invitation, signed by Ben Garza and others, will be personal.

I consider these two moves very significant. I believe that the greatest obstacle that has thus far impeded our unification has disappeared. The opportunity to consolidate is at hand. Let me suggest, therefore, that as soon as Mr. Garza extends an invitation, you name a committee to represent our League at the conference. Please try to be present. I shall do likewise. I intend to leave for Washington on February 15 in my automobile. I will go by Corpus Christi to be present at the conference. The League's committee must be fully authorized to bind the league in any way it deems proper. We must consolidate. I shall try to go to Brownsville this week to talk with you about this and other matters.

The Corpus boys want to adopt a new, short name for the organization in case we all decide to consolidate. I am certain the matter will not make any difference to us. At the conference, it will be necessary to appoint a committee to decide about the name and report to the conference that same day. The members should then appoint a committee to draft the constitution and by-laws, and report at a future conference, when the final changes will be made on all the records.

I had a very frank, plain talk with the Corpus boys and explained matters fully to them. I shall tell you all about it when I see you.

As expected, the Orden Hijos de América from Corpus Christi separated from the organization.

I received a letter from Attorney Canales on February 11, 1929, that stated as followed:

I have your letter of February 9 and a letter signed by Mr. A. de Luna, both with reference to the meeting at Corpus Christi next Sunday. I am enclosing a copy of my answer that explains itself. Be sure to see Mr. Tristán Longoria at La Grulla and Profesor Sáenz.

I do not like the idea of changing our name. This is a foolish notion in my judgment. I do not believe it is essential. Our name is descriptive of our organization, and I like it for that reason. You and I worked hard to get a good name for the organization and we thought this was the best. I am leaving for Premont, expecting to return here tomorrow. I will appreciate hearing from you again.

I went to Brownsville and conferred with Attorney Canales on the consolidation of our organizations. I found him not very willing to fuse our League of Latin American Citizens with the other groups because, ". . . the other two groups have not earned their spurs in the civic-social work in favor of our Raza." I was finally able to convince him that in order to establish a more perfect union among Mexican Americans in Texas, it made sense to form one Mexican-American organization. I have often regretted not following the advice of my friend Canales. Later experiences have convinced me that it would have been better to stay with our original League of Latin American Citizens. The reason is that although the idea of establishing a more perfect union was good, we have faced conflicts and controversies caused by the intrigue and envy of a member of the *Orden Caballeros de América* (now Council No. 2 of our league). These problems have not been good for our league or our Raza. On the contrary, they have caused us great harm and, certainly, do not abide by the spirit of unity that prompted the members of the original League of Latin American Citizens to consolidate with the other groups.

On February 14, 1929, I wrote Attorney Canales and told him the following:

My Dear Antonio:

I am very glad indeed to have talked with you Tuesday night, as I now know just what you have in mind. It makes me feel good to learn of your optimism regarding the labors of our league. It always cheers me up to talk with you and Profesor Sáenz concerning our league and its work.

I believe you should do your utmost to attend the Corpus Christi conference next Sunday. It will be perfectly proper for you to propose that all the other groups join our league and consolidate under our banner. Moreover, you may count upon my cooperation and support. However, I believe we should go with an open mind, ready to hear and to speak. We should be perfectly determined to make any concessions that may be necessary to bring about the end desired, namely, our unification.

On that same day, I sent my friend Ben Garza the following note:

San Antonio, Texas
July 1937

I will probably be present at the conference in Corpus next Sunday. I desire to express the hope that you, the rest of the interested Corpus boys and all the people you have invited to the conference may attend imbued with a conciliatory spirit and be perfectly determined to bring about the consolidation of all intelligent, active and honest Americans of Latin descent. The delegates to this conference must attend fully resolved to make any concession which may be necessary in order to achieve the end desired; namely, the establishment of a real, worthwhile, honest-to-goodness organization of American citizens of Latin extraction.

If each delegate attends the conference with his mind fully made up to have things his own way and not to yield one iota, we will accomplish nothing, and we shall be farther from our goal than ever. Let us get together, my friend. Let us begin to solve the great problems before us. Let us get out of the rut and evolve into a higher level of civilization just as our fellow Anglo Saxon countrymen are doing. Let us convince ourselves that we can only accomplish things by means of a well-organized, solid, powerful organization. Of course, it is possible to evolve as many Mexicans and Mexican Americans have done, but this is a very slow process. Let us unite. Remember: united we stand, divided we fall.

We convened on February 19, 1929, in Corpus Christi, Texas, with representatives from our League of Latin American Citizens that included eight councils, the *Orden Caballeros de América* of San Antonio with one council and a group of Latin American citizens from Corpus Christi headed by Mr. Ben Garza. We consolidated our three groups under the name of United Latin American Citizens. We later added the word "League," and that is why our organization is the League of United Latin American Citizens.

I have provided sufficient evidence on the history of LULAC with the sole purpose of putting things in their place and informing anyone who might be interested in knowing the truth. I also wish to show that I was the **INITIATOR OF THE IDEA AND THE PRINCIPAL FOUNDER** of our **LEAGUE OF UNITED LATIN AMERICAN CITIZENS**. The founders of the organization included persons who were members of the three groups that consolidated, and everyone else that attended the Corpus Christi conference on February 17, 1929, and joined our league. Canales, Garza and Sáenz were the most prominent with their participation, work, and devotion to our league.

My archives are available to anyone who wishes to examine them and accept the truth that I have offered.

San Antonio, TX
July 1937

Notes

INTRODUCTION

[1] I use the term Mexican to identify persons of Mexican-origin, regardless of nativity. When necessary, I use terms such as Mexican nationals and Mexican Americans to denote citizenship status and origin. The following book-length studies inform this introduction: Guadalupe SanMiguel, *"Let All of Them Take Heed": Mexican Americans and the Campaign for Educational for Educational Equality in Texas 1910-1981* (Austin: University of Texas Press, 1987); Mario García, *Mexican Americans: Leadership Ideology, and Identity, 1930–1960* (New Haven, Conn.: Yale University Press, 1989); Cynthia E. Orozco, *No Mexicans, Women, or Dogs Allowed: The Rise of the Mexican American Civil Rights Movement* (Austin: University of Texas Press, 2009); Richard A. García, "Alonso S. Perales, The Voice and Visions of a Citizen Intellectual," In *Leaders of the Mexican American Generation: Biographical Essays*, ed. Anthony Quiroz (Boulder, Colo.: University of Colorado Press, 2015), 85–117; Michael A. Olivas (ed.), *In Defense of My People: Alonso S. Perales and the Development of Mexican-American Public Intellectuals* (Houston: Arte Público Press, 2012); Orozco, *Pioneer of Mexican-American Civil Rights: Alonso S. Perales* (Houston: Arte Público Press, 2020). The Perales family has made available his vast archival collection to the University of Houston. See Alonso S. Perales Papers, 1898-1991, Special Collections, University of Houston (hereafter cited as Perales Papers).

[2] Perales, *En Defensa de Mi Raza*, Vol. 1 and 2 (San Antonio: Artes Gráficas, 1936, 1937).

[3] His closest companions included José de la Luz Sáenz, a teacher and the author of a World War I diary, José Tomás Canales, a co-founder

of LULAC, a former state representative, and a influential member of the Democratic Party, and Fortino Treviño, a childhood friend and fellow founder of LULAC.

[4] Most of the articles appeared in Spanish-language newspapers, the most popular and widely distributed of which was *La Prensa*, the daily from San Antonio. Some of them appeared in English-language newspapers as well.

[5] Dr. Carlos E. Castañeda was a thirty-nine-year-old librarian who helped build the Nettie Lee Benson Latin American Collection. He is also known for a successful career as a historian of the Spanish borderlands while at the Department of History at the University of Texas at Austin, and as a civil rights advocate with the League of United Latin American Citizens. Félix Almaraz, *Knight Without Armor; Carlos Eduardo Castañeda, 1896-1958* (College Station: Texas A&M University Press, 1999); Emilio Zamora, *Claiming Rights and Righting Wrongs in Texas; Mexican Americans and Job Politics during World War II* (College Station: Texas A&M University Press, 2009).

[6] Castañeda, "A propósito del libro 'En Defensa de mi Raza'," *La Prensa*, September 17, 1936, p. 8. The article appeared in volume 1 as "A propósito de Prólogo," or "By Way of a Prologue."

[7] Urbina, "Comentarios sobre el libro *En Defensa De Mi Raza*," *La Prensa*, October 20, 1936, p. 3. Urbina, a thirty-nine-year-old Spanish-language teacher in the public schools of San Antonio, was born in Mexico. He also taught extension courses at the Universidad Nacional Autónoma de México in San Antonio, participated in networks of Mexican government officials and Mexican civic leaders from San Antonio, and served as a political advisor to several local leaders, including San Antonio Mayor Maury Maverick. Manuel A. Urbina, Ancestry.com; Sarita Molinar Bertinato, "Próspero; A Study of Success from the Mexican Middle Class in San Antonio, Texas," PhD Dissertation, Texas A&M University, 2012.

[8] Sauceda, a schoolteacher, owned a printing shop, edited *El Informador Benavidense* and served as an officer of the Comisión Honorífica in the South Texas town of Benavides.

[9] As stated earlier, Benito Juárez is one of the most revered figures in Mexican history primarily because he led the popular opposition against French intervention as the president of Mexico. Cuauhtémoc, also noted earlier, led the last defense against the initial Spanish

onslaught that led to the military conquest of the Aztec empire. Moctezuma, also known as Motecuhzomatzin Ilhuicamina, preceded Cuauhtémoc as the reigning King of the Aztecs who confronted the Spanish forces in the capital of Tenochtitlán.

[10]"Comentarios acerca de la obra En Defensa de Mi Raza," Five-page transcript in Perales Papers. *La Prensa* published additional articles on the 1936 and 1937 volumes, including the following: "Un libro del Lic. Alonso S. Perales," *La Prensa*, September 7, 1936, p. 8; "El segundo tomo de la obra En Defensa de Mi Raza," *La Prensa*, July 11, 1937, p. 2.

[11]Manuel A. Urbina, "Comentarios sobre el libro En Defensa de Mi Raza," *La Prensa*, October 20, 1936, pp. 1, 3.

[12]Perales, "El México Americano y la Política del Sur de Texas" (San Antonio: Privately published, 1931); Weeks, "The Texas-Mexican and the Politics of South Texas," *American Political Science Review* Volume 24, Issue 3 (August 1930), pp. 606-27.

[13]Perales, comp., *Are We Good Neighbors?* (San Antonio: Artes Gráficas, 1948).

[14]Consult the following home-front study that focuses on Mexicans in Texas. Chapter 2 focuses on the issue of unequal recovery. Zamora, *Claiming Rights and Righting Wrongs*.

[15]Gamio, *Mexican Immigration to the United States; A Record of Human Migration and Adjustment* (Chicago: University of Chicago Press, 1930).

[16]Gamio, *The Mexican Immigrant: His Life Story* (Chicago: University of Chicago Press, 1931).

[17]Taylor, *Mexican Labor in the United States: Dimmit County, Winter Garden District, South Texas* (Berkeley: University of California Press, 1930); *An American-Mexican Frontier; Nueces County, Texas* (Chapel Hill: University of North Carolina, 1934).

[18]Muñoz, *La Verdad Sobre los Gringos, Narración Histórica de lo que ha Hecho en Latinoamérica la Aprobiosa Política del Dólar durante los Últimos Veinte Años* (México, DF: Ediciones Populares, 1927). The author published a portion of the 1927 book that addressed the San Diego revolt as a separate publication: *Defendámonos* (México, DF: Ediciones Populares, 1938).

[19]Tenayuca and Brooks, "The Mexican Question in the United States," *The Communist*, Vol. 18 (March 1939), pp. 257-68.

[20] Selden C. Menefee, Orin Cassmore, and John N. Webb, *The Pecan Shellers of San Antonio* (Washington, DC: Work Projects Administration, 1940); Menefee, *Mexican Migratory Workers of South Texas* (Washington, DC: Work Projects Administration, 1941).

[21] Espinoza, *El Sol de Texas / Under the Texas Sun*, Trans., Ethriam Cash Brammer de Gonzales (Houston: Arte Público Press, 2007); Torres, *La Patria Perdida* (México: Ediciones Botas, 1931). The novel by Espinoza first appeared as, *El Sol* (San Antonio: Viola Novelty Company, 1926).

[22] Sáenz, *Los México-Americanos en la Gran Guerra y Su Contingente en pro de la Democracia, la Humanidad y la Justicia* (San Antonio: Artes Gráficas, 1933). Also consult Emilio Zamora, Ed. and Trans., *The World War I Diary of José de la Luz Sáenz* (College Station: Texas A&M Press, 2014).

[23] Gonzales, "Social Life in Cameron, Starr, and Zapata Counties," MA Thesis, University of Texas at Austin, 1930; "Among My People," *Tone the Bell Easy*, Ed. J. Frank Dobie (Austin: Texas Folk-Lore Society, 1932); *The Woman Who Lost Her Soul and Other Stories*, Ed., Sergio Reyna [Houston: Arte Público Press], 2000).

[24] Zamora O'Shea, *El Mezquite* (Dallas: Mathis Publishing Company, 1935).

[25] Fortunately, the Recovering the US Hispanic Literary Heritage Program, an arm of the Arte Público Press from the University of Houston, has contracted with EBSCO Information Service to digitize Spanish-language newspapers from the 1820s to the 1980s, as part of a national effort to recover Hispanic records of historical importance. The Recovery Program is also responsible for securing, processing and making available the Perales Papers.

[26] Marta Perales, "Al pueblo de Alice," two-page handwritten statement that she read at the reinternment of her husband in Alice, October 15, 1960, Perales papers.

VOLUME I

[1] Dr. Carlos E. Castañeda was a thirty-nine-year-old librarian who helped build the Nettie Lee Benson Latin American Collection. He is also known for a successful career as a historian of the Spanish borderlands while at the Department of History, the University of Texas at Austin, and as a civil rights advocate with the League of United Latin American Citizens. Félix Almaraz, *Knight Without Armor; Carlos Eduardo Castañeda, 1896-1958* (College Station: Texas A&M University Press, 1999); Emilio Zamora, *Claiming Rights and Righting Wrongs in Texas; Mexican Americans and Job Politics during World War II* (College Station: Texas A&M University Press, 2009). The Spanish-language terms like "la Raza" and "nuestra Raza" are capitalized throughout this publication to reflect their typical usage and Perales' preference as self-referents in Mexican communities. For Perales, as with most Mexicans, the terms translate into My Race or Our Race, but they express the meaning of The People and Our People. The books and newspaper articles referenced in this publication vary in the use of the terms, and they appear as cited.

[2] Castañeda, like Perales, used the terms Anglos, Anglo-Texans, and whites interchangeably when referring to European-origin persons. The terms, including their Spanish equivalents, were popular among Mexicans.

[3] Castañeda contradicts Perales's earlier reference to seventeen years of political work. Perales, the editor, obviously failed to correct the minor inconsistency or to explain the difference. At any rate, both dates are close approximations of the beginning of Perales' public trajectory as a civil rights leader.

[4] Benito Juárez, the President of Mexico during the French intervention of 1961-67, authored the famous words that called for national unity and reconstruction with mutual respect and democratic rights as basic tenets in a nation of laws. He did this on July 15, 1967 after the defeat of the Hapsburg monarchy, the execution of Emperor Maximilian I (Ferdinand Maximilian Joseph María von Habsburg-Lothringen), and the restoration of the Mexican Republic in 1967. Juárez's complete statement is as follows: "entre los individuos como entre las naciones, el respeto al derecho ajeno es la paz" (Among individuals as between nations, respect towards the rights of others is

peace"). Moisés González Navarro, *Benito Juárez*, 4 vols. (México, D.F.: Colegio de México, 2006-2007).

[5] Castañeda uses the title of the book to complete the thought that Perales, the "selfless fighter," labored "In Defense of the Raza."

[6] When possible, reference notes will cite the source of the book's entry. For instance, Perales' letter to Washer appears in the following: Perales, "Del Público," *La Prensa,* September 8, 1919, p. 6. Some of the entries also originate in the Perales' archives, known as the Perales Papers [previously cited in footnotes to the Introduction]. The Washer record, for example, also appears in the Perales Papers, in its original English-language form. Since Spanish-language newspapers constituted the most important medium for communicating views on issues and events of importance to Mexicans, I often include references to newspaper articles that speak to a larger, related discourse. The following demonstrate the larger discourse on Americanism, including the copy of this entry: Perales, "Del público" (Letter to Washer) *La Prensa* (San Antonio), November 8, 1919, p. 6; "Como inculcan Americanismo en este país," *Evolución* (Laredo), November 11, 1919, p. 2; "A propósito de la labor de americanización," *La Época* (San Antonio), November 16, 1919, p. 6.

[7] Net M. Washer, born in Tennessee to German immigrants, became a prominent businessperson and Mason in San Antonio. Perales depicts Washer as a zealous proponent of Americanization who disregarded the issues of discrimination and segregation as obstacles to the incorporation of Mexicans into US society. Perales was no doubt concerned that Washer's local committee emanated from a national Americanizing initiative and that the San Antonio Chamber of Commerce and the security-conscious Social Defense group of Bexar County had established it a few months earlier. Lois Goldsmith Oppenheimer, "Nathaniel Moses Washer," *Handbook of Texas Online*, https://www.tshaonline.org/handbook/entries/washer-nathaniel-moses-nat; "La campaña para la Americanización de los extranjeros," *La Prensa*, March 16, 1919, p. 1.

[8] The case of discrimination against US soldiers may have involved José de la Luz Sáenz, Perales' long-time friend from Alice and fellow civil rights crusader. Sáenz served with the 90th Division of the American Expeditionary Force and participated, along with Perales, in the founding meeting of LULAC. Sáenz also authored the only known war diary published by a Mexican-origin soldier in any major

war. Emilio Zamora, *The World War I Diary of José de la Luz Sáenz* (College Station: Texas A&M University Press, 2014).

[9] The business achieved greater notoriety in 1943 when Perales and other LULAC members challenged the establishment's discriminatory practice in court. The civil rights leaders used an anti-discrimination concurrent resolution by the Texas Legislature prohibiting discrimination against Caucasians. When the plaintiffs lost the case on an appeal by the owner of the business, Perales and his fellow plaintiffs, joined with Mexican officials in openly calling the Caucasian Race Resolution a bogus attempt to promote the US Good Neighbor Policy at home. They pointed out that the court ruled the resolution did not have the power of law and added that Texas legislators did not intend to prohibit discrimination against Mexicans. According to the critics, the legislators were actually seeking to convince the Mexican Government to include Texas in the international agreement that was sending hundreds of thousands of contract workers to the United States. As far as Perales was concerned, Mexico should continue the Texas ban until its leadership demonstrated a willingness to participate in wartime neighborliness. Emilio Zamora, "José de la Luz Sáenz; Experiences and Autobiographical Consciousness," In Anthony Quiroz, Ed., *Leaders of the* Mexican American Generation, Biographical Essays (Boulder: University of Colorado Press, 2015); Emilio Zamora, *Claiming Rights and Righting Wrongs in Texas; Mexican Workers and Job Politics during World War II* (College Station: Texas A&M University Press, 2009).

[10] Perales occasionally emphasized words or phrases by using capital letters and underlining. The translations retain this treatment.

[11] Roosevelt was asking for unity during WWI and speaking about the duty of a citizen to be fully devoted to the nation on a "fifty-fifty basis." "No Division," *The Tonearm*, Vol. 2, No. 9 (September 2018), p. 57.

[12] "Una magna labor que se inicia," *El Imparcial de Texas* (San Antonio), February 19, 1920, p. 5. Perales quotes from an interview that the *San Antonio Evening News* used in an article on Americanization. The English version of Perales' letter could not be located in the archives of the *San Antonio Express* nor in the Perales Papers. However, the *San Antonio Evening News* and *La Prensa* (Los Angeles) reported on the Maus visit to San Antonio and the research that he was conducting in the Southwest. "Mexicans Must be Taught to

be Americans," *San Antonio Evening News*, February 17, 1920, p. 9; "Examen social de la frontera Mexicana," *La Prensa*, November 13, 1920, p. 2.

[13] Colonel Louis Mervin Maus was born in 1851, graduated from the University of Maryland as a medical doctor, served in numerous military campaigns in places like the US Northwest, Cuba and the Philippines and carried out the duties of the US Assistant Surgeon General and Chief Surgeon of Texas in the early 1900s. He retired from the Army in 1919 and soon thereafter, conducted a study of Mexicans in the American Southwest. The study could not be located, although Perales and newspaper editors generally agreed that Maus offered a positive view of Mexicans against the predominant racist outlook towards them. Maus also urged Mexicans to Americanize to gain Anglo favor. Perales to Maus, March 21, 1927, Perales Papers; Announcement, "Banquete en honor del Coronel L. Mervin Maus," no date, Perales Papers; "Biographical Note," Maus Collection, National Museum of Health and Medicine, http://www.medicalmuseum.mil/assets/documents/collections/archives/2014/OHA%20224%20Maus%20Collection. pdf; Adriana Ayala, "Negotiating Race Relations Through Activism: Women Activists and Women's Organizations in San Antonio, Texas during the 1920s," Ph.D. Dissertation, University of Texas at Austin, 2005.

[14] Although English and Spanish language newspapers regularly reported on official protests by the Mexican government against US military incursions along the Texas-Mexico border and cases of discrimination of Mexicans in Texas, they did not seem to have reported on a legislative bill that favored the segregation of Mexicans. A review of leading newspapers like the *Dallas Morning News*, the *San Antonio Express*, *La Prensa* and *La Revista Mexicana* did not produce results. It is possible that a legislator proposed such a bill, but that it did not find its way through the vetting process or attract the attention of the press. The entry on Governor Ferguson that appears later, however, offers evidence that the idea of subjecting Mexicans to de jure segregation was not a far-fetched idea among the state's leaders.

[15] Crane, "The Ten Points of Americanism," *The Library Journal* (March 1, 1920), p. 214. Crane, a Presbyterian minister of the 1920s, penned short and popular articles intended to uplift and inspire the public with a brand of personal wisdom that he described as common sense. Perales was obviously using Crane's popularity,

especially his individualistic or "boot-strap" sense of upward mobility in a class-based society, to buttress the argument against discrimination towards a group like Mexicans.

[16]"Protesta contra lo aseverado por James Ferguson, Los Mexicanos que vienen a este país son trabajadores fieles y honrados," *La Prensa,* January 7, 1921, pp. 1, 8. Ferguson, a conservative Democrat known for his anti-prohibitionist views and unethical behavior while in office, served as governor between 1915 and 1917. His wife, Miriam Ferguson, was elected to two non-consecutive terms as governor (1925-27, 1933-1935), granting her husband continued influence in state politics. The Senate impeached him for misusing public funds and removed him from office in 1917. Here, Perales is responding to an article that the ex-governor published in the *Ferguson Forum,* on December 16, 1920. The Ferguson's article could not be located. The editors of the recent anthology on Ferguson note the lack of scholarship on the relationship of race to Ferguson's impeachment. William D. Carrigan and Clive Webb, "The Lynching of Persons of Mexican Origin or Descent in the United States, 1848 to 1928," *Journal of Social History,* Vol. 37, No. 2 (Winter 2003), pp. 411-38; and William D. Carrigan, *The Making of a Lynching Culture; Violence and Vigilantism in Central Texas, 1836-1916* (Champaign: University of Illinois Press, 2006). Jessica Brannon-Wranosky and Bruce A. Glasrud, *Impeached: The Removal of Texas Governor James E. Ferguson* (College Station: Texas A&M University Press, 2017). The following articles contributed to the discourse on racism against Mexican immigrants and Ferguson's disdain for Mexicans: "En defensa de México, Réplica a Mr. Ferguson," *El Imparcial de Texas*, December 23, 1920, p. 1. Editorial, "Desahogos rancheros," *La Prensa,"* December 28, 1920, p. 3.

[17]Perales is referring to a case involving a person named Manuel Seguín who, according to Ferguson, killed a White man and injured others with a knife when some Anglo men told him that he could not sit in a section of a railroad car reserved for Whites. The editor of *La Prensa* suggested that Seguín was mentally impaired, a condition that did not keep a court in Georgetown, Texas from condemning him to death. "Tragedia registrada a bordo de un tren de pasajeros," *La Prensa*, December 12, 1920, p. 4; "Un Americano sale a la defensa de los Mexicanos," *El Imparcial de Texas*, January 13,

1921, p. 1; "Fue condenado a muerte el Mexicano Manuel Seguín," *La Prensa*, January 22, 1922, p. 6.

[18] Angeles served in the Mexican Revolution under presidents Francisco I. Madero and Venustiano Carranza and ended his celebrated military career as a general under Pancho Villa, the revolutionary leader of northern Mexico. De la Barra was a diplomat, although he assumed the presidency for a short while in 1911. He chaired the international body that arbitrated the formal dismemberment of the Austro-Hungarian Empire that the Treaty of St. Germain mandated in 1919. Spanish-language newspapers distributed in San Antonio offered readers like Perales continuous coverage of the activities of such historical figures as Angeles and De la Barra. Adolfo Gilly (Comp.), *Felipe Angeles en la Revolución* (México: DF: Ediciones Era, Consejo Nacional para la Cultura y las Artes, 2008); "El señor General Felipe Angeles en acción, afiliase a la reconstrucción Nacional," *El Imparcial de Texas*, January 31, 1918, p. 1; Peter V. N. Henderson, *In the Absence of Don Porfirio: Francisco León de la Barra and the Mexican Revolution* (Wilmington: Scholarly Resources, 2000); "Tribunal Franco Austriaco de arbitraje lo preside un mexicano ilustre, D. Francisco León de la Barra," *La Prensa*, January 31, 1921, p. 2.

[19] Perales' letter to the *Washington Post* is a verbatim translation of the original. Perales, "Protests Against 'The Bad Man'," *The Washington Post*, May 17, 1923, p. 6. The play that he condemned was not without supporters. For instance, Roberto V. Pesqueira, a political figure from Sonora elected twice to the Chamber of Deputies, saw things differently. For him, Mexico was "in vogue" among the intelligentsia in the United States, especially in the influential metropolis of New York. The play, according to Pesqueira, offered a positive depiction of the Mexican, a significant departure from the stereotypical portrayals of ignorant and lazy persons. "Como ha reaccionado la opinión en los Estados Unidos acerca de nuestro país 'El Hombre Malo'," *La Prensa*, September 29, 1920, p. 1; Pesqueira, "Un artículo de crítica," *La Época*, October 31, 1920, p. 3. That the two major Spanish-language papers from San Antonio carried the Pesqueira article and not the one penned by Perales minimally suggests a difference of opinion in his hometown. Perales, however, was not necessarily misrepresenting concerns in the United States and Mexico. Prior critiques of negative represen-

tations in movies and stage productions appeared in the US and Mexico press. Mexican government officials commented on these depictions in 1922 when they warned US movie producers that they would scrutinize and possibly reject their films as they began to expand their cultural influence into Mexico. Examples of the former include the scathing critique of the musical depiction of pre-Colombian life in Mexico by the Chicago Opera Company and the observation by a leading newspaper from Los Angeles that the Mexican government and its consular offices were vigorously protesting the pejorative depictions of Mexicans. "De nuestro corresponsal en San Antonio," *El Heraldo de México*, June 9, 1918, p. 3; Miguel Necoechea, "De arte musical Americano," *Las Novedades* (New York), January 17, 1918, p. 26; "Mexico's Ban on Mexican Movie Villains Forbids All Pictures it Considers Propaganda," *The New York Times*, February 11, 1922.

[20]This entry could not be located in surviving Spanish-language newspapers, but a copy is in the Perales Papers at the University of Houston Special Collections and Recovering the US Hispanic Literary History Program archives.

[21]Eight armed and unidentified persons apparently took Villarreal Zarate out of the jail, lynched him and shot him on November 9. Local authorities discovered the body about five miles from the South Texas town of Weslaco. *El Heraldo de México* also reported a demonstration in Breckenridge, west of Fort Worth, by 300 hooded persons calling themselves the White Owls. They threatened violence on Mexicans and Blacks if they did not leave town. The White Owls accused them of taking jobs from Whites and adding to the ranks of the unemployed. They also distributed posters among local businesses and work sites in urban centers and rural sites that stated, "We only hire White people." The workers apparently left and others stayed away causing the farmers to face difficulties finding anyone to harvest their crops. "Es muy justa y enérgica la nota de protesta de Obregón por el linchamiento de un Mexicano en Texas, y por otros atentados de que han sido víctimas nuestros compatriotas en los Estados Unidos," *El Heraldo de México* (Los Angeles), November 16, 1922, p. 1; "Después del linchamiento de Elías Villarreal Zarate, se expulsa a los nuestros de otro pueblo," *El Heraldo de México*, November 17, 1922, p. 1; "Los Rangers de Texas están investigando lo del linchamiento," *Tucsonense* (Tucson), November

23, 1922, p. 1. Spanish-language newspapers gave wide coverage to the issue of violence against Mexicans and Mexican Americans, especially when directed at youth in legal custody. The following are additional examples: "El atropello de Mexicanos en EE.UU. causa una protesta," *La Prensa,* November 16, 1922, p. 1; "Otro Mexicano iba a ser lynchado," *El Heraldo de México,* November 26, 1922, p. 1.

[22] Perales obviously assumed that his readers were sufficiently informed about Mexican history that they would know the full name and significance of the historical figures that he notes with a single name. Cuauhtémoc, also known as Guatimozín, was the last Aztec emperor when Spanish forces established colonial rule in 1520. Miguel Hidalgo y Costilla was the parish priest from Dolores Hidalgo, Guanajuato credited with initiating the war for independence in 1910.

[23] "La ignorancia como causa de los prejuicios raciales," *La Estrella* (Las Cruces), September 8, 1923, p. 1. Benito Juárez was a member of the Zapotec people who became the Chief Justice of the Supreme Court, the President of Mexico and the head of the official opposition against French intervention between 1861 and 1867.

[24] The saying that Perales used to underscore differences reads as follows: "no porque todos somos del mismo barro, lo mismo de cazuela que jarro." My translation of the entry differs slightly from the following: Nicolás Kanellos, et. al. Ed., *Herencia, The Anthology of Hispanic Literature of the United States* (New York: Oxford University Press, 2002), pp. 152-53.

[25] Juárez, Hidalgo y Costilla, Cuauhtémoc and de la Barra have been previously identified. Santiago Ramón y Cajal, a Spanish scientist, shared the 1906 Nobel Prize in Physiology or Medicine with the Italian Camilo Golgi for their discoveries of the structure of the nervous system.

[26] Perales, "Sufragio México Americano," *La Prensa,* June 25, 1924, p. 3. A copy of the Spanish-language article also appears in the Perales Papers.

[27] Perales makes use of the popular saying, "De lo dicho a lo hecho hay mucho trecho," literally meaning that great distance separates a stated purpose from its actualization. It suggests a wait and see attitude. The English-language saying "Things are easier said than done" is close to the figurative meaning of the saying in Spanish.

28"Conferencias en pro del mejoramiento de los mexicanos; Las harán sobre educación, gobierno y derechos políticos," *La Prensa*, August 2, 1924, p. 10. A translated copy of the article in *The San Antonio Light* leaves out parts of the original. The deleted material, however, does not substantially alter the meaning in the Spanish version. The titles, on the other hand, suggest divergent purposes. The editors of *La Prensa* reported that the speakers sought the social advancement of Mexicans while their counterparts at *The San Antonio Light* announced that they were promoting Americanization. The different interpretations underscore the concern that Perales and other leaders in Mexican communities expressed with Americanization programs that called for their cultural incorporation but on an unequal social basis. The editors of *The San Antonio Light* did not necessarily endorse such a program of action, but the title of their article reflected the controversial idea of Americanization without changes in the social structure. The Spanish-language title also announces that Perales and Sáenz would be speaking about the entire Mexican community. The English version informs readers that they will be teaching "US Ways to Border Aliens." This too suggests difference in perspective as well as the kind of cultural distance that keeps observers from understanding the Mexican communities. On the other hand, if Perales or another bilingual person translated the title of the article into English, the translator may have been consciously attributing ideas to the English-language readers to reflect their biases and make the article more realistic. Assuming that the audience was versed in both languages, the translator may have also sought to demonstrate political differences through this heuristic juxtaposition. Rivaling interpretations notwithstanding, the exchange made for a rich and assumptively embedded dialogue on language, identity, politics and power. "Border Aliens to Be Taught US Ways; Orator of Mexican Descent will Speak in Interest of Americanization," *The San Antonio Light*, August 1, 1924, p. 22.

29This entry could not be located in the available Spanish-language papers. A copy, however, is in the Perales Papers. The Spanish-language press, including *La Prensa* and *El Monitor* (Falfurrias), carried accounts of the presentations by Perales and Sáenz during their speaking tour.

[30] Copies of the newspaper that published this entry, *El Monitor*, could not be located. The Perales Papers, however, contain a copy of the article in Spanish.

[31] This is the first time that Perales uses the term "ideal" as a theoretical allusion to social perfection that lacks explicit grounding, but that obtains contextual meaning from its frequent association with goals like social justice, constitutional protections and effective unity throughout the text.

[32] This article could not be located in Spanish-language newspapers but it appears in Spanish in the Perales Papers.

[33] Perales, "Opiniones de un México Americano; La evolución de los México Americanos," *La Prensa*, October 11, 1924, pp. 3, 5. This article also appears in the Perales Papers.

[34] Perales uses a general reference to "Cotón azul" that also means work clothes.

[35] The article that Perales quotes could not be located in the available English-language newspapers of San Antonio.

[36] The saying that Perales notes suggests sending foreigners, or Mexicans, on a marathon for high timber. It means that they would have to quickly decamp, or vacate their places and head for presumably safer cover with no guarantee that they would not be pursued.

[37] "Opiniones del pueblo; El ideal de los México Americanos," *La Prensa*, October 13, 1924, pp. 3, 7.

[38] This entry first appeared in *The Washington Post* as a letter to the editor and later as a translated article in *La Prensa*. Perales, "Mexican Peon Defended as Honest, Trustworthy and Efficient," *The Washington Post*, September 5, 1926, p. S2; "Calurosa defensa de los trabajadores Mexicanos; La hace un abogado de Texas al ver que se atacó a los braceros de nuestra raza en un diario de Wash DC," *La Prensa*, September 9, 1926, p. 2. Perales' letter to the editor was a response to an editorial: "Restrict the Peons," *The Washington Post*, August 24, 1926, p. 6. The last sentence in the text that appears in italics only appears in the Spanish-language version. The rest of Perales' English-language letter to the editor matches the article in *La Prensa*.

[39] "Se pide justicia en el caso de Raymondville," *La Prensa*, November 3, 1926, p. 5. The letter from Perales to Governor Ferguson addressed the issues of violence against young Mexicans in legal custody, a recurring topic in the letters and articles that he published in Spanish and English-language papers. He makes special note of

the case of Tomás Núñez and his two sons. The incident began with the arrest of the brothers and a subsequent visit to the Willacy County jail by the elder Nuñez where the Sheriff arrested him as well. Newspaper reports do not explain the cause of the arrests. According to the Sheriff and constables who transported the prisoners to the Cameron County jail in Brownsville, unknown persons ambushed them. The prisoners died in the shooting while the officers survived without injury. They claimed that the prisoners tried to escape during the shooting and that the alleged shooters killed them. "México protesta por la muerte de Mexicanos en Raymondville, Texas," *El Cronista del Valle* (Brownsville), September 15, 1926, p. 1; "Aprehensión de empleados del condado Willacy," *El Cronista del Valle*, January 8, 1927, p. 1; Perales, "Tribuna del público," *La Prensa*, January 21, 1927, p. 3; "Están investigando las autoridades federales la muerte de Mexicanos en el condado de Willacy, Texas," *La Prensa*, February 2, 1927, p. 1.

[40]Perales is acknowledging newspaper accounts that the governor's report to Secretary of State Frank B. Kellogg would defuse "international complications" because of previous assumptions that the deceased were Mexican nationals. In other words, he understood that US officials were more interested in averting a conflict with Mexico than in determining that the deaths were "assassinations," that is, wanton killings reserved for Mexicans and Mexican Americans in South Texas. Perales would also lament that the Mexican government typically lobbied on behalf of Mexican nationals but not Mexican Americans. He probably based this on a Grand Jury report that claimed that at least three of the deceased were US citizens. On the other hand, an article in *The Brownsville Herald*, noted that the elder Nuñez was a Mexican citizen. This had led the Mexican Consulate at San Antonio to assign one of their attorneys, Manuel J. Gonzales, to sue the alleged killers for $50,000 on behalf of the Nuñez family. "Nuñez Killing Basis for Suit," *The Brownsville Herald*, February 11, 1926, p. 1; "Report Men Killed in Willacy County were Citizens of US," *The Brownsville Herald*, October 23, 1926, p. 1. See note 39 for additional information on the Núñez case.

[41]The entry appears in its entirety in *El Cronista del Valle* and in abbreviated form in *La Prensa*. "Enérgica protesta del licenciado Alonso S. Perales," *El Cronista del Valle*, February 3, 1927, p. 1;

"Hay disgusto en McAllen," *La Prensa*, February 3, 1927, p. 1. The first statement of protest by the Mexican Consul noted by the editors of *La Prensa* and *El Cronista del Valle* appeared earlier, while a subsequent article addressed the housing covenant in McAllen, an issue that continued unabated for at least one more month. The protest by Consul Treviño suggested that the appearance of signs refusing service to Mexicans in some South Texas businesses as well as the McAllen covenant were responses to Mexico's decision to build a dam on the *Rio Salado* (in the northern Mexican state of Nuevo León) which empties on the Rio Grande River. Texas farmers reportedly claimed that the dam would reduce their water supply. "Sección editorial; La viril actitud del consul Treviño," *El Cronista del Valle*, January 1, 1927, p. 3; "Una protesta del consul de México en McAllen," *El Cronista del Valle*," January 29, 1927, p. 1, "Una justa defensa de los Mexicanos," *El Heraldo de México*, March 5, 1927, p. 3.

[42] This article also appeared in the weekly from McAllen. "Protesta de un México Texano," *Diógenes*, February 5, 1927, page unknown.

[43] An English-language version of the major part of this entry is in the Perales Papers as the copy that Perales sent Senator Morris Sheppard. In other words, only the copy sent to the senator has survived. The letter could not be located in its entirety in Spanish-language papers, although some parts are available in *La Prensa*. "Carta enviada al Presidente Coolidge protestando contra los asesinatos de Raymondville," *La Prensa*, May 6, 1927, p. 1; "Una carta dirigida a Mr. Coolidge sobre el caso Núñez," *La Prensa*, May 6, 1927, p. 1; "Interesante carta dirigida al presidente Coolidge," *El Cronista del Valle*, May 7, 1927, p. 1. The weekly from McAllen, *Diógenes*, also published a copy of the letter from Perales to Senator Sheppard. Perales, "Carta abierta, Al márgen de los crímenes de Raymondville," January 22, 1927, p. 1, 2.

[44] The other two casualties, Deputy Constable L. E. Shaw and Deputy Sheriff Lewis May, had been responsible for overseeing two Mexican dances on September 5 in Mexiquito, the Mexican side of town. After the dances were over, they heard a shot and, upon investigating, became the target of unknown shooters who seemed to have drawn the officers into an ambush. A day after the initial shooting, the rest of the police officers rounded up a large number of young Mexican males who had attended the dances. According to the

County Sheriff, the Núñez brothers admitted to have done the shooting and they implicated Gonzalez and Solar. According to the report of the Grand Jury, the Núñez brothers led the officers to a place where they claimed to have hidden the arms that they had used to kill Shaw and May. The second shooting, almost a mirror image of the first ambush, did not seem like a planned execution to the members of the Grand Jury. "Officers of Willacy County Exonerated," *The Brownsville Herald,* September 18, 1926, pp. 1, 2.

[45] The president's letter could not be located.

[46] "U.S. 'Big Stick' in Nicaragua," *San Antonio Light*, January 8, 1927, pp. 1, 3; "Liberals Move Towards the Capital of Nicaragua," *San Antonio Express*, January 8, 1927, pp. 1, 3. Perales refers to President Coolidge's decision to implement a US arms embargo directed at revolutionary groups in Nicaragua and to send troops to the Central American nation ostensibly to "protect American lives and property." The president also reportedly warned Mexico against appropriating oil properties.

[47] The English-language letter to Senator Sheppard does not include the following paragraphs that also appear in Perales' entry. In other words, I translated Perales' entry beyond this point.

[48] The following article addresses the peonage cases involving Teller as well as the Nuñez case: Alicia A. Garza, "Raymondville Peonage Cases," *Handbook of Texas Online*, accessed February 24, 2018, http://www.tshaonline.org/handbook/online/articles/pqreq.

[49] A copy of the letter to Senator Sheppard appears in the Perales Papers.

[50] "El Lic. Perales defiende a los braceros Mexicanos," *La Prensa,* March 1, 1927, p. 7. This is an expanded version of the letter that Perales sent to the McAllen Real Estate Board appearing in the previous entry titled "A Protest Against a Real Estate Company."

[51] Editorial published in *El Heraldo de* México in Los Angeles, California, on March 1927. Perales, "Una justa defensa de los Mexicanos," *La Prensa*, March 5, 1927, p. 3.

[52] Perales, "Una carta a Mr. Coolidge sobre el caso Núñez," *La Prensa*, May 6, 1927, p. 1.

[53] This paragraph and the following one are verbatim copies of parts of a statement made by President Coolidge that Perales translated in his article. "Coolidge Presents Policy to World," *The Washington Post*, April 26, 1927, p. 2.

[54] Perales, "Honremos la memoria de los heroes de origen Mexicano," *El Cronista del Valle,* July 20, 1928, p. 1. *La Prensa* carried the same article in its July 23, 1928 issue.

[55] "Mas gestiones a favor de los Mexicanos, las hizo en Washington el licenciado Alonso S. Perales ante un senador y diputado de Texas," *La Prensa,* May 8, 1929, p. 1.

[56] "El Lic. Alonso, S. Perales hace unas oportunas indicaciones de gran utilidad a la juventud," *La Prensa*, September 12, 1929, p. 1.

[57] The third, fifth and sixth paragraphs in Kellogg's address are verbatim copies of sections that appeared in *The Washington Post* and *The New York Times*. The rest of the quoted material appears in the previously noted article in *La Prensa* and in Perales' entry. "Kellogg in Speech Lauds Peace Pact," *The Washington Post*, February 19, 1929, p. 1; "Kellogg Opposes Penalty for Pact," *The New York Times*, February 19, 1929, p. 4.

[58] "Brillante defensa de la Raza Mexicana hizo el Lic. Perales en Washington, declaró ante el comité de inmigración," *La Prensa*, February 4, 1930, p. 1. The book entry appears in the following: Hearings before the Committee on Immigration and Naturalization, House of Representatives, Seventy-First Congress, On the bills HR 8523, 8530, 8702, To Limit the Immigration of Aliens to the United States and for Other Purposes (Washington, DC: Government Printing Office, 1930), January 28 and 30, 1930, pp. 179-89. Like the entry, the article in *La Prensa* includes an almost verbatim account of the hearings. A newspaper from the Rio Grande Valley also reported on the testimony by Perales and other members of LULAC. "Brillante defensa de la raza Mexicana," *El Cronista del Valle*, February 21, 1930, p. 4.

[59] Representative John C. Box from Texas had submitted an immigration restriction bill to include Mexico in the National Origins quota system, a legislative measure that allocated numbers of allowed immigrants from mostly southern and eastern nations according to a percentage of their nationals already living in the United States. The bill sought to amend the Johnson-Reed initiative that became the Immigration Act of 1924. The 1924 law established a national origins quota but exempted Western Hemisphere nations from the restrictive system. Although the bill failed, Congress legislated immigration preferences that intended to regulate the immigrant flow from Mexico and other non-quota sources of immigration. The Immigration and

Nationality Act of 1965, also known as the Hart-Celler Act, assigned a quota to Mexico after its enactment in 1968. The Box bill amplified the voice of anti-immigration groups like nativists, eugenicists and organized labor. William G. Hartley, "United Immigration Policy; The Case of the Western Hemisphere," *World Affairs, Vol. 135, No. 1 (Summer 1972), pp. 54-70.* Racial thinking also motivated the restrictionists. Box, for example, offered the following justification for his bill: "Another purpose of the immigration laws is the protection of American racial stock from further degradation or change through mongrelization. The Mexican peon is a mixture of mediterranean-blooded Spanish peasant with low-grade Indians who did not fight to extinction but submitted and multiplied as serfs. Into that was fused much Negro slave blood. This blend of low-grade Spaniard, peonized Indian, and Negro slave mixes with Negroes, mulattoes, and other mongrels, and some sorry whites, already here. The prevention of such mongrelization and the degradation it causes is one of the purposes of our laws which the admission of these people will tend to defeat." Mae M. Ngai and Jon Gjerde, Eds., *Major Problems in American and Ethnic History; Documents and Essays* (Boston: Wadsworth/Cengage Learning, 2013), p. 286.

[60] Information on Mata, the Mexican surgeon, could not be located.

[61] Green may have been acknowledging relations with a North American indigenous group when he claimed a common origin with Perales.

[62] José Tomás Canales, co-founder of LULAC and a former State Representative, also gave testimony. Hearings before the Committee on Immigration and Naturalization, House of Representatives, Seventy-First Congress, pp. 169-179.

[63] The rest of the entry appears as the introduction of an extended research statement that Perales entered into the record of the hearings. Perales, in other words, does not include in his book the seven-page single-spaced research statement that he submitted as an attachment to his testimony. The purpose of the Perales statement was to underscore that Mexicans, contrary to popular opinion, were not inferior. In both Mexico and the United States, they had demonstrated a capacity to learn, build communities and produce important figures in history. Perales, however, conceded a racial hierarchy of worth and essentially posited that Mexicans, unlike other less endowed peoples, could contribute to the development of society if

given a chance. In other words, in his rush to vindicate Mexicans, Perales partly justified the racial edifice that confined his people in a marginalized condition. Hearings before the Committee on Immigration and Naturalization, House of Representatives, Seventy-first Congress, 182-89.

[64] Hearings before the Committee on Immigration and Naturalization, House of Representatives, Seventy-First Congress, p. 191. The Committee accepted the telegram from Clemente Idar and Manuel Gonzales a day after Perales' testimony.

[65] The editor has made minor editing on the stilted language of the telegram from Idar and Gonzales to William Green, the head of the American Federation of Labor and a close associate of Idar. Idar served as an AFL organizer beginning in 1919 while Gonzales worked as a legal advisor to the Mexican consulate of San Antonio since at least the late 1920s. See the following book by Zamora for information on the political careers of Idar and Gonzales: *The World of the Mexican Worker in Texas* and *Claiming Rights and Righting Wrongs in Texas.*

[66] "Fue un acontecimiento la convencion De La Liga De Ciudadanos en Edinburg, El licenciado Perales citó casos concretos en que no se hacía justicia en Texas a los latinoamericanos siendo interrumpido por los licenciados Gonzales y Canales," *La Prensa*, May 7, 1931, p. 2.

[67] Robertson, a WWI veteran, railroad and land developer and Cameron County Sheriff, was already an established figure in the Rio Grande Valley at the time of the LULAC conference. Verna J. McKenna, "Samuel Arthur Robertson," *Handbook of Texas Online,* accessed July 05, 2018, http://www.tshaonline.org/handbook/online/articles/fro32.

[68] Abney was a citrus farmer and a popular candidate for the position of mayor that the LULAC organization from Hidalgo County endorsed in 1931. Couch was a judge, banker and reformer from Hidalgo County. Guerra had a distinguished career in public service, at one time serving as the Presiding Judge of the 139th District Court of Hidalgo County, from 1954 to 1980. He was an insurance salesman with a budding political career in 1931; Lozano was an attorney and LULAC member from San Antonio; Loftin worked for the San Antonio ISD as a teacher. Information on Brown and McWhorter is not available. "Las elecciónes del 7 de abril," *El Defensor* (Edinburg), April 3, 1931, p. 1; "Fidencio M. Guerra,"

Obituary, *Austin American Statesman,* https://www.legacy.com/ obituaries/statesman/obituary.aspx?n=fidencio-m-guerra&pid= 2934832; "EdCouch," accessed August 5, 2017; http://kenanderson.net/delta/ed_couch.html; Verna J. McKenna, "Robertson, Samuel Arthur," *Handbook of Texas Online,* accessed September 28, 2016, http://www.tshaonline.org/handbook/online/articles/fro32; December 18, 2004; J. O. Loftin, Ancestry.com.

[69]Guerra may have been the same thirty-year old person who, according to the Census, owned a food store in Edinburg with her husband José. Lubbock, the daughter of a cattle salesman and school principal was twenty-six, a singer and a stage performer. Information on the "García and Herrera" women was not available. "Celia Guerra," Ancestry.com; Teresa Mary Lubbock, Ancestry.com;

[70]Consult the following for a newspaper report on the death of Quintanilla: "Interviene el consulado en un juicio, Tratase de que se haga justicia en la muerte," *La Prensa,* May 14, 1933, p. 2.

[71]The 1930 case against the Del Rio school district is the first known legal challenge against the segregation of Mexican children in Texas. The plaintiffs, Jesús Salvatierra and other parents, claimed that school officials denied their children the benefits accorded "other White groups." By the time of the 1931 LULAC Convention, the court had declared that the school had segregated Mexican children, although it accepted the defense's major argument that the school was obligated to treat them differently because it made pedagogical sense to give them separate instruction to accommodate their alleged lack of English proficiency and irregular attendance. The plaintiffs lost their appeal before the Court of Appeals in San Antonio. Perales was most probably reflecting on the possibility of taking the case to the highest court when he spoke. This did not occur. Perales, along with other LULAC leaders that included José Tomás Canales and Manuel C. Gonzales, served with the team of lawyers representing the parents. LULAC also supported the plaintiffs with public campaigns that informed the public and generated funds for the legal costs of the case. Cynthia E. Orozco, "Del Rio ISD v. Salvatierra," *Handbook of Texas Online,* accessed February 13, 2018, http://www.tshaonline.org/handbook/online/articles/jrd02. For a more substantial treatment of the issue of school segregation and the role that LULAC played in addressing the issue, consult Guadalupe San Miguel's *"Let All of Them Take Heed": Mexi-*

can Americans and the Campaign for Educational Equality in Texas (Austin: University of Texas Press, 1987).

[72]"El discurso del Lic. Perales en la gran fiesta De la Raza efectuada en el auditorio," *La Prensa*, October 15, 1933, p. 3. The text is prefaced by a statement that indicates that the speech was erudite and covered important topics that had a positive effect on the attendees.

[73]Lozano was the editor of *La Prensa* and a major political figure, primarily among "Los Mexicanos de Afuera," or the Mexicans in the exterior. The San Antonio daily folded in the 1950s, although his family continues to publish another newspaper in Los Angeles, *La Opinion*. See the following for an account of his binational leadership in the 1920s: Emilio Zamora, "Las Escuelas del Centenario in Dolores Hidalgo, Guanajuato; Internationalizing Mexican History," In *Recovering the Hispanic History of Texas*, Edited by Mónica Perales and Raul Ramos (Houston: Arte Público Press, 2010), pp. 38-66.

[74]The celebration of El Día de la Raza in Latin America is typically a tribute to the cultural amalgam of indigenous people and Europeans. The process theoretically began with the arrival of Europeans and the subsequent conquest over the vast territory extending from the southern tip of the continent to the current U.S. South, Southwest and West. In Latin America, the commemoration gives primary attention to the cultural mixing as an on-going and profound experience in the making of an all-encompassing and binding hemispheric identity as *La Raza*, or the people. The celebrations outside present-day Mexico—like San Antonio—took on the added purpose of reinforcing Mexican cultural and racial ties to the history of America, in the original and broad sense of the word. Perales interprets this history as a Hispanophile and, in the process, commits the same error of omission that he laments in the article by Wells that minimizes the importance of indigenous peoples in the amalgamation process. At the same time, he utilizes his triumphant sense of history to defend "the worth" of Mexican people.

[75]The source that Perales cites could not be located.

[76]Herbert G. Wells, *The Outline of History, Being a Plain History of Life and Mankind*, Vol. II (New York: The Macmillan Company, 1920), p. 166.

[77]The letter to Johnson does not appear in the Perales Papers or in any Spanish and English-language newspapers.

[78] According to a Master's thesis, San Antonio constructed two women's centers, although its author did not indicate if officials integrated Mexican women into the Anglo or African American groups. Articles in the *Southwestern Historical Quarterly* and the *Handbook of Texas* offered little help. The authors acknowledged the difficulties that Blacks faced in the NYA programs, but said nothing about how Mexicans fared. Deborah Lynn Self, "The National Youth Administration in Texas, 1935-1939," Master's Thesis, Texas Tech University, 1974; Christie Lynne Bourgeois, "Stepping over Lines: Lyndon Johnson, Black Texans, and the National Youth Administration, 1935-1937," *Southwestern Historical Quarterly*, Vol. 91, No. 2 (October 1987), pp. 149-52; Kenneth E. Hendrickson, "National Youth Administration," *Handbook of Texas Online*, accessed July 16, 2017, http://www.tshaonline.org/handbook/online/articles/ncn04.

[79] Perales added a note at the end of this article that read as follows: "The author published another article on the same topic in November 1933." Perales, "Tribuna del público, oportunidades educativas que debemos aprovechar," *La Prensa*, August 30, 1935, p. 3.

[80] "Se reunió la comisión de salubridad, Se discutieron en la junta las condiciones del barrio oeste de la ciudad," *La Prensa*, November 3, 1935, p. 2.

[81] The newspaper article with the quote that appeared in the entry could not be located. Local newspapers, however, carried several articles and editorials on the public health issues and the failure of the City Health Department to do much about them. The following is representative of the critical editorials that appeared beginning during the early part of October: "Disease Common Enemy," *San Antonio Light*, November 2, 1935, p. 9.

[82] The term *corrales*, or corrals, refers to congested living areas on the west side of San Antonio that included small frame houses or *jacales*, rudimentary structures constructed with assorted building material bound and plastered with sod or adobe. Poor Mexican families typically lived in homes that encircled an open area, suggesting a corral structure. The term *corrales* spoke to the physical circle-like structure of neighborhoods as well as to the figurative demarcation of an enclosure that contained mobility. Studies that interpret life and work on the west side include the following: Selden C. Menefee and Orin C. Cassmore, *The Problem of Underpaid and Unemployed Mexican Labor* (Washington, DC: Government Printing Office, 1940); Julia

K. Blackwelder, *Women of the Depression; Caste and Culture in San Antonio, 1929-1939* (College Station: Texas A&M University Press, 1984); Zaragosa Vargas, *Crucible of Struggle; A History of Mexican Americans from Colonial times to the Present Era (New York: Oxford University, 2011).*

[83]"Otra protesta con respeto a las pensiones, La fórmula del concilio 16 de la liga de ciudadanos unidos latinoamericanos," *La Prensa*, November 15, 1935, p. 1. Perales was probably seconding a protest by another Mexican American organization, El Club Democrático. "Distinción en las pensiones a mexicanos, Protesta por ella El Club Democrático del condado de Bexar," *La Prensa*, November 14, 1935, p. 2. Perales criticizes the state version of the New Deal program that was supposed to provide old age assistance. The Texas Legislature established the Old Age Assistance Law in 1936 to provide financial support to needy persons over the age of sixty-five. According to Governor James Allred, approximately 300,000 citizens over 65 lived in Texas, but only half of them qualified. The state agency received approximately one-half of the funding from the federal government to help approximately 15,000 persons who met eligibility requirements. The age requirement was set at sixty-five, but the actual disbursements were unequal. A legislative report noted that assistance from the Old Age Assistance Program, "shall not exceed $30 per month and shall be granted in such amounts as will provide a reasonable subsistence in keeping with the accustomed standard of living of the applicants." This meant that state officials disbursed unequal amounts to eligible persons, that is, persons with poorer abilities to sustain themselves received lower monthly amounts. According to the governor, the Old Age Assistance Program gave out between $16 and $20 per person during its first year of operation. Additional analysis of the program is necessary to determine the different levels of support according to the socio-economic status and racial background of eligible persons. Perales may have been especially concerned that the Texas Relief Commission had reduced the scope of its work and sent away an undetermined number of needy people, forcing as many as 40,000 aged persons to turn to the Old Age Assistance Program for help between June and November 1935. Mexican origin persons no doubt were among them. Vivian Elizabeth Smyrl, "Texas Department of Human Services," *Handbook of Texas Online*, accessed

September 30, 2016, http://www.tshaonline.org/handbook/online/articles/mct06; Governor's address on State Unemployment Compensation, 44th Legislature, 3rd Session (HB 26, SB 5), September 28, 1936, pp. 290-91, Legislative Reference Library of Texas, http://www.lrl.state.tx.us/scanned/govdocs/James%20V%20Allred/1936/mess1.pdf.

[84] This entry did not appear in local papers, suggesting that Perales did not always make use of newspapers to publicize his views and challenges injustices. In this instance, he was sharing with his readers of an account of his civic engagement work before the Civil Service Commission on behalf of Manuel Urbina, a popular teacher, minister and political figure from San Antonio. Urbina claimed that a police officer named Mike Livo had unjustly arrested him and made disparaging remarks to an audience of Mexicans who had gathered at a local park to hear the minister criticize Italy for waging its colonial war against Ethiopia between 1935 and 1939. The editor of *La Prensa* reported that Perales made an impassioned final statement in defense of Urbina and the Mexican community. The Commission cleared the police officer of all charges. "El oficial de policía Mike Livo fue absuelto, Se le acusaba de tres cargos en relación con un incidente en la Plaza Milam," *La Prensa*, November 14, 1935, p. 8.

[85] Perales, "La Asociación de Padres y Maestros," *Actualidad*, December 1935, Perales Papers. The following are examples of other articles on the popular topic of Parent Teacher Associations: "Latin Americans Talk on Schools," *San Antonio Express*, July 24, 1934, p. 16; "Se instaló un nuevo concilio de los Lulacs and Kenedy, TX," *La Prensa*, December 1, 1935, p. 16; "Las labores realizadas por las comisiónes del concilio 16 de los Lulacs," *La Prensa*, December 23, 1935, p. 8; "The Pauline Nelson Faculty and the Parent-Teacher Association," *San Antonio Light*, March 9, 1941, Part Three, p. 5.

[86] "En la corte del distrito se ventila un juicio en contra del consejo escolar," *La Prensa*, January 30, 1936, p. 1. African Americans sued the San Antonio School Board to compel it to expend bond money on a high school on the South side of the city. The plaintiffs, led by C. C. Hudson, had submitted a petition for a bond election and the construction of a high school for the predominantly African American side of town. Days before the election, the school Board issued an "official statement" declaring that the school would be built. Once the

bond issue carried, the Board decided that the "official statement" was not binding and that it could exercise its regular authority to expend the proceeds of the bond as they saw fit. The District Court decided against the plaintiffs. They appealed, but the Board had spent most of the money before the Court of Civil Appeals had heard the case. The higher court essentially decided against the plaintiffs by noting that since the remaining bond money was not sufficient to build the Black high school, "the contended-for project cannot now be substantially carried out from the remaining proceeds of this bond issue." It is not possible to tell the extent to which the Mexican American leadership influenced the Board or the District Court, but the case no doubt frayed their relations with the African American community, especially since the board members reneged on their promise and favored one minority group over another. Hudson v. San Antonio, 95 S.W. 2d 673 (Tex. 1936), https://casetext.com/case/hudson-v-san-antonio-ind-sch-dist, Accessed July 4, 2018.

[87] Perales, "Concurso para embellecer solares," *La Prensa*, April 11, 1936, p. 8. This entry is Perales' translation of a major part of a proclamation by the mayor of San Antonio that first appeared in the *San Antonio Express* on March 1, 1936. The four paragraphs of the resolution originate in the English-language paper. "Centennial Yards Contest to Promote Beautification of City, A Proclamation," *San Antonio Express*, March 1, 1936, Real Estate and Classified Section, p. 1.

[88] "A propósito de la convención de la asociación anti-tuberculosis del estado de Texas *La Prensa*, April 14, 1936, p. 1. Tuberculosis disproportionally affected Mexican-origin persons in Texas during the 1930s, especially in places like South Texas and large urban areas where they were concentrated. They registered the second highest number of deaths from the disease, next to Anglos. Their tubercular death rate of 212.8 (per 100,000) in Texas exceeded related figures for Anglos and Blacks at 34.3 and 98.2, respectively. For an excellent study on health issues and health policies along the Mexico-US border, see: John McKiernan Gonzalez, *Fevered Measures; Public Health and Race at the Texas-Mexico Border, 1848-1942* (Durham: Duke University Press, 2012). McKiernan Gonzalez attributes the figures to George Cox, *The Latin American Health Problem in Texas* (Austin: Texas State Department of Health, Division of Maternal and Child Health, 1940), 6-7.

[89] Perales, "Una excitativa a prominentes asociaciones Americanas en favor de los Mexicanos," *La* Prensa, April 27, 1936, p. 8. An English-version copy of the article is in the Perales Papers, however, it is difficult to read due to the deteriorated condition of the paper. The editor of *La Prensa*, often acknowledged Perales' participation in the Pan-American efforts to improve understanding in the hemisphere. He supported Pan-Americanism, especially beginning in the middle 1930s when President Roosevelt began to promote the Good Neighbor Policy to build wartime solidarity in the Americas in the event that the United States entered the war. Perales, however, also criticized Anglo Pan-Americanists for overlooking the need for improved understanding with Mexicans in the United States. His call for an expanded Pan-Americanism became even more pronounced during the war when he took a more active role in connecting the local cause of equal rights with the call for wartime unity in the Americas. Dr. George I. Sanchez, also a LULAC officer and a Professor of Education at the University of Texas at Austin, famously captured the shared civil rights critique when he noted that White Pan-Americanists were "interested in the Mexican across the border but not in the one across the tracks." Emilio Zamora, *Claiming Rights and Righting Wrongs in Texas, Mexican Workers and Job Politics during WWII* (College Station: Texas A&M University Press, 2009), p. 101. For a closer examination of Perales' work on behalf of hemispheric unity and civil rights, see the following: Emilio Zamora, "Connecting Causes; Alonso S. Perales, Hemispheric Unity, and Mexican Rights in the United States," In *Defense of My People: Alonso S. Perales and the Development of Mexican-American Public Intellectuals*, Ed., Michael Olivas (Houston: Arte Público Press, 2012), pp. 287-314; Zamora, "Alonso S. Perales: In Defense of My People," *Southwestern Historical Quarterly*, Vol. CXXIV, No. 2 (October 2020), pp. 110-34.

[90] Perales is referring to instances when *farmers* contracted Mexicans to harvest their crops with the understanding that they would pay them a share of the harvest or a dollar equivalent. This is different from contractual arrangements by which tenants or sharecroppers rented the land and paid a rental fee with a share of the crops at the end of the season. See the following studies of Texas agriculture and Mexican workers for discussions on the land rental arrangement as a

form of labor exploitation: David Montejano, *Anglos and Mexicans in the Making of Texas, 1836-1986* (Austin: University of Texas Press, 1987); Emilio Zamora, *The World of the Mexican Worker in Texas* (College Station: Texas A&M University Press, 1993).

[91] Perales did not make this letter public. The Poetry Club from Thomas Jefferson High School, however, did publish the poems (noted below). Perales' concern over the first poem is understandable given the depiction of Mexican tortilla makers as dirty. The negative portrayal no doubt acquired added meaning with a possible suggestive cue in the persons of the Mexican women who regularly set up food booths in local parks, much like the similarly vilified "Chili Queens" that Perales and others defended elsewhere. The second poem also debased Mexicans but it used history to explain a seeming fall from grace into depravity. The Mexican, the descendant of the once "great men of Spain" that Perales admired had now degenerated to lowly workers laboring in the shadows of the Alamo, popularly known as the shrine of Texas liberty and the symbol of political and cultural independence from Mexico. The idea that young Anglos were learning and speaking with such disdain must have also troubled the ordinarily hopeful Perales. Raymond White, "Tortilla Makers," and "Peons," *If Crickets Hear* (San Antonio: The Poetry Club, 1935-6), pp. 65-66.

The Tortilla Makers

Sound of the slap-slap
>of dirty hands of dirty women
>>Making tortillas—
Smell of fresh-ground meal,
>ground in a stone bowl
>>to make tortillas—
Sound of Mejicanos gurgling cheap wine
>made a day before
>>to eat with tortillas—
Smell of peons and horses and peons
>who work for fifty cents a day
>>to feed dirty children
>>>With dirty tortillas
>>from Haymarket Plaza.

Peons

Peons work in the shadow
>of the Alamo
for
>. . . fifty centavos a day.
Grandes hombres de Espana [sic]
(the great men of Spain)
built
>the Alamo
built its walls, unfalling walls,
now calling but softly
>of the spirit of Spain
>of the spirit of the cottonwoods,
ever musing—musing
>on
peons who work
>for
. . . fifty centavos a day in the shadow
>of
. . . . . the Alamo.

[92]"Lulacs in Annual Convention," *The Laredo Times*, June 7, 1936, pp. 1, 6; "Ayer se abrió la convención," *El Tiempo de Laredo*, June 7, 1936, pp. 1, 2.

[93]Educational reformers from San Antonio established the first such organization in 1934 as a federation of over forty organizations. It originated as the Committee on Playgrounds and School Facilities of LULAC Council 16 and quickly expanded into nearby places like Del Rio. Differences of opinion led the Liga to split from LULAC and to dissolve in the late 1930s, although it registered a comeback after the war. The organization led the Mexican-led effort to reform education in San Antonio and the state. Cynthia Orozco "School Improvement League," *Handbook of Texas Online*, accessed August 12, 2017, http://www.tshaonline.org/handbook/online/articles/kaswm.

[94]Valls was a popular figure in South Texas beginning in the early 1900s when he assumed the position of District Attorney for the 49th District Court in Laredo. After thirty-five years as a District Attorney, he served as the judge for the same court until his passing in

1941. Valls prosecuted cases of international importance involving adherents to the irredentist movement associated with the 1915 Plan de San Diego and murder suspects connected to Mexican officials such as President Elias Plutarco Calles. He self-identified as a Latin American and often attributed his success to a close relationship with Mexican-origin persons, including influential figures in predominantly South Texas towns like Laredo. Perales often referred to him as a critic of racial discrimination and a supporter of the Mexican American civil rights cause. Stanley C. Green, *John Valls and the History of the Laredo Bar* (Laredo: Border Studies, 1991).

[95] Perales is referring to Mexicans who joined the Texas Rebellion of 1836 and served in public office during and after the revolt. Their full names are Juan Nepomuceno Seguín, José Antonio Navarro, José Francisco Ruiz, Plácido Benavides, Juan Antonio Badillo, Gregorio Esparza, Antonio Fuentes, José María Guerrero, José Toribio Losoya, and Andrés Nava. Roberto R. Calderón, "Tejano Politics," *Handbook of Texas Online*, accessed August 12, 2017, http://www.tshaonline.org/handbook/online/articles/wmtkn.

[96] This entry did not appear in the available newspapers or the Perales Papers.

[97] Perales, "Las próximas elecciones y el porvenir de nuestra niñez," *La Prensa*, July 9, 1936, p. 3.

[98] Perales, "Las proximas elecciones y el porvenir de nuestra Raza," La Prensa, July 12, 1936, p. 8.

[99] Perales, "El México-Americano y las recientes elecciones," *La Prensa*, August 4, 1926, p. 4.

[100] This entry could not be located in the available newspapers or the Perales Papers.

[101] Weeks, "The Texas-Mexican and the Politics of South Texas," p. 627.

[102] Perales' entry provided the document in English.

[103] Perales' entry provided the documents in English.

[104] The English version of this entry was secured from the following: *Complete Texas Statutes, Chapter 18, Compulsory Education* (Kansas City: Vernon Law Book Company, 1928), pp. 375-76. Article 2892a appeared in the following: Supplement to the 1928 Texas Statutes, Public Education (Kansas City: Vernon Law Book Company, 1931), p. 314.

[105] Perales made a Spanish-language copy of the statutes available to the Mexican public to underscore the need to keep the children in school and the legal responsibility of school officials to ensure equal access to a public education. The low enrollment record of Mexican students must have also motivated Perales. This was a well-known issue that at least one researcher from the University of Texas, Herschel T. Manuel, addressed. According to Manuel, arguably the most important researcher on the educational experience of Mexican children between the 1920s and the 1930s, no more than sixty percent of the school-age Mexican youth attended any grade in Texas public and private institutions in the late twenties. Most of them attended segregated schools. Their attendance record was significantly lower than Whites and Blacks in absolute and proportional numbers. Mexican children also registered an enrollment decline beginning in the fourth grade in both urban and rural schools. Four months after Manuel's speech at the 1931 LULAC convention, he and Perales spoke at a San Antonio event sponsored by the Professional Women in Obstetrics to secure funding for a desegregation fight on behalf of the Comité Pro-Defensa Escolar de Del Rio, Texas. Manuel reportedly discussed his research findings and stated that state officials were not enforcing the law on compulsory education. Perales added that the segregation of Mexican-origin children also violated the constitution of the United States and Texas and the 1848 Treaty of Guadalupe Hidalgo that ended the war between Mexico and the United States. Manuel, *The Education of Mexican and Spanish-Speaking Children in Texas* (Austin: The Fund for Research in the Social Sciences, the University of Texas, 1930), pp. 91-94; "Terminó la convención en Edinburg," *La Prensa*, May 6, 1931, p. 1; "La segregación escolar es contra la Constitución de Estados Unidos y de Texas también," *La Prensa*, September 8, 1931, p. 1. For a reading on the historical legal challenge against racial discrimination in Del Rio, see the following: Cynthia Orozco "Del Rio ISD v. Salvatierra," accessed August 12, 2017, http://www.tshaonline.org/handbook/online/articles/jrd02.

[106] This entry could not be located in the Spanish-language papers.

VOLUME II

[1] Urbina, "Comentarios sobre el libro En Defensa De Mi Raza," *La Prensa*, October 20, 1936, p. 3.

[2] The quote attributed to Washington could not be located.

[3] The Assyrians kidnapped Daniel, a biblical figure of great faith, around 605 BC. He won favor with King Belshazzar of Babylon with his superior intellect. When the pagan king mocked Daniel's God and a mysterious hand appeared writing a message on the palace wall, he called on the sage from Judah to interpret the writing. Daniel refused offers of wealth and status, but read the warning to the alarmed king. Urbina was reminding Spanish-language readers that they could place their hope for a better future in the nation's egalitarian tradition, based on the views of figures like Washington and Christian principles. Readers could also take this to mean that egalitarianism embodied the Mexican cause for equal rights and repudiated racial thinking. Daniel 5:1-30.

[4] Urbina refers to an attempt by El Paso city officials to classify Mexicans as a race and the major unprecedented protests by Mexican Americans who feared that it would encourage further discrimination. City officials, no doubt encouraged by similar measures in other Texas cities, defended their action by noting that the US Bureau of the Census had called for the re-classification. Legal action led the city to rescind the order and encourage a broader statewide coalition that included protests by Perales and Local No. 16. The larger effort, also led by Mexican-American leaders from El Paso, also levelled successful protests against federal agencies, including the Bureau of the Census. According to the historian Mario García, upwardly mobile, US-born Mexicans, some of whom were associated with LULAC, led the protest actions largely because they feared their re-classification encouraged additional racial discrimination and undermined their integrationist efforts. Mario T. García, "Mexican American and the Politics of Citizenship: The Case of El Paso, 1936," *New Mexico Historical Review*, Vol. 59, 2 (April 1, 1984), pp. 187-204.

[5] A copy of this entry could not be located in the available newspapers.

[6] The saying, "Para muestra, basta un broche," proposes that the adorning broach (or button) matches or exceeds the existential

worth or beauty of the attire. Sáenz suggests that the Perales' already accomplished life is a reliable indication of what he will continue to achieve. The use of "broche," a fastener that is of higher quality than a "button," grants Perales even greater stature. A more colloquial and provisional translation of the saying could be, "The proof is in the pudding."

[7]Sauceda was a forty-eight-year-old Mexican national who owned a printing shop, edited *El Informador Benavidense* and served as an officer of the Comisión Honorífica in Benavides. The town of Benavides is located in Duval County, between Laredo and Corpus Christi. Mexican consulate officials usually assisted Mexican Nationals establish Comisiones Honoríficas as government-affiliated organizations. US Bureau of the Census, 1940, Duval County, Benavides, Texas, Profesor Juan Sauceda, Vol. 2, p. x, Benavides 1940 Census.

[8]As stated earlier, Juárez is one of the most revered figures in Mexican history primarily because he led the popular opposition against French intervention as the president of Mexico. Cuauhtémoc, also noted earlier, led the last defense against the initial Spanish onslaught that led to the military conquest of the Aztec empire. Moctezuma, also known as Motecuhzomatzin Ilhuicamina, preceded Cauhtémoc as the reigning King of the Aztecs who confronted the Spanish forces in the capital of Tenochtitlán.

[9]A copy of the English version of the letter is in the Alonso S. Perales Papers. In all such cases, the editor has revised the original with minor edits. The Perales Papers contain other letters that address the Falfurrias incident.

[10]Maximiliano Hinojosa was a thirty-five year old grocery clerk from Falfurrias. He was born in 1893 and served in the 90th Division of the American Expeditionary Force during World War I. US Bureau of the Census, 1930, Ancestry.com.

[11]This is a near verbatim copy of the English-language letter in the Perales Papers.

[12]Perales' letter refers to *Diógenes,* a newspaper from McAllen that mostly escaped the attention of archivists. The Hispanic Literary Heritage Program, an archival recovery initiative of Arte Público Press, has recovered a few copies of its articles. They are part of the Perales Papers that the Hispanic Literary Project has collected and processed for public use. Like *Diógenes,* numerous Mexican dailies and week-

lies that Perales used in his essays have been lost. This means that his book and his papers rescued material when he reproduced articles from papers that are now missing. According to the masthead of at least one of the issues Perales preserved, the weekly appeared in print for the first time on October 1927. Conrado Espinoza, the author of the novel *El Sol de Texas,* served as its editor.

[13] Perales offers the following reference in his entry: *Diógenes,* August 18, 1928. The article also appeared in *La Prensa,* August 25, 1928, p. 3 and in *El Cronista del Valle,* August 23, 1928, p. 3.

[14] Perales notes that this entry appeared in *Diógenes,* August 18, 1928. It also appeared in *La Prensa,* August 28, 1928, p. 3.

[15] This entry, according to Perales, appeared in *Diógenes,* September 1, 1928. Perales again provides reference information on his entry. The article also appears in *La Prensa,* August 25, 1928, p. 3 and in *El Cronista del Valle,* September 7, 1928, p. 3.

[16] The article could not be located. Handman was a Professor at the University of Texas at Austin. He made important contributions to the study of Mexicans in San Antonio. Max S. Handman, "Social Problems in Texas," *The Southwestern Political and Social Science Quarterly,* Vol. 5, No. 3 (1924): 255-63; "The Mexican Immigrant in Texas," *The Southwestern Political and Social Science Quarterly,* Vol. 7, No. 1 (1926): 33-41; "Economic Reasons for the Coming of the Mexican Immigrant," *American Journal of Sociology,* Vol. 35, No. 4 (1930): 601-11.

[17] The two paragraphs authored by Maus appear in Volume I.

[18] Foster, *A Gringo in Mañana-Land* (New York: Dodd, Mead and Company, 1924), p. 321.

[19] *Ibid.,* pp. 321-22.

[20] *Ibid.,* p. 322.

[21] The point here is that Mexican dignitaries demonstrated the capacity of the Mexican people by achieving great success in film (Del Rio, Vélez, Torres, Novarro), aviation (Carranza), and art (Cobarrubias).

[22] Perales states that this entry appeared in *Diógenes,* September 8. 1928. La Prensa also published it on August 27, 1928, p. 3.

[23] According to Perales, his letter to Manuel appeared in *Diógenes,* December 20, 1930. It also appeared in Spanish as "La segregación de escolares Mexicanos será combatido por La Liga de Ciudadanos Latinoamericanos," *La Prensa,* December 12, 1930, pp. 1, 5.

[24] Perales notes that the entry originated in *Álbum de La Raza*, (San Antonio) January 15, 1934. This issue of the periodical is unavailable.

[25] According to a reference note by Perales, this entry also appeared in *Álbum de La Raza,* January 15, 1934.

[26] The excerpt attributed to Dr. Binder could not be located. Binder, a leading sociologist of the early 1900s, wrote extensively on progress and leadership. See the following for works that Perales may have used: *The New Encyclopedia of Social Reform,* with William D. P. Bliss (New York: Funk and Wagnalls, 1908); Major Social Problems (New York: Prentice-Hall, 1920); *Health and Social Progress* (New York: Prentice-Hall, 1920); *Principles of Sociology* (New York: Prentice-Hall, 1928).

[27] *El Porvenir* (Publication of the Student Adult Association of the Sidney-Lanier School, San Antonio), May 28, 1934.

[28] The document indicates that it was taken from "Regresó de México el Lic. Perales," *La Prensa,* August 20, 1934, p. 6.

[29] *La Prensa,* January 9, 1936.

[30] *La Prensa,* January 25, 1936.

[31] The translation of the letter can be found in the Perales Papers and appears here in verbatim form.

[32] *La Prensa,* October 14, 1936.

[33] Valls, a reformer who served as District Attorney and judge in Webb County, most probably claimed "Latin blood" because his father was born in Spain. Culturally, however, he identified with Mexicans, beginning with his birth in Bagdad, Tamaulipas and close friendships with Mexicans from Mexico and Texas. Mexicans reciprocated, judging the admiring and endearing nickname that they gave him, "Don Juanito Valls."

[34] The translation of this entry can be found in the Perales Papers and appears here in verbatim form.

[35] Mr. Maverick, a New Dealer and strong supporter of LULAC, represented the 20th district of Texas in the House of Representatives from January 3, 1935, to January 3, 1939. Richard B. Henderson, "Maverick, Fontaine Maury," *Handbook of Texas Online,* accessed November 11, 2017, http://www.tshaonline.orghandbook/online/articles/fma83.

[36] This "explanatory note" appeared in the book's entry but not in the translated version in the Perales Papers. Brown, the city health officer from Marfa became the State Health Officer in 1933 and served

until 1937. James E. Peavy, *History of Public Health in Texas* (Austin: Texas State Department of Health, 1974), p. 58.

[37] The Perales Papers includes the English-language letter from the mayor and appears here in verbatim form.

[38] This translated copy can be found in the Perales Papers.

[39] The Perales Papers contains the English version of the telegram.

[40] An English-language version of this letter is in the Perales Papers. It appears here as a verbatim copy.

[41] *La Prensa,* October 19, 1936.

[42] Teresa Palomo Acosta, "Cleofas Calleros," *Handbook of Texas Online,* accessed November 12, 2017, http://www.tshaonline.org/handbook/online/articles/fcadb.

[43] *La Prensa,* October 20, 1936.

[44] *La Prensa,* October 21, 1936.

[45] The entry is available in English in the Perales Papers.

[46] *La Prensa,* November 1, 1936.

[47] *La Prensa,* October 18, 1936.

[48] *La Prensa,* November 24, 1936.

[49] *La Prensa,* November 26, 1936.

[50] Article 2900 allowed for "Separate Schools." The full provision reads as follows. "All available public school funds of this State shall be appropriated in each county for the education alike of white and colored children, and impartial provisions shall be made for both races. No white children shall attend schools supported for colored children, nor shall colored children attend schools supported for white children. The terms 'colored race' and 'colored children,' as used in this title, include all persons of mixed blood descended from Negro ancestry. Texas, *1925 Revised Civil Statutes and Revised Criminal Statutes of Texas* (Austin: A. C. Baldwin & Sons, 1925), p. 795.

[51] Texas, *Penal Code of the State of Texas,* Adopted at the Regular Session of the Thirty-ninth Legislature, 1925 (Austin: A. C. Baldwin & Sons, State Printers, 1925), p. 102. Bruce A. Glasrud authored an article-length study on Jim Crowism. Although useful, the article limits its attention to Black-White relations and disregards the forms of segregation affecting the more numerous minoritized Mexican population in Texas. The laws that defined racial segregation in Texas reached fruition during the early 1900s. Human bondage, early segregationist statutes and modern forms of labor

control like sharecropping had set the stage for a caste system that became increasingly visible in the growing towns and cities of Texas. Glasrud, "Jim Crow's Emergence in Texas," *American Studies,* Vol. 15, No. 1 (Spring 1974), pp. 47-60.

[52] Penal Code of the State of Texas, "Separate Coach Law," p. 374.

[53] Allred to Blalock, July 25 1934, Perales Papers. Blalock had requested an official opinion on whether Mexicans could participate in the White Primary of the Democratic Party on July 28. Allred responded by quoting from a resolution that the State Convention of the Democratic Party approved in Houston on May 24, 1932. Perales only quoted three paragraphs from the resolution.

[54] When Perales notes that the Director of the Bureau of the Census is confirming an opinion that Mexicans are White, he is referring to the October 15, 1936 telegram that appears earlier in the text. Austin to Maverick, Perales Papers.

[55] Maverick to Perales, November 25, 1936. Maverick attached the telegram in his letter to Perales.

[56] The telegram from de la Garza is in the Perales Papers.

[57] Allport's quote could not be located.

[58] The Perales Papers does not include a translation of this entry, however, it does contain copies of at least 12 articles or speeches that Perales delivered on paying the poll tax to improve Mexican political representation in San Antonio and throughout the state. An important column by a *San Antonio Light* writer with the pseudonym of Don Político reveals the importance of the poll tax for Mexicans in San Antonio. According to Don Político, 90% of the Mexican poll tax holders voted in the local elections of 1940, while Whites and African Americans voted at 80% and 60%, respectively. Bexar County Whites (130,000) outnumbered Mexicans (82,000) and African Americans (18,000) in 1930, and they were more financially able to pay the poll tax and vote in greater numbers. The higher voting participation rate among Mexicans, however, represented a potential that no doubt explains why Perales was so encouraged to promote voting as a means to produce change. He may have also believed that the poll tax and voting campaigns organized by Mexican leaders like him had already leveraged spaces for their participation in San Antonio politics, a development that he sought to preserve and expand. Don Político, "Poll Tax Still Curtails Negroes," *The San Antonio Light,* January 30, 1941, copy in the Perales Papers.

59 *La Prensa,* January 7, 1937.
60 Durán Carbajal was a forty-year old Mexico-born physician with a private practice in San Diego, Texas. He and his wife Emma, also born in Mexico, had eight children, all born in Texas. According to the 1940 Census report, Durán Carbajal was in the process of becoming a naturalized citizen. US Bureau of the Census, 1940, Ancestry.com.
61 The article from *La Prensa* as well as the English-language copy of the letter to the Mayor of San Angelo are in the Perales Papers.
62 Johnston was a thirty-seven year old grocery store owner at the time of the racial incident. Johnston and his twenty-seven year old wife, Aurora, were born in Texas. US Bureau of the Census, 1930, Ancestry.com.
63 Although we do not know how the incident was resolved, Johnston expressed his appreciation for the widespread response to the proposed segregation of Mexicans, suggesting a favorable resolution. Johnston thanked the consulate offices from San Antonio, Houston, Galveston, Dallas and El Paso, as well as the editors of *La Tribuna* (Piedras Negras, Coahuila), *El Mundo* (Del Rio), *Los Novedades* (Kingsville) and *La Prensa* (San Antonio). He also acknowledged the special role played by LULAC representatives, especially Perales. "Nuestro agradecimiento," *El Latino,* January 15, 1937, p. 1.
64 This entry could not be located in the Spanish-language press or the Perales Papers.
65 Senator Hugo Black, a Democratic Senator from Alabama, introduced the wage-hour legislation in 1932, while William Connery, a Democratic Representative from Massachusetts, proposed corresponding legislation and held congressional hearings on the Bill. President Roosevelt entered the contentious debate over succeeding proposals and finally signed a compromise bill establishing the Fair Labor Standards Act (FLSA) of 1938. It followed the passage of the National Recovery Act (1933) that had given the president authority to regulate commerce and wages. The 1938 initiative sought to reduce unemployment by guaranteeing a minimum wage in industries involved in interstate commerce. It also provided for overtime pay and protections for youth involved in "oppressive child labor." Although we still do not know the extent to which the NIRA benefitted the Mexican-origin work force, Mexican farmworkers did not fare well under the law. Southern Congressmen, concerned that the

NIRA would upend industrial and racial patterns, and Roosevelt, willing to once again compromise the labor and civil rights of non-White labor, made sure that the law did not extend labor protections to Black and Brown farmworkers. The 1938 strike by the CIO-affiliated pecan-shelling union of San Antonio offers an example of an additional form of discrimination affecting minority workers in the arbitration process. Despite the fact that the pecan shelling industry participated in interstate commerce and the workers were entitled to twenty-five cents an hour, employers paid piece-rate earnings that were equivalent to less than six or seven cents an hour. The strike settlement, negotiated by CIO leaders and supervised by the Texas Industrial Commission, called for an immediate salary increase that did not meet the legal amount. The CIO and employers agreed to the settlement while the latter subsequently mechanized the industry, released thousands of workers and practically destroyed the union. Despite the employer subterfuge that violated the intent of the law to reduce unemployment, no one seems to have brought legal action against the pecan shelling industry. Mark Linder, "Farm Workers and the Fair Labor Standards Act: Racial Discrimination in the New Deal," *Texas Law Review,* Vol. 65 (1987), pp. 1335-1393; Richard Croxdale, "Pecan-Shellers' Strike," *Handbook of Texas Online,* accessed July 01, 2018, http://www.tshaonline.org/handbook/online/articles/oep01; and Gabriela González, "Carolina Munguia and Emma Tenayuca: The Politics of Benevolence and Radical Reform, 1930s," *Frontiers: A Journal of Women's Studies,* Vol. 24 (2003), pp. 200-209.

[66]The movement to end the exploitation of child labor and to regulate their participation in industrial employment began soon after WWI. By 1937, the Supreme Court had ruled against child labor and Congress had approved a congressional amendment that the majority of the states certified. The previously noted FLSA lent support to the Child Labor Amendment, but the constitutional campaign had not yet secured the required number of state ratifications to succeed. Sec the following Senate's resolution announcing that the ratification by twenty-eight states of the proposed amendment to the Constitution was not sufficient. The Senate amended the resolution to secure additional support but this attempt also failed to reach the required number of states. US Senate, "Child Labor Amendment," Report No. 788, 75th Congress, 1st Session, June 15, 1937. See the following for

an excellent review of Mexican-origin workers in the Great Depression: Zaragosa Vargas, Chapter 7, "Mexican American Labor Rights in the Great Depression," in *Crucible of Struggle: Mexican Americans from Colonial Times to the Present Era* (New York: Oxford University Press, 2017).

[67] Navarro, Ruiz, Menchaca, Seguín and other "Latin" historical figures appeared in the publication, suggesting that the protest convinced the author to be inclusive. Frederick C. Chabot, *With the Makers of San Antonio, Genealogies of the Early Latin, Anglo American and German Families with Occasional Biographies, Each Group Being Prefaced With a Brief Historical Sketch and Illustrations* (San Antonio: Artes Gráficas, 1937).

[68] Robert Wagner, Democratic Senator from New York, and Henry Steagall, Democratic Representative from Alabama, authored the Wagner-Steagall Bill that created the US Housing Authority in the Department of the Interior. The 1937 Act, which provided subsidies to local governments for public housing, lasted two years. Housing reformers influenced the Harry Truman and Lyndon Johnson administrations to expand the government's role in public housing, including urban renewal programs that razed minority homes in the name of slum clearance and public housing for the poor. Local clearance projects began soon thereafter. The San Antonio Housing Authority, established in 1937, constructed the Alazán-Apache Courts between 1939 and 1942, primarily in response to the political agitation over the deplorable housing conditions on the West side of the city. Robert B. Fairbanks, Ed., *The War on Slums in the Southwest: Public Housing and Slum Clearance in Texas, Arizona, and New Mexico, 1935-1965* (Philadelphia: Temple University Press, 2014); Donald L. Zelman, "Alazán-Apache Courts," *Handbook of Texas Online,* accessed June 28, 2018, http://www.tshaonline.org/handbook/online/articles/mpa01.

[69] The authors of the anti-communist resolution may have been referring to the Alien Registration Act, known as the Smith Act, which Congress enacted as a federal statute in 1940. The resolution reflected LULAC's conservative political outlook and its opposition to the significant CIO gains among Mexican workers in the American Southwest, especially in San Antonio. Vargas, "Crucible of Struggle," Chapter 7.

70"Atrevido Juego Puñales," *Las Novedades* (Kingsville), June 25, 1937, p. 1. The only surviving copy of the article is in the Perales Papers. The author's name may be a pseudonym for Alonso S. Perales. Aside from the shared initials of the first and last names, the alias literally reads as the daring play of knives, possibly meaning that Perales sought to convey the daring use of words in place of swords.

71The Wagner bills refers to the series of legislative bills that concluded with the passage of the National Labor Relations Act of 1935. Also known as the Wagner Act, the law established the National Labor Relations Board, the agency responsible for guaranteeing workers the right to organize, bargain collectively and strike. The law did not extend its labor guarantees to domestic and farm workers. Also, see Note #56.

72This entry does not appear in the existing Spanish-language papers nor the Perales Papers. It was dated July 1937.

73This entry, dated March 6, 1937, does not appear in the Spanish-language press. An English version of the article appears in the Perales Papers with the title "Honorable Mayor and City Commissioners, Ladies and Gentlemen." Perales, the author, did not identify the park. It may have been the Koehler Pavilion, a 1937 addition to Brackenridge Park built under the Works Progress Administration.

74Hearings before the Committee on Immigration and Naturalization, House of Representatives, Hearing No. 70.I.5, February 21—April 5, 1928 (Washington, DC: Government Printing Office, 1928), pp. 98-99. This entry does not appear in the available Spanish-language newspapers nor in the Perales Papers. Perales was a co-founder of LULAC in 1929. Here, he is referring to the organization's predecessor, the League of Latin American Citizens, of which he was the leading founder.

75This entry is one of several that *La Prensa* published to underscore the importance of Perales' leadership. "Elogios al Lic. A. Perales por la labor desarrollada en pro de La Raza Mexicana," June 18, 1929, p. 2.

76This entry and the subsequent one do not appear in the Spanish-language press nor in the Perales Papers. Perales letter refers to the communication by Manuel Gonzales and Clemente Idar noted earlier. The letter from Gonzales and Idar to William Green, President of the American Federation of Labor, had disparaged Canales, Garza and Perales by stating that LULAC had not authorized them to speak for the organization. Gonzales had a long-standing personal feud with Perales that may have originated in their differences over the participation of Mexican nationals in LULAC, a point of debate between them that emerged during LULAC's special convention of 1934 addressed in this publication. Idar, the first official Mexican organizer in the AFL, most probably wanted Perales to take a stronger stand against immigration from Mexico, a stand that gained public and labor support during the hard times of the Depression. As noted earlier, Perales refused to support open border advocates and restrictionists as long as they continued to use racialized arguments to support their views.

[77] This entry could not be located in the available Spanish-language newspapers nor in the Perales Papers. The editors of *La Prensa*, however, carried an article that reported on the special conference held in Corpus Christi. "Los concilios de los 'Lulacs' en Corpus Christi," *La Prensa*, March 30, 1934, p. 4.

[78] The letter from Manuel could not be located in the Spanish-language papers nor does a copy exist in the Perales Papers.

[79] This entry could not be located in the Spanish-language press nor in the Perales Papers. An introductory article on the White Man's Associations, however, is available. Christopher Long, "White Man's Union Associations," accessed July 02, 2018, http://www.tshaonline.org/handbook/online/articles/vcw02. A book-length study on African American unionism offers a treatment of racism in East Texas during the early 1900s. Ernest Obadele-Starks, *Black Unionism in the Industrial South* (College Station: Texas A&M University Press, 2001).

[80] A copy of the letter could not be located.

[81] *The Palms* (Published quarterly by the Students of Our Lady of the Lake College, San Antonio, Texas) Vol. XI (March 1936): pp. 53-54.

[82] This entry could not be located elsewhere. The delegation representing LULAC Council 70 from New Braunfels authored the petition that the editors of *La Prensa* noted on July 8, 1937. Additionally, Manuel Gonzales wrote a letter to the mayor of New Braunfels on behalf of LULAC protesting the claims and the mayor responded to Gonzales with a denial of the charges. The outcome of the case is unknown. "Por la lucha racial en N. Braunfels," *La Prensa*, July 8, 1937, pp. 1, 2; "Enérgica protesta de los mexicanos, Ha llegado a un grado extremo el prejuicio racial en regiones de Texas," *El Continental* (El Paso), July

9, 1937, p. 1; "Según dice el mayor de New Braunfels, Acerca de particular envío una carta al licenciado Manuel C. Gonzales," *La Prensa,* July 13, 1937, p. 1; Perales, "Arquitectos de nuestros propios destinos, Somos buenos vecinos," *La Prensa,* August 6, 1950, p. 3.

[83] This entry could not be located in the newspapers or the Perales Papers.

[84] This article appeared in *Diógenes* (McAllen) and *El Fronterizo* (Rio Grande City), on July 2, 1927.

[85] This entry is in English and appears here as a verbatim copy.

[86] Perales entered the following note in the text of the letter: "Ben was referring to my request that he do everything possible to persuade the Corpus Christi Council of the Orden Hijos de América and the Orden Caballeros de América to join our League."

[87] The letters that follow appear as entries in English.

[88] Perales did not provide an English-language translation of this entry.